Fundraiser in Chief

Presidents and the Politics of Campaign Cash

Brendan J. Doherty

University Press of Kansas

For Robyn

Published by the University Press of Kansas (Lawrence, Kansas 66045), which was
organized by the Kansas Board of Regents and is operated and funded by Emporia
State University, Fort Hays State University, Kansas State University, Pittsburg State
University, the University of Kansas, and Wichita State University

Library of Congress Cataloging-in-Publication Data

Names: Doherty, Brendan J., author.
Title: Fundraiser in chief : presidents and the politics of campaign cash /
    Brendan J. Doherty.
Description: Lawrence : University Press of Kansas, 2023. | Includes index.
Identifiers: LCCN 2022021912 (print)
    LCCN 2022021913 (ebook)
    ISBN 9780700635320 (cloth)
    ISBN 9780700634057 (paperback)
    ISBN 9780700634064 (ebook)
Subjects: LCSH: Campaign funds—United States—History—20th century. |
    Campaign funds—United States—History—20th century. | Presidents—United States.
Classification: LCC JK1991 .D636 2023 (print) | LCC JK1991 (ebook) | DDC
    324.7/80973—dc23/eng/20220815
LC record available at https://lccn.loc.gov/2022021912.
LC ebook record available at https://lccn.loc.gov/2022021913.

British Library Cataloguing-in-Publication Data is available.

Printed in the United States of America

10 9 8 7 6 5 4 3 2 1

The paper used in this publication is acid free and meets the minimum requirements of
the American National Standard for Permanence of Paper for Printed Library Materials
Z39.48-1992.

Contents

Preface

A burst of important changes to campaign finance dynamics during Barack Obama's reelection campaign and second term as president sparked the idea for this book. In 2011 and 2012, Obama set records for the amount of time he spent fundraising for his reelection bid. While most previous presidents had primarily held separate fundraising events for their own reelection campaign committee and their national committee, Obama integrated his fundraising efforts for both entities from the beginning of his run for a second term. Super PACs were becoming increasingly prominent actors, and Obama, who had vocally criticized these groups, decided to headline fundraising events for Super PACs during the 2014 midterm election cycle. Obama also chose to fundraise almost exclusively for the benefit of national party committees instead of individual candidates for office as the midterm elections approached, a pronounced departure from the practices of prior presidents. Additionally, a Supreme Court decision and little-noticed congressional action in 2014 would combine to enable political parties to raise large amounts of money through expanded, complicated joint fundraising committees. These newly enlarged committees, which would be central to fundraising efforts both during the 2016 presidential campaign and throughout Donald Trump's four years as president, would raise renewed questions about the role of money in American politics.

Collectively, these changes heralded dramatic shifts in the campaign finance system that was set up in the 1970s and restructured in 2002. I had examined presidential fundraising in two chapters of my 2012 book, *The Rise of the President's Permanent Campaign*. The combination of these new developments and additional questions that had been prompted by my prior research led me to embark on this book project. "Money is the mother's milk of politics," declared Jesse Unruh, who served as speaker of the California State Assembly.[1] Most studies of money in politics have relied on Federal Election Commission data on the

amounts of funds raised and spent by campaigns, political parties, and other entities. This book approaches presidential fundraising from a different perspective
by analyzing how seven presidents elected under the modern campaign finance
regime—Jimmy Carter, Ronald Reagan, George H.W. Bush, Bill Clinton, George
W. Bush, Barack Obama, and Donald Trump—allocated their scarce time to the
task of raising campaign cash for their own reelection bids and their fellow party
members. To do so, I built an original data set of presidential fundraising efforts
by systematically reviewing a wide range of sources that shed light on how presidents spend their time. As I conducted this research, I learned of and reviewed additional records of presidential activities that enabled me to expand my data set to
include more fundraising events that were closed to the press than I had found for
my previous book. The result is the most comprehensive record available of presidents' efforts to raise campaign funds for themselves and their political allies.

The primary proposition of this book is that fundraising is a frequently used
yet underexamined tool of modern presidential leadership. This project analyzes
presidential resource allocation strategies and seeks to shed light on a series of
related questions. How much of their time do presidents dedicate to fundraising?
For whom do they raise campaign cash, and what priorities are revealed by their
efforts? How do their fundraising strategies relate to the incentives established
by the evolving campaign finance landscape? Under what circumstances do they
exclude the media from their fundraising activities? Finally, what controversies
result from presidential fundraising, and what implications arise for presidential
leadership and the American political system?

I set forth an argument about why presidential fundraising has evolved and
contend that changes in the campaign finance landscape and strategic responses
to those developments by presidents and their fellow party members have led to
a number of unintended consequences. Under the current disjointed campaign
finance system in which Super PACs raise funds in unrestricted amounts, it is
both rational and controversial that more tightly regulated campaigns and party
committees seek creative ways to circumvent contribution limits in order to raise
the funds they believe they need to be electorally competitive. My primary goal is
that readers will understand the important role that fundraising has come to play
in the efforts of modern presidents to bring this country closer to their view of a
more perfect union.

I have been fortunate to benefit from much assistance and support as I have re-
searched and written this book. Through the years, many people have shared valuable advice, insights, opportunities, and data that have helped with this project. I
would like to thank Julia Azari, Terri Bimes, Lara Brown, Bruce Buchanan, Justin
Buchler, Bruce Cain, Jim Caraley, Jeff Cohen, John Dearborn, George Demko,
Daniel DiSalvo, George Edwards, Richard Ellis, Matt Eshbaugh-Soha, Donald
Fowler, Daniel Galvin, Jessica Gerrity, Matt Grossmann, Dave Hopkins, Gary

Jacobson, Matt Jarvis, David Karol, Robin Kolodny, Martha Joynt Kumar, Ray La Raja, Marylena Mantas, Chris Marston, William Mayer, Sidney Milkis, Michael Nelson, Eric Ostermeier, Jack Pitney, Nelson Polsby, Sean Savage, Gordon Silverstein, Geoffrey Skelley, Doug Sosnik, Robert Spitzer, Jon Rogowski, Justin Vaughn, Martin Wattenberg, Stephen Weatherford, and Jacob Wirz. I'm also quite appreciative of John Woolley and Gerhard Peters, whose American Presidency Project is a remarkable resource that was my starting point as I compiled much of the data used in this book. Additionally, I owe a particular debt of gratitude to Mark Knoller, formerly of CBS News, who tracked presidential activities for decades and who kindly answered many questions over the years as I built my data set of presidential fundraisers.

I am fortunate to work alongside a remarkably collegial group of civilian and military faculty in the United States Naval Academy's Political Science Department. I am grateful for their support, and would especially like to thank my department chairs—Dave Richardson, Howard Ernst, Matt Testerman, Priscilla Zotti, Ellie Malone, and Gale Mattox—as well as my now-retired colleague in American politics Steve Frantzich. I am also quite appreciative of the dedicated staff at the Naval Academy's Nimitz Library, including Donna Goda, Linda McLeod, and JoAnne Danchik. Additionally, I am thankful for the support for my research provided by multiple Senior Grants from the Naval Academy Research Council, as well as a Volgenau Fellowship made possible by the generosity of Naval Academy alumnus Dr. Ernst Volgenau. I am also grateful for two research sabbaticals, one at the very beginning of this project and the other at its conclusion, which were essential to my being able to dedicate the time to formulate and complete this project. While the Naval Academy offered support for my research efforts, I would like to note that the views expressed in this book are solely those of the author and are not those of the Naval Academy, the US Navy, or the Department of Defense.

While this book is almost entirely composed of new analysis and prose, in limited instances I have used select wording or anecdotes that appeared in my previously published research in *Political Studies Quarterly* and *The Forum: A Journal of Applied Research in Contemporary Politics*. I thank those editors for their earlier support of my work.

I have been fortunate to work again with the talented team at the University Press of Kansas. David Congdon has been a remarkably thoughtful, supportive, and patient editor. I'd also like to thank Erica Nicholson, Derek Helms, Karl Janssen, Michelle Asakawa, Fred Woodward, Chuck Myers, Kim Hogeland, and Kelly Chrisman Jacques for their encouragement and guidance. Additionally, I am grateful to Jeffrey Crouch and an additional anonymous reviewer whose thoughtful feedback on the manuscript improved this book.

I am thankful beyond words for the love and support of all of my family. My parents, Jack and Wendy Doherty, taught me to love books and to hope to write my own one day. My sister, Kate, offered much encouragement over the years, as did my family by marriage, the Altmans. My children urged me to write this book even though they wished I were writing a book full of magic and adventure in a faraway land. My wife, Robyn, to whom this book is dedicated, is the best partner I could ever imagine. Quite fortunately for me, she is one of the most talented writers I know, and her insightful edits made this book far better than it would have been otherwise.

1

Fundraising as a Presidential Leadership Tool

"There are two things that are important in politics. The first is money, and I can't remember the second."

—Mark Hanna, campaign manager to William McKinley

"They call him the fund-raiser in chief. The money man. The closer. The Democratic Party's biggest draw, elder statesman, marquee attraction. Put him on the bill. Lead him to the podium. Wallets will open."

—*New York Times* article on Bill Clinton's fundraising, June 25, 2000

In the fall of 2018, President Donald Trump crisscrossed the country to raise money for himself and for his fellow Republicans who would soon face the voters in midterm elections. One nine-day stretch exemplified many dynamics of modern presidential fundraising. He began by headlining a fundraiser on September 26 in New York for Trump Victory, a joint fundraising committee that benefited his own reelection campaign and the Republican National Committee (RNC). The next day in Washington, DC, he sought to shore up the fortunes of Republican members of the House of Representatives as the featured speaker at a fundraiser that benefited both the National Republican Congressional Committee (NRCC) and a joint fundraising committee called Protect the House, which shared its proceeds with twenty-six congressional candidates, fourteen state Republican parties, two political action committees, and one national party committee.[1] Four days later, Trump traveled to Johnson City, Tennessee, to fundraise for the Republican candidate for that state's open Senate seat. On the following day in Southaven, Mississippi, he headlined a fundraiser jointly benefiting Mississippi's two Republican senators. Two days later, on October 4, he took part in a fundraiser in Minneapolis that benefited both the NRCC and the Minnesota Republican Party. All five of these fundraising events were closed to the press.

Trump's fundraising sprint bore many of the hallmarks of recent presidential money-raising efforts and illuminated his strategic priorities. In the almost

1

half-century since the modern campaign finance system was created in the 1970s, presidential fundraising has become a far more frequent and complicated endeavor, as presidents have devoted substantial amounts of time to raising money for specific candidates and for increasingly complex and nationalized fundraising committees. Like his recent predecessors, Trump raised money for individual Senate and House candidates, state parties, political action committees, and multiple national party committees. Unlike any other modern president, he chose to raise money for his own reelection campaign during his first two years in office, dramatically accelerating the trend of progressively earlier starts to reelection fundraising. Two of his five events had no local beneficiary, illustrating the increasing frequency of so-called ATM state fundraising—when out-of-state beneficiaries receive campaign funds instead of that state's own candidates or party committees.[2] Trump's fundraising was also marked by a lack of transparency, as members of the media are frequently excluded from presidential money-raising events. Finally, fundraising efforts like these spark numerous controversies, including allowing wealthy donors to buy access to the president, whether time spent fundraising distracts a president from the official duties of the office, and, in a controversy unique to Trump, the propriety of the president personally profiting from fundraisers held at commercial properties that he owns.

Winning elections is the essential starting point in American politics, and fundraising has become an increasingly important instrument of modern presidential leadership. Recent presidents have faced escalating campaign costs, a shifting campaign finance landscape that has empowered outside groups to raise previously unseen amounts of money, frequent legislative gridlock in Washington, and competitive elections that in any cycle could switch party control of Congress, the White House, and statehouses across the country. Presidents fundraise to win a second term in the Oval Office, to help their party hold the White House in the following election, to win majorities in the House and Senate, to defend those majorities, to minimize looming electoral losses, to elect likeminded governors, to influence the redistricting process, and to aid other party members. The president is the most effective fundraiser in the American political system. In a campaign environment in which candidates and political parties must raise millions of dollars in the increments in the low thousands that are prescribed by campaign finance law, the president's fundraising efforts for himself and for his, and someday her, fellow party members are in great demand.

The central premise of this book is that fundraising is a frequently used yet underexamined tool of modern presidential leadership. Presidential fundraising should be viewed as an instrument of presidential power, akin to signing statements, executive orders, veto threats, public speeches, and more. Presidents allocate their scarce time to fundraising as a means to an end. In order to understand more clearly how modern presidents exercise leadership and seek to move the country closer to their vision of a more perfect union, this book analyzes their priorities and the strategies they employ as they devote themselves to fundraising.

This book draws upon an unprecedented amount of empirical evidence about the extent to which modern presidents have dedicated themselves to political fundraising. In so doing, I advance the argument that a campaign finance system has emerged that is now far removed from the imperatives that members of Congress responded to when they worked to create a new campaign finance regime in the 1970s. Public funding for presidential elections became irrelevant as campaign costs rose dramatically, and presidents consequently devoted more and more time to fundraising. Presidents and their parties have been incentivized to seek creative legal ways to circumvent federal contribution limits in order to raise funds in increasingly greater amounts. First, they exploited rules that allowed unlimited soft money donations to political parties. Later, after those unlimited contributions to national party committees were banned, the empowerment of groups such as Super PACs that are not subject to contribution limits spurred presidents and their parties to make use of complicated joint fundraising committees that could engage in high-dollar fundraising. These approaches changed substantially over the course of the presidencies of Jimmy Carter, Ronald Reagan, George H. W. Bush, Bill Clinton, George W. Bush, Barack Obama, and Donald Trump. But a reliably recurring theme has been the desire of presidents and their parties to adapt to an evolving campaign finance landscape by finding innovative ways to raise the funds they believe they need to be electorally competitive.

These most recent dynamics have played out during a period characterized by what political scientist Frances Lee has called "insecure majorities." The Republican takeover of the Senate in 1980 brought the GOP their first majority in that chamber in twenty-six years. This ushered in a biennial battle for control of the upper chamber of Congress and sparked Republican hopes for a takeover in the House of Representatives as well. By 1994, Republicans had not held the majority of House seats for forty years, which led two political scientists to publish a book that year titled *Congress' Permanent Minority?: Republicans in the U.S. House.*[3] However, historic midterm election gains that year gave control of both chambers of Congress to the Republicans for the first time in four decades and signaled the beginning of an era without long-lasting congressional majorities in either the House or the Senate.[4]

Power in Washington has become increasingly insecure in recent years. A discontented electorate voted a new party into power in seven of the eight federal election cycles from 2006 to 2020. Majority control switched to the opposition party in the House, the Senate, or both in 2006, 2010, 2014, 2018, and 2020, while the party that held the White House changed in the elections of 2008, 2016, and 2020. Only in 2012 did election results affirm the status quo instead of ushering a party to an increased position of power. With most elections offering the prospect of regaining or losing control of at least one chamber of Congress, as well as many high-stakes gubernatorial races across the country, presidents and their parties have a good deal to gain or lose in any particular election.

Changes in the campaign finance landscape and the recent era of electoral

competitiveness have played key roles in modern presidential fundraising practices. Voters who have felt poorly served by their elected leaders have repeatedly
voted to change the party in power in Washington. Presidents and their allies
know that the competitive nature of congressional and presidential elections in
any cycle could switch party control of the White House, Congress, and statehouses across the country. This has incentivized presidents to focus on fundraising for the next election in hopes of tilting the political balance of power in their
favor. Given these dynamics, presidents are in great demand to raise funds in
support of their own reelection bids and to help their fellow party members in
competitive races across the country.

These evolving dynamics raise important issues about presidential leadership
and the workings of the American campaign finance system. Presidential fundraising sits at the intersection of campaigning and governing. Presidents who devote
their scarce time to fundraising do so at the expense of other important presidential priorities. In a campaign finance system that was designed to limit corruption
or the appearance of corruption, the appearance of corruption now abounds. Super
PACs and other nominally independent groups have been empowered by their
ability to raise unlimited contributions to support or oppose any particular set of
political candidates. And presidents and their parties have responded by creating
complicated joint fundraising committees that enable them to hold events where
the price of admission is hundreds of times the amount that one could contribute
to an individual candidate. The result is a disjointed campaign finance system that
no one would have designed from the ground up. In this system, it has become
increasingly rational for presidents to spend substantial amounts of their time raising money for themselves and for their parties in the hopes of electoral gains that
will reshuffle the governing deck in their favor.

PRESIDENTIAL FUNDRAISING RARELY STOPS

Presidential fundraising is not an occasional enterprise. Instead, it has become a
frequently used instrument of presidential leadership that takes place throughout
a president's time in office. The periods between elections in the American political system are relatively brief, and the stretches of time when presidents are not
actively campaigning have become shorter in recent decades. Federal elections
take place every two years, with all members of the House of Representatives
and about one-third of all senators on the ballot, and nominating contests are held
months in advance of the November general election. In midterm elections, thirty-
six states elect their governors. Two states, New Jersey and Virginia, elect their
governors in a president's first year in office, and three others, Kentucky, Louisiana, and Mississippi, do so during the third year of a president's term.[5] Major
cities across the country choose their mayors on a patchwork of dates, including
New York City's high-profile contest during a president's first year in office. And

special elections for the House of Representatives and the Senate can occur at any point in a president's term. For example, in Trump's first year in office there were six special elections for the House of Representatives and one for a Senate seat.[6] A president inclined to help his fellow party members in an upcoming election need not wait long for an opportunity to do so.

In April of 2013, just over two months after Obama was sworn in for his second term as president, he spoke about the relatively brief period of time for governing between elections:

> Now, this year, we have a window. Just completed one election. We would like to see some governing done in Washington before the next election starts. . . . And so my hope is, is that we can get some governing done this year. . . . And my hope is, is that we're going to see more and more Republicans who say, you know what, I didn't come here just to fight the President or demonize Nancy Pelosi, I came here to get some stuff done. And they will be greeted with great enthusiasm by me and I think by Nancy, if we could get some more stuff done right now. But, realistically, I could get a whole lot more done if Nancy Pelosi is Speaker of the House.[7]

Where was Obama when he was discussing productive governing during the brief window of time between elections? He was speaking at a fundraising event in San Francisco that raised $2.5 million for House Democrats who were seeking to reclaim the majority they had lost to the Republicans in the 2010 midterm elections.[8] As Obama spoke about potential progress during a limited period for governing, he was raising campaign funds for midterm elections that would take place nineteen months in the future.

Presidential fundraising begins soon after the nation's chief executive is sworn in, continues throughout the first term, and doesn't let up in the second term once the president's own reelection bid is in the rearview mirror. Figure 1.1 depicts the number of fundraising events that presidents participated in by year from the start of Carter's presidency in 1977 through Trump's final full year in 2020. The figure reveals some relatively consistent patterns within terms. Fundraising during midterm and presidential election years was more frequent than fundraising during a president's first and third years in office in seven of these eleven presidential terms. The first year of a president's term offered the lowest number of fundraisers for five of these seven presidents, all except Carter and Reagan. The greatest number of first-term fundraisers came in the reelection year for each of the three Democratic presidents—Carter, Clinton, and Obama. In contrast, the first-term high-water mark came in the midterm election year for Reagan, George H. W. Bush, and George W. Bush, and in the third year in office for Trump, whose reelection fundraising in 2020 was curtailed by the COVID-19 pandemic.

Fundraising in odd-numbered years, which don't coincide with presidential or midterm elections, has been less frequent than in most even-numbered years,

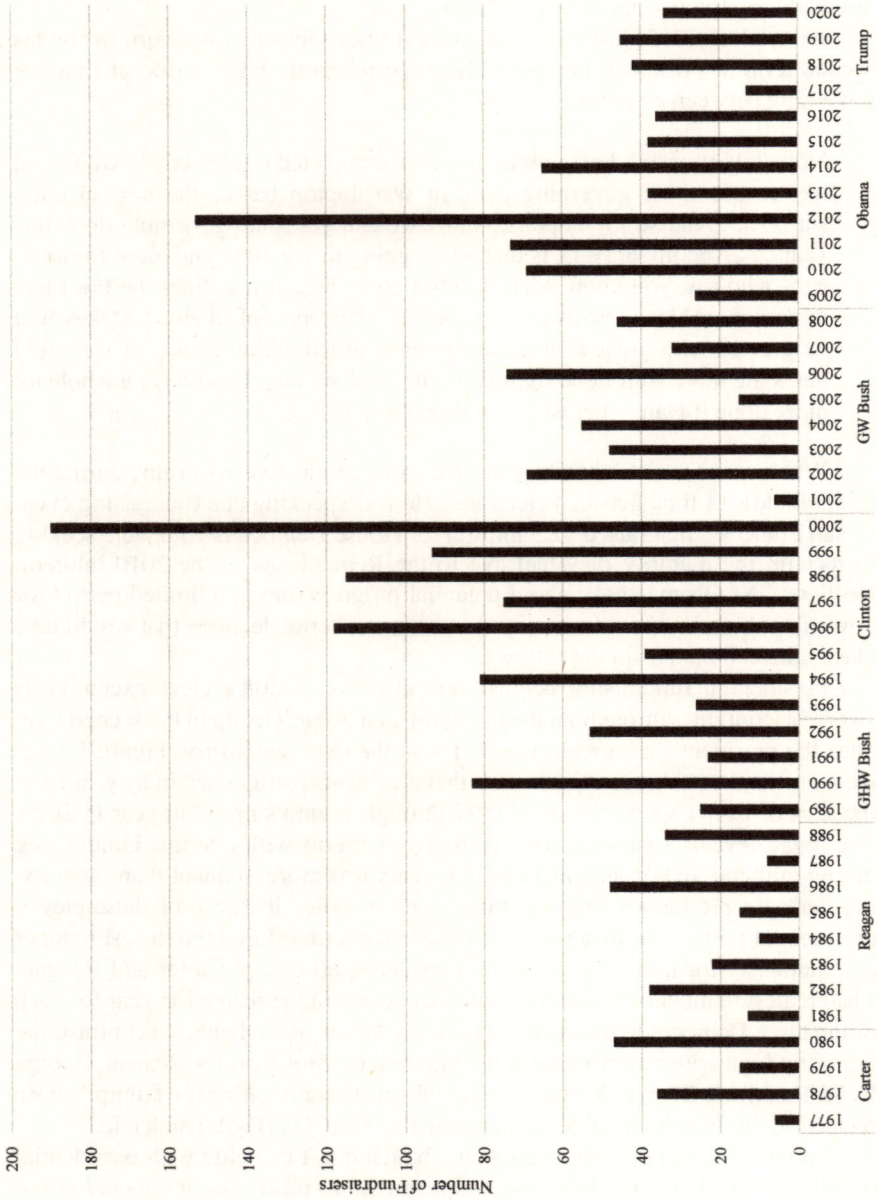

Figure 1.1: Presidential Fundraising Events by Year, 1977–2020 *Sources*: Data compiled by the author from the *Public Papers of the Presidents*, the Digests of Other White House Announcements, White House schedules and press briefings, Reagan's personal diary, and Associated Press and other news articles.

but it is still quite important. Raising campaign cash early in an election cycle can be particularly valuable in the eyes of both political scientists and political professionals. One study by Robert Biersack, Paul Herrnson, and Clyde Wilcox found that early fundraising by challengers seeking House seats predicted future fundraising success. In an April 1983 Associated Press article that discussed Reagan's plans to fundraise for Senate elections that were almost eighteen months away, a Republican cited the importance of early fundraising, declaring, "One early dollar is worth $3 at the end."[9]

Fundraising in nonelection years matters for a president's reelection bid as well. In October 2019, Trump's reelection campaign and the RNC had a combined $158 million in cash on hand, thanks in part to Trump's unprecedented early reelection fundraising. One Democratic campaign adviser captured the incumbent's advantage this way: "Trump and the Republicans are bankrolling an enormous amount of money, and they have no competitive primary." Another Democrat concurred, explaining, "There's two separate elections going on, and the really unfortunate part is Trump is the only one involved in the general election today." Fundraising early in an election cycle can provide a president with a significant resource advantage. This is also the case in congressional races, where early fundraising can scare off other potential candidates and decrease the possibility of having to wage a hard-fought campaign. A president's help raising that early money is very much in demand.[10]

The individual year that saw the greatest number of fundraisers was 2000, when Clinton's unrivaled 190 fundraisers during his final year in office included thirty-three that aided first lady Hillary Rodham Clinton's unprecedented run for the US Senate. The second-highest number of fundraisers came as Obama sought reelection in 2012. Every one of Obama's 153 fundraisers that year benefited the Obama Victory Fund, a joint fundraising committee that divided its proceeds among Obama's reelection campaign, the Democratic National Committee (DNC), and a number of Democratic state parties. The year with the third-greatest number of presidential fundraisers was 1996, Clinton's reelection year. Two-thirds of his 118 fundraisers that year aided the DNC, which provided much financial support for Clinton's bid for a second term, while just five benefited his own campaign committee due to the limits on fundraising that were a condition of the public funding program, as will be discussed in chapter 2.

While the years with the greatest numbers of fundraisers draw the eye, the key takeaway from Figure 1.1 is that fundraising has become a regular enterprise for the presidents who have been elected since the advent of the modern campaign finance system in the 1970s. While there have been occasional extended hiatuses from presidents' personal involvement in fundraising due to various crises—such as the capture of American hostages in Iran in late 1979, the terrorist attacks on September 11, 2001, and the outbreak of the COVID-19 pandemic in 2020—fundraising has become a frequently used element of presidential leadership. And while fundraising for a president's own reelection bid has tended to draw the most media attention, presidents have spent even more time raising campaign funds for their fellow party members. Of the 2,190 fundraising events that presidents collectively participated in from 1977 through 2020, just over a quarter supported their reelection campaign committee or their party's national committee in the president's third or fourth years in office, when the national parties focus much of their energy on aiding a president's bid for another term. Almost three-quarters of all presidential fundraisers supported others' elections bids, as presidents served as the electoral leader of their party, regularly assuming the role of the fundraiser in chief.

THE DEMAND FOR PRESIDENTIAL FUNDRAISING

Presidents seeking to exercise leadership are frustrated on many fronts. The public expects presidents to be heroic leaders who can bend the arc of history. But a fragmented constitutional system replete with veto points and an international scene where coordination is difficult and the costs of action can be high make it difficult for a president to enact much of his agenda. There is one important activity, however, at which presidents tend to excel, and which helps presidents to achieve their other goals—raising campaign cash. The president, in good political times and bad, is the single biggest fundraising draw in American politics.

Presidential fundraising is an arrow in a party's quiver, and the party that doesn't hold the White House has no figure who is able to serve as a comparable fundraising draw. "Getting the president of the United States brings you more money than any other political fundraiser," declared Amy Walter of the Cook Political Report. RNC chair Michael Steele described the challenge of fundraising for his party without the help of a sitting president during the initial portion of Obama's presidency as "hard has hell. It's just a heck of a lot easier when you've got a president sitting down the hill from you to help with [raising money]." A spokesperson for the NRCC in 2013 concurred, explaining, "Any time you have the presidency as a political party, that's just something the other party can't match. And the same was true a few years ago when Republicans had the presidency." Indeed, after Republicans reclaimed the White House following Trump's 2017 inauguration, an Associated Press article declared, "Trump's fundraising prowess is the engine of the Republican National Committee and a lifeline for every Republican planning to rely on the party for financial help during next year's congressional races."[11]

Even unpopular presidents are in substantial demand as fundraisers. In September 1994, Clinton traveled to Minnesota to raise money for that state's Democratic nominee for a US Senate seat. An aide to that Senate candidate, when asked whether the relatively unpopular president's visit would help or hurt the campaign, replied, "I doubt he's much of a help, nor does he do any harm, but he helps raise money and that's what we need."[12] Twelve years later, when the unpopular president living in the White House was a Republican, a 2006 *Los Angeles Times* headline declared, "Bush Still a Fundraising Magnet for GOP Donors" and summarized his situation this way:

> President Bush's approval rating has been no higher than the low 40s for four months. Independents have been running from him for a year. Conservatives, angered by his failed nomination of Harriet E. Miers to the Supreme Court, are now steaming over his administration's decision to let a company based in Dubai operate port facilities in six American cities. And on Thursday, with speedy stops in Indiana and Ohio, he helped raise more than $1.6 million for Republican campaigns. No one gathers political money quite like the president of the United States. Any president of the United States. And Bush's political allies are taking advantage of his ability to turn out the most loyal Republicans, despite the controversies that swirl about him, Vice President Dick Cheney and issues such as the war in Iraq.[13]

Why are all presidents, regardless of their popularity, highly sought after as fundraising draws? The confluence of sharply increasing campaign costs and the contribution limits imposed by campaign finance law combine to produce great demand for presidential fundraising. Figure 1.2 depicts the substantial rise in money spent by all candidates in presidential and congressional elections during presidential election years from 1976 through 2020. The total amounts spent in presidential elections rose steadily from 1976 through 1996. Expenditures then increased more steeply once candidates started opting out of the public funding program and its accompanying spending limits, first in 2000 for the nominating process, and then in 2008 for the general election, as discussed in chapter 2. If expenditures in 1976 had risen at the rate of inflation, candidates would have spent just $491 million in 2016 and $529 million in 2020. Those totals fell far short of the $1.5 billion spent by all candidates in 2016 and the more than $4 billion spent in 2020. Because the data include spending by all presidential candidates, not just the parties' eventual nominees, the total for 2020 includes the billion dollars spent by Mike Bloomberg in his failed bid for the Democratic presidential nomination.[14] Even before the sharp rise in money spent in 2020, the increase in spending had been substantial.

When presidents fundraise for their own reelection bids, they worry about being outspent by their competitors—both the occasional candidates who self-fund their campaigns, like Bloomberg in 2020, and candidates who can raise substantial amounts of money from others. Presidents have both responded to and contributed to the increasing costs of campaigning as they have spent increasingly substantial amounts of time on reelection fundraising.

Similarly, total spending by congressional candidates has risen at a rate far greater than inflation as well. If the $115 million spent in 1976 by all candidates had increased at the rate of inflation, candidates would have spent $479 million in 2016 and $516 million in 2020. The actual totals in those years were almost $1.6 billion

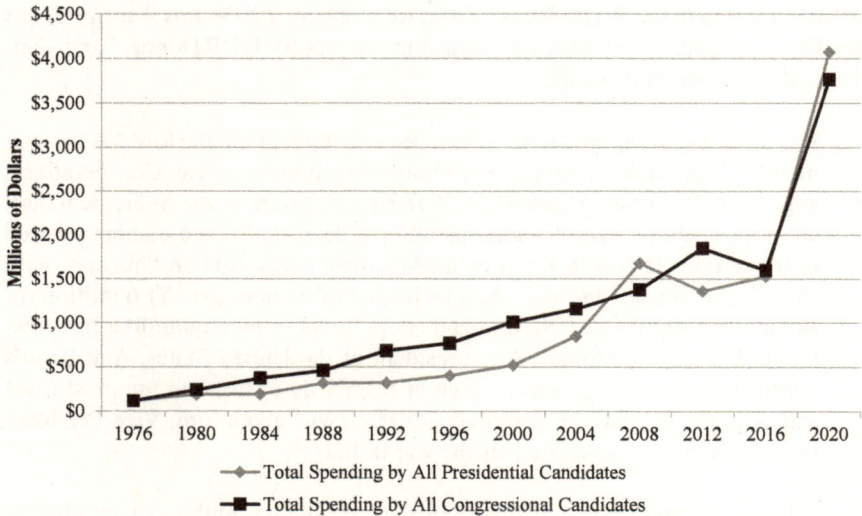

Figure 1.2: Total Candidate Spending in Presidential and Congressional Elections during Presidential Election Cycles, 1976–2020
Sources: Nelson W. Polsby, Aaron B. Wildavsky, Steven E. Schier, and David A. Hopkins, Presidential Elections: Strategies and Structures of American Politics, 15th ed. (Rowman & Littlefield, 2019), 50; Federal Election Commission, "Statistical Summary of 24-Month Campaign Activity of the 2019–2020 Election Cycle," April 2, 2021, https://www.fec.gov/updates/statistical-summary-24-month-campaign-activity-2019–2020-election-cycle/.

and more than $3.7 billion, respectively. These congressional campaign expenditure totals can vary from year to year depending on a number of factors, including how many seats are competitive, and thus see contested campaigns and substantial spending. The specific states that hold Senate elections in a given year matter as well, since it costs more money to run an effective statewide campaign in populous states like California, Texas, and Florida than it does in states with fewer voters and smaller media markets such as South Dakota, Vermont, and Wyoming. But regardless of variation from year to year, the clear trend over time has been a dramatic increase in the aggregate amounts of money spent in congressional contests.

What do these increased totals mean for individual House and Senate candidates? The inflation-adjusted mean expenditure of a House candidate rose from almost $272,000 in 1974 to almost $1.7 million in 2018. The mean expenditure for a Senate candidate increased from close to $2 million in 1974 to more than $12 million in 2018.[15] These averages include the totals spent in many noncompetitive contests; the amounts spent in hotly contested races can be much higher. Since all 435 House seats along with thirty-three or thirty-four Senate seats are on the ballot every two years, a large number of congressional candidates spend much time raising substantial amounts of money in every election cycle.

Candidates for federal office must raise these increasing amounts of campaign funds in the increments in the low thousands mandated by campaign finance law. From 1974 through 2002, the maximum contribution an individual could make to a congressional or presidential campaign was $1,000 for a nominating contest and another $1,000 for a general election. This amount was raised to $2,000 per election and mandated to rise with inflation by the Bipartisan Campaign Reform Act of 2002 (BCRA), which was more commonly known as the McCain-Feingold law, after its two principal sponsors in the US Senate, Arizona Republican John McCain and Wisconsin Democrat Russell Feingold. By 2020, the individual contribution limit had risen to $2,800 per election.[16]

Raising millions of dollars in campaign funds in the increments in the low thousands required by campaign finance law takes a great deal of time, as candidates and office holders must reach out to a large number of contributors for financial support. Ernest "Fritz" Hollings described in his Senate farewell speech how these dynamics played out in the 1990s:

> The main culprit, the cancer on the body politic, is money: Money, money, money. When I ran 6 years ago, in 1998, I raised $8.5 million. That $8.5 million is $30,000 a week, every week, for 6 years. If you miss Christmas week, you miss New Year's week, you are $100,000 in the hole and don't you think we don't know it and we start to work harder at raising money.[17]

When a House or Senate candidate gets fundraising help from the president, that can go a long way toward alleviating those pressures. On March 12, 1998, Clinton did this for Hollings, who was facing a competitive race for reelection that fall, when the president headlined a fundraising dinner for the senator at a private home in Washington, DC, with about fifty paying guests in attendance.[18]

These fundraising pressures have only increased in recent decades. Reporting in 2013 indicated that newly elected members of Congress had been advised that they should devote four hours per day to raising money, either in person at fundraising events or by phoning potential donors in sessions that are known as call time. Party leaders closely monitor members' fundraising progress. This pressure leads some members to hold their first reelection fundraiser before they are even sworn in for their first term, and many others start soon after they officially become members of Congress.[19] Representative Steve Israel of New York served in the House for sixteen years. In 2016, just after he announced his retirement from Congress, he calculated, "I've spent roughly 4,200 hours in call time, attended more than 1,600 fund-raisers just for my own campaign and raised nearly $20 million in increments of $1,000, $2,500 and $5,000 per election cycle."[20] Israel, who chaired the Democratic Congressional Campaign Committee for four years, was thanked by name by Obama at nineteen different fundraising events that appeared on Obama's White House website, attesting to his central role in fundraising for House Democrats.[21]

Similarly, Senator Chris Murphy of Connecticut, who previously served in the House, explained that he had spent four to five hours per day making fundraising calls for his House campaigns. Murphy declared:

Today, more than ever before, the one question you have to ask when you are deciding whether to run for the United States House, the United States Senate is, are you willing to become a telemarketer for 24 months? Are you willing to sit on the phone and ask your friends and, just slightly worse than that, absolute strangers to give you thousands of dollars to run for office?[22]

One anonymous first-term lawmaker in 2013 described the time spent fundraising memorably: "It may not be exactly like the Bataan Death March, but there are some similarities."[23] When Barbara Mikulski decided in early 2015 to retire from the Senate instead of running for another term in 2016, she said that she asked herself how she wanted to spend the last two years of her term. "Do I spend my time raising money, or do I spend my time raising hell?"[24]

Presidential and congressional candidates have felt particular pressure in recent years to spend more time raising money because of the threat posed by groups such as Super PACs that are legally independent from campaigns and parties. These entities can accept contributions in unlimited amounts and then spend that money without notice in any House, Senate, or presidential race. A former chair of the Federal Election Commission attested in 2014 that "candidates increasingly have to focus on the fact that they have the potential to be outspent" by Super PACs. This assessment aligns with the research of Eric Heberlig and Bruce Larson, who found that that Super PACs have "induced incumbents to rachet up their fundraising as a strategic response to this new uncertainty in the electoral environment." Or, as Trump put it in 2015 when talking about US senators, "Most of their life is fundraising."[25]

These dynamics place the fundraising services of the president in great demand. A president, regardless of his popularity, is his party's most potent fundraiser. The president's role as party leader is an extra-constitutional one. Political parties are not mentioned in the Constitution, and in *The Federalist Papers*, James Madison contended that our constitutional system's institutional structure would minimize the problematic elements that stem from political factions.[26] But parties emerged early in the history of the new republic, with presidents at their head. Politics is a team sport, and presidents serve as captain of their team.

As campaign costs have grown in recent decades and as the pressure to raise funds has increased tremendously, a president's financial help has become all the more important. In 2013 White House deputy press secretary Josh Earnest declared, "I think the most tangible way that an incumbent president of either party, frankly, can benefit his party's prospects in congressional races is to try to help them raise money."[27] Clinton adviser Harold Ickes sounded a similar note in the months before the 1998 midterm elections. "The basic thing the president can do is raise money, and that's what this guy is doing."[28] Later that year, Michigan state attorney general Jennifer Granholm introduced the president at a state party fundraiser by sharing a top-ten list that included praise for Clinton's commitment to raising "Mo' money. Mo' money. Mo' money."[29] She colloquially captured a frequent dynamic for presidents in the modern campaign finance era who have embraced their role as their party's fundraiser in chief.

STUDYING FUNDRAISING THROUGH THE LENS OF THE PRESIDENT'S TIME

Most studies of campaign fundraising have drawn on data from the Federal Election Commission on donations to and expenditures by candidates' campaign committees, political parties, political action committees, and other political entities. A number of enlightening books by scholars such as Herbert Alexander, Anthony Corrado, David Magleby, and Michael Malbin have examined campaign finance issues in various specific election cycles.[30] Other studies have examined the characteristics of political donors, the political and constitutional issues related to campaign finance reform efforts, and the ways in which campaign finance rules affect both who chooses to run for office and the dynamics of partisan polarization that result from those choices.[31] All of these studies have shed important light on the issue of money in politics. Rather than approaching fundraising dynamics by examining the donors who give to a campaign or party, the total amount contributed, or the constitutional issues related to money in politics, this book focuses on the extent to which a president devotes his limited time to the pursuit of campaign funds. Presidents and their aides know that there are more demands on a president's time than can be accommodated, and they must carefully weigh how much time a president should devote to fundraising and other campaign efforts, meeting with advisers at the White House, negotiating with members of Congress, interacting with foreign leaders, and more.

A number of senior Democratic and Republican White House officials have testified to the importance of the president's time. Henry Kissinger described, "One of the most important challenges of modern government: to husband the President's time—his most precious commodity."[32] Jimmy Carter sounded a similar note, asserting, "In the life of a president, it's necessary to establish priorities, because the demands on one's time and one's attention are very severe."[33] More recent officials have made the same case. Josh Bolten, who served as White House chief of staff to George W. Bush, declared, "The most valuable asset in any White House is not money, it's the president's time." Another Bush aide explained, "There are so many claims on the president's time. They will come from policy people, the legislative people, the national security people, the public diplomacy people, Congress, agencies . . . everybody wants a piece of the president's time."[34] Indeed, in George W. Bush's administration, the White House schedule was planned in five-minute blocks, highlighting the importance of strategic decisions about the president's time.[35] Clinton chief of staff Mack McLarty crystalized why the allocation of the president's time matters. "The president's time is, in many ways, his most valuable commodity because it's finite. It reflects his priorities. It reflects what he's trying to get done with the country."[36]

This is a study of presidential resource allocation strategy: how much of their scarce time presidents devote to fundraising, for whom they do it, what priorities are illuminated by their efforts, how their fundraising strategies relate to the evolving campaign finance landscape, under what circumstances they fundraise behind closed doors, and the resulting implications for presidential leadership and the American political system. In order to understand more clearly how modern presidents exercise leadership, it is important to analyze how they use this scarce resource. All presidents must make difficult choices about how to allocate their time. These decisions reveal a great deal about their priorities, and recent presidents have increasingly prioritized fundraising as an instrument of presidential leadership.

Although presidents attending fundraising events is only part of the constellation of campaign fundraising efforts, it is a vital element. Fundraising efforts by surrogates such as the vice president or the first lady, through direct mail, and, in recent elections, via the internet do not involve commitments of presidential time. But these efforts, while important, only go so far, and the president's direct involvement is unique. Presidents have particular appeal to high-dollar donors, those who can write the most substantial checks to a campaign, political party, or other political entity. Mike McCurry, who served as White House press secretary during Clinton's reelection bid, explained the essential role of the president in reelection fundraising. "Frankly he had to put a lot of time into it. The single best ingredient you've got [in fundraising] is face time with the president, the picture, the personal note."[37] But presidents who spend substantial time fundraising from large donors spark concerns about the influence of money in the American political system and a host of other controversies, which are discussed in detail in chapter 6.

This book is one of the relatively few studies that examine this important but underexamined element of modern presidential leadership. It does so more comprehensively and with an unprecedented amount of data about the extent to which presidents devote themselves to fundraising. Several illuminating studies have analyzed presidential fundraising efforts only in the months immediately preceding an election, just in the election year itself, or only in specific election cycles but have not systematically examined all presidential fundraising efforts. Additionally, most previous studies relied only upon the record of presidential fundraising in the *Public Papers of the Presidents of the United States*, which does not include events that are not open to the media and thus omitted important presidential activity.

The most prominent study of the president's fundraising efforts is Jeffrey Cohen et al.'s 1991 article in the *American Political Science Review*, which analyzed presidential campaign appearances, including both rallies and fundraisers, in midterm Senate elections from 1966 through 1986.[38] That study focused only on the traditional campaign season from Labor Day through Election Day, a practice that captures many campaign rallies but misses the majority of presidential party fundraising, which takes place throughout a two-year election cycle. Similarly, both Matthew Hoddie and Stephen Routh's and Matthew Lang et al.'s studies of campaigning and fundraising in midterm elections covered just the period from August 1 of the election year onward.[39] Matthew Eshbaugh-Soha and Sean Nicholson-Crotty focused their analysis of presidential midterm campaign efforts from 1994 through 2006 on the time from June 1 until Election Day, while Rob Mellen and Kathleen Searles in two different studies examined presidential campaign efforts in midterm House races throughout the entirety of the election year, but not during the previous year.[40] The most comprehensive effort along these lines is Michael Julius's book analyzing presidential campaigning and fundraising from the start of the year through Election Day in every midterm election year from 1954 through 2014.[41]

All of these studies shed valuable light on the president's fundraising, but none provides a complete picture of these efforts. Figure 1.1 makes clear that a full understanding of a president's fundraising efforts requires examination of activities throughout his term in office, not just in the months or year closest to the election, since presidents fundraise throughout their four or eight years in office. While several studies have employed this more complete view of fundraising efforts, one by Patrick Sellers and Laura Denton relied solely on the *Public Papers of the Presidents of the United States* and thus did not examine many presidential fundraisers that are closed to the media.[42] Two others drew upon data from journalist Mark Knoller that included closed-press fundraisers, but each covered only a single election cycle—1999–2000 for Gary Jacobson et al.'s study of Clinton's fundraising in his final two years in office, and 2001–2002 for Paul Herrnson and Irwin Morris's examination of George W. Bush's efforts on behalf of candidates in House races.[43]

Two broader studies have attempted to address fundraising efforts throughout a president's term in office. Daniel Galvin did so in a qualitative manner as part of his sweeping study of the efforts of presidents from Eisenhower through George W. Bush to build their party's organizational capacity.[44] And I analyzed the contours of presidential fundraising in two chapters of my previous book, *The Rise of the President's Permanent Campaign*, which examined the ways in which presidents handle electoral concerns throughout their terms in office.[45] This book builds on unanswered questions from that work and draws upon a unique and newly expanded data set of presidential fundraising events in every year of a president's term in order to tackle questions about the ways in which our nation's chief executives have used fundraising as a tool of modern presidential leadership.

This study begins with Carter, as he was the first president to be elected during the evolving campaign finance regime established by the Federal Election Campaign Act of 1974 (FECA). Carter and his successors all made strategic choices that took into account the restrictions, requirements, and incentives established by FECA and thus operated within a common, though evolving, institutional environment. The forty-four-year period from 1977 through 2020 includes four Republican presidents—Reagan, both Presidents Bush, and Trump—who collectively held the White House for twenty-four years, and three Democratic presidents—Carter, Clinton, and Obama, who served as president for twenty years of this study. The data set includes political fundraisers for the benefit of candidates, party organizations, and political action committees (PACs), including both traditional PACs and Super PACs. Understanding the ways in which presidents have allocated their scarce time to fundraise sheds new light on this important aspect of modern presidential leadership.

THE MANY FORMS OF A PRESIDENTIAL FUNDRAISER

There are many varieties of presidential fundraising events. Presidents raise campaign cash for themselves and their fellow party members in intimate sessions with relatively few high-dollar donors and in gala events with thousands of attendees. They take place in hotel ballrooms, at the homes of wealthy supporters, in upscale restaurants, in sports arenas, outdoors under tents, and in Broadway theaters. They occur minutes from the White House and all across the country. Twenty-two percent of the 2,190 presidential fundraising events from 1977 through 2020 took place in Washington, DC, itself. Many of those were held in hotels near the White House. In 2012 Barack Obama attended dozens of fundraisers at DC hotels such as the Jefferson, the W, and the Mandarin Oriental.[46] Trump's preferred destination for DC fundraisers was his own hotel on Pennsylvania Avenue.

Presidents also headline fundraising events in much larger venues that can accommodate many more people. In April 1987 Ronald Reagan was the featured speaker at the annual joint House-Senate fundraising dinner. Close to 3,800 Republican donors gathered at the Washington Convention Center to hear a series of Republican speakers and watch a "light show, which also flashed green outlines of the Statue of Liberty, the Liberty Bell, and other scenes of Americana to the accompaniment of 'America' and 'Proud to Be an American.'" Tickets to the black-tie dinner cost $1,500 apiece, and the menu included "salmon florentine, filet mignon, Chocolate Decadence cake and a 1982 Chateau Ste. Michelle chardonnay." During his speech, Reagan alluded to the inflation that had slowed during his presidency when he told the assembled donors, "You should take gratification in knowing that if it weren't for us [Republicans], what we're paying tonight might be the normal price for dinner." The event raised $6.5 million, which at the time made it the most profitable fundraising event on record.[47]

Thirteen years later, Bill Clinton helped the DNC raise even more money from a larger number of people at a Washington, DC, event with an intentionally different feel. At the sold-out MCI Center, home to the city's NBA and NHL teams, donors got to watch performances by Stevie Wonder, Lenny Kravitz, and Robin Williams, in addition to speeches by Clinton and Vice President Al Gore, who was running to succeed Clinton in the White House. To contrast the event with the black-tie fundraisers often held by both parties, the Democrats chose a more casual theme. DNC spokesperson Jenny Backus said, "You're not going to see goat cheese here. You're going to see good old-fashioned blue jeans, cowboy boots and barbecue." Indeed, both Clinton and Gore wore blue jeans and boots that night. Donors contributed or raised from others between $50 and $500,000 to attend, and the event brought in more than $23 million, setting a new record for the most lucrative fundraising event.[48]

Presidents also fundraise with relatively small numbers of people in private homes near the White House. A 1996 *Washington Post* article declared, "One axiom of [the] fund-raising business is that the size of the check is in inverse proportion to the size of the room."[49] In 1999 a spokesperson for Gore explained, "We wanted to have just 25 in each dinner because the more you get into a room, the less intimate it becomes."[50] In 1998 Clinton took part in a fundraiser for California Senator Barbara Boxer hosted by Smith and Elizabeth Bagley, who had inherited part of the R. J. Reynolds Tobacco Company fortune. Clinton joked about how often he'd attended events at their home in the Georgetown neighborhood of Washington, DC, saying, "First of all, I want to thank Smith and Elizabeth. I'm going to have to start paying a portion of the property tax on this home if I come here many more times this year."[51]

Presidential fundraisers often take place in beautiful homes located in elite enclaves around the country as well, including Martha's Vineyard, New York City, the Hamptons, Palm Beach, and San Francisco. For example, in May 2012 Obama took part in a fundraiser at the Los Angeles home of actor George Clooney, where attendees paid $40,000 apiece. Famous guests at the event, which raised about $15 million, included Barbra Streisand, Tobey Maguire, Robert Downey Jr., and Jeffrey Katzenberg. In February 2020 Trump headlined a fundraiser at the home of billionaire Oracle founder Larry Ellison in Rancho Mirage, California. Guests paid between $100,000 and $250,000 per couple for an event that included a photo with Trump, a round of golf on Ellison's private course, and, for the higher-dollar donors, a roundtable with the president.[52]

These events in the homes of the wealthiest of the wealthy can lead to criticism and charges of hypocrisy. In October 2014 Obama took part in two DNC fundraisers in New York City with two billionaires, then traveled by helicopter from Manhattan to the Greenwich Polo Club in suburban Connecticut. From there, he went to a fundraiser for Senate Democrats at the home of another billionaire named Rich Richman. On that same day, House Democrats sent out a fundraising email under Obama's name arguing, "If Republicans win, we know who they'll be fighting for. Once again, the interests of billionaires will come before the needs of the middle class." The *New York Post* story covering Obama's fundraising that day noted the clashing interests. The headline read: "Obama slams billionaires at the home of a guy named Rich Richman."[53]

Not all fundraisers are so glamorous. On July 21, 1980, Carter took part in an outdoor fundraiser under a tent in Kentucky followed by two in Texas—first, a low-dollar event in a train station that was intended to draw a large crowd and register new voters; then a more exclusive high-dollar fundraiser at the home of a wealthy supporter of the Democratic Party. The Associated Press offered the following description of these three events in an article headlined "With Carter Fundraisers, What You Get Is What You Pay For":

> For $10, you get to stand up for more than three hours in a shoulder-to-shoulder crowd waiting for the president of the United States to promise "peace through strength" and recite the concerns of his "party of compassion." If you can fight your way through the mob, you can buy a plate of cheese nachos with hot peppers and refried beans for another $1.50. But at least it's air conditioned. For $500, you get to stand in stifling heat under a yellow-and-white-striped carny tent, eat Kentucky-style barbeque and fresh corn and hear the president of the United States boast about his party of compassion and promise to try and keep the peace. And for $2,500, you get a buffet dinner of salmon mousse with dill dressing, hot crab souffle over toast, molded chicken tureen and a variety of hors d'oeuvres served on a flagstone terrace surrounding the pool outside a Texas mansion. And you can hear the president of the United States talk about a compassionate party committed to the needs of its people. It was all in a day's fundraising for President Carter, who ran through his litany three times at separate political events Monday to help the national and state Democratic parties net an estimated $700,000 for the upcoming fall campaign.[54]

The five reelection fundraisers Obama took part in on March 16, 2012, further illustrate the variety of these events. The first two events were held at the Palmer House Hilton hotel in Chicago. Obama spoke to 600 donors who had given at least $2,500 each before addressing a smaller gathering of sixty people who had contributed at least $10,000 to his reelection campaign and the DNC. Obama then flew to Atlanta, Georgia, for three more reelection fundraisers. The first was at a private home. The second was at actor Tyler Perry's television studio, where attendees paid just $250—part of the Gen44 program aimed at involving younger voters in Obama's reelection campaign. The day ended with a high-dollar fundraiser at Perry's home where the forty guests, including Oprah Winfrey, had each donated $35,800. The Republican National Committee was quick to criticize Obama, saying that his events "resemble a movie theatre schedule: 1:20, 2:35, 6:35, 8:25, & 9:20. More evidence that the president is in full campaign mode." Obama's five fundraising events that day raised more than $4.5 million for his reelection campaign and the DNC.[55]

Presidential fundraisers sometimes take a creative approach. In 1998 Clinton took part in a New York City fundraiser in a Broadway theater, where guests watched a special performance of the hit play *The Lion King* and heard from the president. Reagan appeared at multiple fundraisers with celebrities, including a 1982 event with Marie Osmond and another in 1983 with Tammy Wynette. George H. W. Bush took part in a 1992 fundraiser at the Burbank, California, estate of entertainer Bob Hope. In 2015 Democrats held a New York City fundraiser at a special performance of the Broadway musical *Hamilton*, and Obama spoke at the conclusion of the show. While a president was the headliner of each of these events, offering such additional attractions for donors can make for memorable and profitable political fundraisers.

In 2020 virtual fundraising via Zoom became popular with many candidates during the COVID-19 pandemic. On July 21, 2020, Trump took part in a virtual fundraiser that brought in $20 million for the Trump Victory joint fundraising committee, which benefited Trump's reelection campaign committee, the RNC, and numerous state parties. Democratic presidential nominee Joe Biden participated in many Zoom fundraisers in 2020. One news account described the appeal of these events to Biden's team. "These virtual events typically took less than 90 minutes of the candidate's time, could raise millions of dollars and cost almost nothing. Mr. Trump has almost entirely refused to hold such fund-raisers. Aides say he doesn't like them." Indeed, the July 2020 virtual fundraiser was the only such event that Trump took part in. He reportedly preferred in-person events, particularly those held at his own properties in Palm Beach and Miami, Florida; Bedminster, New Jersey; Washington, DC; and elsewhere.[56]

Although presidential fundraisers can take place in a variety of venues near the White House or in far-flung locales, one commonality is that the amount raised is only shared with the public if the organizers choose to disclose it. Federal campaign finance laws require detailed reporting of the identity of contributors and the amounts of donations to campaigns and political parties. But there is no reporting of whether the money was raised at an in-person fundraiser, in response to a direct mail fundraising appeal, online, or in some other manner. Campaign staff sometimes proudly tout the money raised at a specific fundraising event, but the amount raised is often difficult to ascertain, especially when attempting to do so years or decades after a fundraiser took place. Even when organizers do not disclose how much money a certain event raised, a president's decision to take part in a fundraiser for a particular beneficiary is a signal of that president's strategic fundraising priorities.

OUTLINE OF THE BOOK

Presidents are goal-oriented actors who seek to make circumstances more favorable for and receptive to their leadership. This book sets out to offer a systematic examination of fundraising as an important yet understudied tool of modern presidential leadership in the more than forty years since the establishment of the modern campaign finance system in the 1970s.

In chapter 2 I examine the escalation and complication of presidential fundraising. The chapter first focuses on reelection fundraising efforts by every president from Carter through Trump to highlight the increasing amounts of time that presidents have dedicated to seeking funds for their reelection bids. I then situate these trends in the context of the changing campaign finance landscape and analyze the emergence of groups such as Super PACs, as well as the increasing prevalence of complicated joint fundraising committees that presidents and their parties have created to work around the limits on contributions imposed by campaign finance laws. These developments highlight the tension between lower-dollar fundraising, which can take more of a president's scarce time, and higher-dollar fundraising, which can be less time-consuming but sparks more concerns about potential corruption.

In chapter 3 I analyze the nationalization of presidential fundraising. The chapter presents evidence about the relative increase in presidential fundraising for national beneficiaries and the corresponding decrease in fundraisers held for state parties and solely for individual beneficiaries. I also examine a geographic component of nationalized fundraising—the rise of ATM states. These are places where presidents travel to fundraise for out-of-state beneficiaries rather than local candidates and party committees. I advance an argument about the ways in which specific evolving campaign finance rules account for these dynamics and discuss the implications of nationalized fundraising.

Chapter 4 offers a panoramic assessment of the fundraising priorities and strategies of the seven presidents from Carter through Trump. It begins by highlighting the divergent fundraising patterns when a president is seeking another term and when a president is not on the ballot. I then analyze the relative priorities that presidents have placed on fundraising for Senate races, House contests, campaigns for governors' seats, and other parts of their party. The chapter also investigates the extent to which presidential fundraising is defensive—trying to aid incumbents and candidates running for open seats previously held by the president's party—and offensive—helping challengers to incumbents of the other party and candidates seeking open seats that had been vacated by the other party.

Chapter 5 focuses on fundraising transparency by analyzing when and under what circumstances presidents exclude the media from their fundraising events. I contend that fundraising behind closed doors can be a form of hidden-hand leadership that allows presidents and their fellow party members to reap the financial benefits of a president's fundraising prowess while avoiding some of the potential political costs. I also discuss the ways in which presidential popularity and media pressure for increased transparency often but not always play into the dynamics of limiting press access to fundraisers.

Finally, in chapter 6 I examine many controversies that are sparked by presidential fundraising practices and consider the future prospects for the president's role as fundraiser in chief. I argue that changes in the campaign finance landscape and strategic responses to those changes by presidents and their fellow party members have led to numerous unintended consequences. What has resulted is a disjointed campaign finance system that is far removed from the aims of campaign finance reform efforts. In this system, Super PACs raise funds in unrestricted amounts, presidents and their parties work to circumvent contribution limits, and the appearance of corruption abounds.

For those readers who are eager for further understanding of the intricacies of presidential fundraising, the appendix discusses the sources examined and the principal factors considered as I constructed the record of presidential fundraising that underpins the analysis in this book.

2

Escalation and Complication

"I believe in raising money. I believe people ought to contribute."

—Bill Clinton, September 25, 2000

"Trump to headline a $580,600-per-couple fundraiser, the most expensive of his reelection bid."

—*Washington Post* headline, February 13, 2020

On May 29, 1980, Jimmy Carter headlined his first two fundraisers for his reelection campaign. First, donors paid $250 to attend a lunch event with the president in Columbus, Ohio. Carter then traveled to Cleveland, where the price of admission to the evening fundraiser was $150 per person.[1] Carter took part in a total of six fundraisers for his reelection campaign, as well as thirty-one for the Democratic National Committee (DNC) during the third and fourth years of his term, for a total of just thirty-seven such fundraisers that directly or indirectly benefited his efforts to win a second term in the White House. The decades since Carter's limited involvement in low-dollar fundraising for his reelection campaign have ushered in substantial changes in the campaign finance legal landscape and an accompanying transformation of presidential fundraising from an occasional enterprise into a vital and frequently used instrument of presidential leadership.

When Barack Obama held his 220th and final fundraiser for his reelection campaign committee on October 11, 2012, in Miami, Florida, tickets for the star-studded event featuring actress Eva Longoria and singer Sheila E. ranged from $500 to $40,000 per person.[2] Most prior presidents had primarily held separate fundraising events for their own reelection campaign committee and their national committee, but Obama integrated his fundraising efforts for both entities from the beginning of his reelection bid. The proceeds from every fundraiser for his reelection campaign went to a legal entity called the Obama Victory Fund (OVF). This joint fundraising committee initially benefited both Obama's reelection campaign and the DNC, and it was later expanded to include multiple Democratic state parties as well. Additionally, Obama headlined three other fundraisers in his third year in office for just the DNC. These 223 events that benefited his reelection campaign directly or indirectly far outpaced the similar efforts of his five immediate predecessors.

Donald Trump succeeded Obama in the White House and began his reelection fundraising far earlier in his term than had his predecessor. Obama declared his candidacy for a second term and began his record-setting efforts to raise money for his reelection bid in April of his third year in office. This marked the earliest start of a president's reelection fundraising in the modern campaign finance era. That record did not stand for long, however, as Trump filed the paperwork to establish his reelection campaign committee on January 20, 2017, the day he took office. He then headlined his first reelection campaign committee fundraiser on June 28 of his first year in the White House, just over five months into his presidency. No other president in the modern campaign finance regime in place since the 1970s took part in fundraising events for his reelection bid in his first two years in office. Tickets for Trump's kickoff reelection fundraising event in 2017 cost $35,000 apiece, and the dinner raised an estimated $10 million.[3] The price of admission for Trump's reelection fundraising events would go much higher; in 2020, he headlined multiple fundraisers where the price of admission was $293,300 per person.[4]

This dramatic escalation in the frequency, the price of admission, and the initiation of presidential fundraising efforts has been accompanied by increasing complication as well. In 2012, the first presidential election during the Super PAC era, the first $5,000 of a contribution from an individual at an OVF fundraising event went to the Obama campaign itself. At the time, the maximum legal individual contribution to a campaign was $2,500 for the nominating contest and another $2,500 for the general election. The DNC received any additional amount up to $30,800, which was the maximum legal contribution per year by an individual to a national political party committee. At some events where donors gave more than $35,800, the additional money was then directed to state parties that would use it to help Obama's reelection effort and other Democratic candidates for office. At some events, the price of admission was $75,800; in those cases, the $40,000 above the amount that benefited the reelection campaign committee and the DNC was divided, with $10,000 going to each of four state party organizations in key Electoral College battleground states.[5]

By the time of Trump's presidency, campaign finance had become even more high-dollar and complex. A 2014 Supreme Court decision removed the aggregate limits on an individual's donations to federal candidates and party committees during a particular election cycle. Additionally, congressional action that same year allowed parties to raise substantially larger sums of money for their national conventions, legal costs, and expenses related to their party headquarters building. These changes led candidates and parties to establish complicated joint fundraising committees. Both Democrats and Republicans set up committees that included different combinations of national and state party committee accounts, allowing them to raise money in far greater increments.[6]

While federal law during the 2016 election cycle limited a donor's contributions to a presidential campaign to just $2,700 for the nominating contest and another $2,700 for the general election, complicated joint fundraising committees enabled numerous party committees to benefit from much larger contributions. Obama headlined multiple fundraising events that year for the Democrats' Hillary Victory Fund, which benefited the campaign of Democratic presidential nominee Hillary Clinton, the DNC, and thirty-eight state party committees.[7] Republicans in 2016 opted for a fund named Trump Victory that benefited the Trump campaign, the Republican National Committee (RNC), and twenty-one state parties.[8] The maximum contributions to these joint committees shifted throughout the election cycle, as each was reorganized multiple times to change which specific state and national party committees were beneficiaries, but reporting in June 2016 indicated that the Hillary Victory Fund could accept contributions up to $358,800 whereas an individual could donate up to $449,400 to the Trump Victory committee.[9]

In the 2020 election cycle, both the Republican and Democratic nominees for the presidency again utilized complicated joint fundraising committees. The Trump Victory committee was reorganized in March 2017 so that it benefited both Trump's reelection campaign and the RNC, but no state parties, during the early portion of Trump's presidency.[10] In January 2020 the committee was expanded so that its funds were allocated to the Trump campaign, the RNC, and twenty-two state Republican parties. In September 2020 the committee was restructured again so that it would benefit the campaign, the RNC, and forty-six state parties.[11] Trump participated in multiple fundraisers in 2020 where the price of admission per couple was $580,600, or $290,300 per person. That amount was more than fifty times the $5,600 that an individual could legally contribute to the Trump campaign itself for both the nomination and general election campaigns in the 2020 election cycle.[12]

These complicated legal entities enable presidential campaigns and political parties to raise campaign funds in amounts far greater than the contribution limits mandated by law. While there are limits on how much an individual can contribute to a campaign, a national party, and a state party, there are no limits on the amounts of money that a state party can transfer to a national party or vice versa.[13] A 2016 study by the Center for Public Integrity described what it called a "shell game," as state parties regularly transferred the money received through these complicated joint fundraising committees to a national party committee. An official at the Campaign Legal Center described the practice as "effectively a form of legalized money laundering."[14] In 1976 the Supreme Court asserted in *Buckley v. Valeo* that limits on the amounts donated to campaigns and parties were justified by the desire to prevent "corruption and the appearance of corruption spawned by the real or imagined coercive influence of large financial contributions on candidates' positions and on their actions if elected to office."[15] The increasing prevalence of complicated legal fundraising entities has allowed presidents to collaborate with political parties to work around and effectively eviscerate the contribution limits that are intended to bind them.

These changing dynamics illustrate that presidential fundraising has evolved a great deal since Jimmy Carter's initial $250 per person reelection fundraising lunch in May of his fourth year in office. The four decades from Carter's reelection bid to Trump's witnessed a revolution in campaign finance dynamics. While the Federal Election Campaign Act of 1974 established the core rules of the current campaign finance system, critical changes since have altered the rules and created a new legal landscape in which organizations not legally affiliated with campaigns and parties—Super PACs and similar groups—are less regulated and thus more empowered to easily raise large sums of money that are used to influence political campaigns. In an era of competitive presidential elections and rising campaign costs, the public funding program has become irrelevant for successful presidential campaigns. As presidents have planned their fundraising strategies, they have responded to the evolving incentives of the campaign finance system.

This chapter analyzes important developments in presidential fundraising that have resulted from the evolving legal campaign finance regime over the past four decades. Presidents have escalated their role in fundraising and partnered with political parties to create complicated legal entities that enable them to receive contributions far in excess of the limits imposed by federal law. A disjointed campaign finance system has resulted that is a far cry from the regime that Congress originally created in the 1970s. These rapidly evolving dynamics have important implications for how the president allocates his scarcest resource—his time—as well as for questions of power, influence, and the appearance of corruption in American politics.

THE ESCALATION OF PRESIDENTIAL FUNDRAISING

The escalation and complication of fundraising by sitting presidents between 1977 and 2020 are both seen quite clearly in presidents' efforts to secure a second term in the White House. Figure 2.1 depicts the number of first-term fundraisers headlined by Presidents Carter through Trump for their reelection campaign committee, as well as fundraisers for the Democratic or Republican National Committee in the third and fourth years of their first term in office. For every president except Trump, all reelection fundraisers also were held in their third or fourth years as president. Trump took part in sixteen reelection fundraisers in his first two years in office, which are included in his total in Figure 2.1.

The first important takeaway is that Obama's efforts were far more substantial than those of his predecessors and successor. He headlined 223 fundraisers for his reelection campaign committee, the DNC, or both in his third and fourth years in office—a number more than twice as great as the president ranking second—Bill Clinton, with 110 such fundraisers. Obama's total was almost two and a half

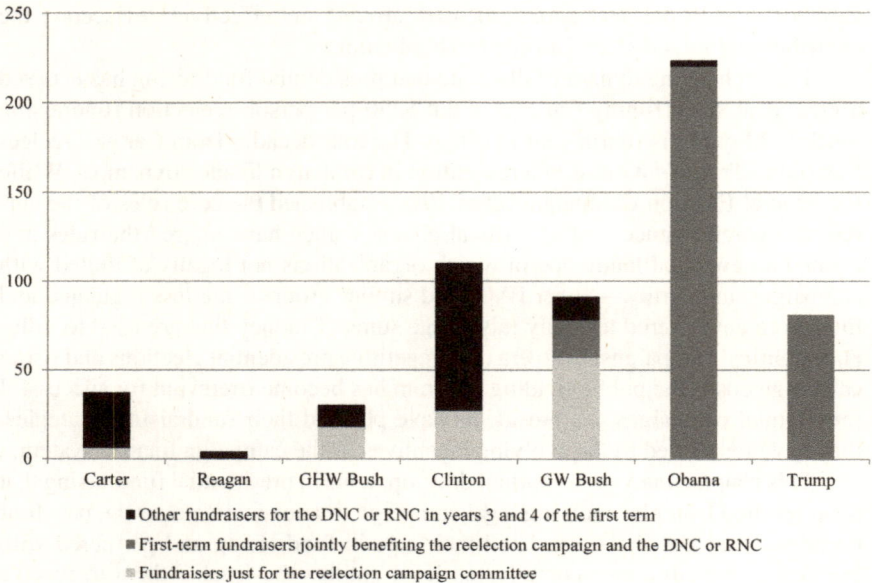

Figure 2.1: Presidential Fundraisers for Their Reelection Committee, and for Their National Committee in Years 3 and 4 of Their First Term, 1979–2020
Sources: Data compiled by the author from the *Public Papers of the Presidents*, the Digests of Other White House Announcements, White House schedules and press briefings, Reagan's personal diary, and Associated Press and other news articles.

times that of George W. Bush, close to three times that of Trump, six times that of Carter, more than seven times that of George H. W. Bush, and almost fifty-six times higher than that of Ronald Reagan.

Focusing primarily on Obama's efforts can obscure the fact that the rise in presidential reelection fundraising played out over the course of multiple presidencies. Jimmy Carter, Ronald Reagan, and George H. W. Bush all spent relatively little time fundraising for their reelection campaign committee and their respective national committee in the third and fourth years in the White House. Carter's total of thirty-seven such fundraisers in 1979 and 1980 was followed by Reagan's four in 1983 and 1984, and then by the first President Bush's thirty such events in 1991 and 1992. Bill Clinton's total of 110 such fundraisers in 1995 and 1996 was more than triple George H. W. Bush's commitment. While George W. Bush's ninety-one such events in 2003 and 2004 did not eclipse Clinton's record, Bush's number exceeded the combined totals of Carter, Reagan, and the first President Bush. Obama's 223 such fundraisers would far outpace the efforts of his five most recent predecessors. Trump's eighty-one such fundraisers didn't approach Obama's record and also trailed Bush's total from sixteen years earlier, in part because of restrictions on in-person fundraising during the COVID-19 pandemic. Additionally, as described in more detail below, the empowerment of complicated joint fundraising committees following a Supreme Court decision and congressional action in 2014 allowed Trump to raise money in larger amounts at fewer events than had his predecessors. This change led to less criticism about fundraising taking too much of a president's time, but more concerns about potential corruption.

Why Include National Committee Fundraising?

While a president's fundraising for his campaign committee is at the heart of his reelection efforts, examining his third and fourth year efforts on behalf of the DNC or RNC yields a more complete picture and enables clearer comparisons across presidencies. Both Obama and Trump held reelection fundraisers that jointly benefited their campaign committee and respective national party committee from the beginning of their reelection bids. In contrast, earlier presidents mostly or always fundraised separately for their campaign committee and then for the DNC or RNC. These party fundraising efforts during their reelection cycle clearly had much to do with advancing their prospects of a second term in the White House.

For example, in 1995 and 1996 Bill Clinton headlined just twenty-seven fundraisers for his reelection committee; twenty-two of these events took place in 1995, the year before the election. Clinton limited his efforts for his own reelection committee because of spending limits that came with participating in the public matching funds program during the nominating contest. The cap on pre-convention spending in the 1996 campaign by candidates who chose to take part in the government's voluntary public funding program was $37.1 million.[16] But Clinton also attended eighty-three additional fundraisers for the DNC in 1995 and 1996. After the Clinton-Gore campaign had raised the maximum amount of money it could legally spend, Clinton turned his attention to helping the DNC further, which used the money to help reelect Clinton and support other down-ballot Democrats. Not all of Clinton's DNC fundraising helped his own campaign, but a great deal of it did, as the DNC used the money to air television issue advertisements and organize get-out-the-vote efforts.[17] While including Clinton's DNC fundraising leads to the consideration of some efforts that benefited his fellow party members, focusing only on Clinton's reelection campaign committee fundraising but not his events for the DNC would miss a substantial portion of his commitment to raise money for his reelection bid.

In 2003 and 2004 George W. Bush exceeded Clinton's fundraising for his reelection campaign committee, but not for his national committee. As the first sitting president to opt out of public matching funds for the nominating contest, Bush was not limited in the amount that he could raise for his reelection campaign committee before his party's national convention, as Clinton had been. Thus, in the third and fourth years of his first term, Bush headlined an unprecedented fifty-seven fundraisers for the Bush-Cheney reelection campaign, as well as twenty-one events that jointly benefited both his reelection campaign committee and the RNC, plus an additional thirteen fundraisers for the RNC. This combined total of ninety-one such fundraisers did not break Clinton's record, but it far surpassed the efforts of Carter, Reagan, and the first President Bush.

National party fundraising has long been an important part of recent presidents' reelection efforts. Some presidents raised funds jointly and simultaneously for both their reelection campaign committee and for their national party, while others raised money for first one and then the other. Because of this, including fundraisers for the DNC and RNC that presidents headlined in their third and fourth years in office facilitates the clearest apples-to-apples comparisons across presidents.

Beginning Reelection Fundraising Increasingly Early

As recent presidents have spent more of their time fundraising for their reelection bid, these efforts have begun earlier and earlier in their terms. Figure 2.2 indicates when each of the seven presidents from Carter to Trump first attended a fundraiser for their reelection campaign committee, as well as how long before Election Day that event took place. The clear takeaway is that successive presidents began raising money for their reelection bid progressively earlier. Carter's reelection fundraising didn't begin until May 1980, but his efforts to raise funds were supposed to kick off in December 1979. After American diplomats were taken hostage in Iran, Carter decided not take part in the fundraisers in late 1979 and in the initial months of 1980. Instead, he asked Vice President Walter Mondale and First Lady Rosalynn Carter to headline what would have been his first reelection fundraising event in early December 1979.[18] Carter, who at first sought to avoid electoral politics during the hostage crisis, would not attend a reelection fundraiser until May 29, 1980, just over five months before Election Day. In spite of this, the planned December 1979 start to fundraising indicates when the campaign believed the president needed to begin his personal efforts to finance his reelection bid.

Reagan's reelection fundraising practices were an anomaly, as I found no record of Reagan headlining a fundraising event to benefit his own reelection campaign committee. As will be explained later in the chapter, Reagan's lack of reelection fundraising was due to the rules of the public funding program, which limited the amount of funds the campaign could raise, and the campaign's success raising money in ways that did not involve the president's personal participation.

Reagan's successor took a different approach. George H. W. Bush's first fundraiser for the Bush-Quayle '92 committee took place on October 31, 1991, just over a year before the 1992 election and a month earlier in his term than the planned start of Carter's fundraising in early December 1979. The next four pres-

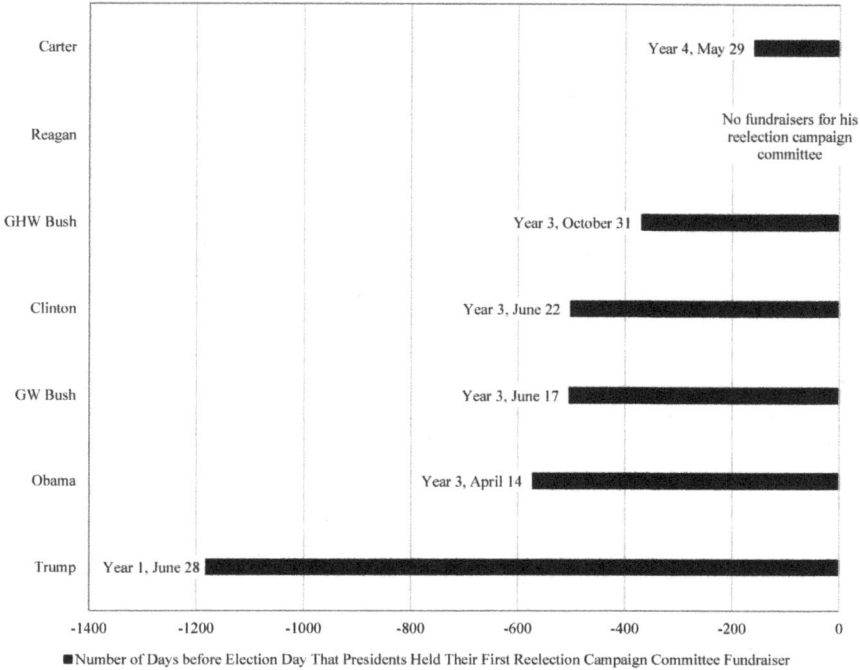

Figure 2.2: Timing of Presidents' First Reelection Campaign Committee Fundraisers
Sources: Data compiled by the author from the *Public Papers of the Presidents*, the Digests of Other White House Announcements, White House schedules and press briefings, Reagan's personal diary, and Associated Press and other news articles.

idents would begin raising money personally for their reelection campaigns even earlier in their terms. Clinton's first fundraiser for the Clinton-Gore campaign committee took place on June 22, 1995, almost a year and a half before the 1996 election, and more than four months earlier in his term than George H. W. Bush's first reelection fundraiser had been. George W. Bush's initial reelection campaign fundraiser was held on June 17, 2003, just a few days earlier than Clinton's start eight years before. And Barack Obama outdid his predecessors' early starts, beginning his reelection fundraising on April 14, 2011, almost a year and seven months before Election Day in 2012.

Trump continued this trend and accelerated it dramatically. After filing the paperwork to establish his reelection campaign committee on January 20, 2017, the day he took office, Trump then took part in his first reelection campaign committee fundraiser on June 28, 2017. The event took place just over five months into his presidency, more than three years and four months before Election Day in 2020. Presidents often hope to amass a substantial campaign war chest early in order to scare off potential primary challengers and build up a financial advantage that they can use against the other party. Trump's early start allowed him to do this to an extent unrivaled by other recent presidents. Federal Election Commission (FEC) filings revealed that the Trump campaign and the RNC had jointly raised more than $127 million during 2017 and 2018.[19] Those totals came at the end of Trump's second year in office—a year and a half after Trump started headlining reelection fundraisers, and more than three months before the point in Obama's term when he had begun his own personal joint reelection fundraising efforts with the DNC.

Presidents had long been hesitant to begin their explicit reelection efforts too early in their term. When Reagan's team filed paperwork in October 1983 establishing his reelection campaign committee, the president himself declared that he still had not decided whether to run. He explained that he would likely let the American people know whether he would be a candidate for another term "possibly by the first of the year," almost three years after his inauguration as president. Why would Reagan delay? White House chief of staff James Baker expressed confidence at the time that Reagan would indeed run for a second term, but explained, "I think he gains a little additional time to handle the tough job of being president and governing this nation without having everything he does be judged as purely political."[20]

Similarly, when George H. W. Bush established his reelection campaign committee in October 1991, he wrote in his letter to the FEC, "Although I am not yet formally declaring my candidacy for the Republican nomination for the office of president . . . I am hereby authorizing this organization as my principal campaign committee." When Bush headlined his first reelection fundraiser on October 31, 1991, news stories reported that he did not plan to officially announce his candidacy until after he gave his State of the Union address in 1992, the election year itself. This led the Associated Press to describe Bush's trip to Houston for his first reelection fundraiser this way: "President Bush arrived in his adopted hometown on Thursday for a glitzy kickoff of a re-election campaign he doesn't acknowledge exists."[21]

Trump's decision to file paperwork for his reelection committee on the day he was inaugurated in 2017 came with a similar initial disclaimer that this step did "not constitute a formal announcement of my candidacy for the 2020 election."[22] Although Trump would declare that he was running for reelection at a rally in June 2019, by that point he had already headlined twelve Trump Victory fundraisers and held more than sixty campaign rallies. When asked at the time of his first campaign rally in February 2017 if it was too soon to hold a rally, he replied, "Life is a campaign."[23]

As of this writing in early 2022, Joe Biden has not yet established his reelection campaign committee and has not held a reelection fundraiser. A reporter asked at a White House press conference in March 2021 whether Biden would run for a second term, noting that Biden had not followed Trump's lead in setting up his reelection campaign committee at the start of his term. Biden responded, "My plan is to run for reelection. That's my expectation." He added that Trump had created his reelection committee so early because he "needed to."[24] Advisers to Biden told reporters that he would not file paperwork to establish his reelection campaign committee until after the 2022 midterm elections, returning to the common practice before Trump's presidency.[25]

The presidents who were elected since the establishment of the modern campaign finance system in the 1970s have come to devote substantial amounts of their scarce time to reelection fundraising and have begun these efforts progressively earlier in their term in office. This escalation in reelection fundraising has been accompanied by complication as well. Obama and Trump both fundraised in an era characterized by joint fundraising committees, Super PACs, and high-dollar fundraisers. These dynamics represented a drastic departure from the campaign finance environment created by the post-Watergate campaign finance reforms. What has changed? How did the institutional landscape shift to one in which presidential fundraising is characterized by both escalation and complication?

WHAT EXPLAINS THE ESCALATION AND COMPLICATION OF PRESIDENTIAL FUNDRAISING?

To understand how we progressed from a world in which Carter infrequently attended low-dollar fundraising events for his reelection campaign to one in which presidents headline large numbers of high-dollar reelection fundraisers for complex joint fundraising committees with multiple beneficiaries, we must examine the competitive nature of presidential elections and presidents' strategic responses to the changing campaign finance regime. Presidents since the 1970s have operated in a period that has witnessed an evolution from a system in which public funding provided most of the financial resources a president seeking reelection would need, to one in which presidents devote substantial time and effort to help fund their campaigns and party organizations in an effort to keep up with newly empowered and well-funded independent groups. As the campaign finance landscape shifted, strategic presidents who feared defeat in a reelection bid adapted their practices to the evolving rules of the system. They escalated their reelection fundraising efforts and did so through the medium of complicated legal entities that allowed presidents to raise money in much larger increments that circumvented contribution limits in increasingly creative and controversial ways.

The Risk of a President Losing a Reelection Bid

The three consecutive two-term presidencies of Clinton, George W. Bush, and Obama might lead a casual observer of American politics to assume that sitting presidents possess such formidable electoral advantages that they have little need to fear defeat as they seek a second term. But this seeming stability masks the competitive nature of presidential reelection bids. A string of three two-term presidents is a rarity that has only occurred at one other time in American history—the trio of two-term Virginian presidents in the early 1800s: Thomas Jefferson, James Madison, and James Monroe.[26]

Political scientist Nelson Polsby often proclaimed that there are two types of politicians: paranoids and losers. Elected officials who appear to face little risk of losing their seat seem unnecessarily paranoid that they might indeed lose, as they work hard to win reelection even while facing no clear and present electoral threat. Those who stop being paranoid no longer do what they need to in order to stay in office, and their complacency contributes to their electoral defeat. Presidents are goal-oriented political actors who are well aware that there is no guarantee that they will win a second term in the White House, and thus they work hard to give themselves the best chance of success. The period immediately preceding the three two-term presidencies of Clinton, George W. Bush, and Obama was particularly tumultuous, as three of the previous four presidents—Gerald Ford, Carter, and George H. W. Bush—faced primary challengers as they sought their party's nomination for another term. Each was then ousted from office in the general election. In 2020 Trump became the first president in twenty-eight years to lose a bid for a second term.

Recent decades also have witnessed many presidential elections decided by relatively close margins in the Electoral College, including those in 1976, 2000, 2004, 2016, and 2020. In one indicator of the competitiveness of many presidential elections, when Obama won a second term in 2012, he became the first president since Dwight Eisenhower to win at least 51 percent of the popular vote twice.[27] Additionally, some presidents who ended up winning reelection comfortably had no reason to feel assured that they would, as presidents' public standing can shift dramatically and quickly. Reagan's job approval in the Gallup poll stood at just 40 percent in the summer of 1982, and just 39 percent of the public approved of the job Clinton was doing in the summer of 1994. Both went on to win reelection by substantial margins just over two years later. In contrast, George H. W. Bush's job approval soared to 89 percent during the 1991 Gulf War but dropped to 37 percent in October 1992, just weeks before he lost his bid for a second term.[28] A president's fortunes can change substantially, and strategic presidents have learned to take little for granted when it comes to their reelection bids.

Earlier in this chapter, Figure 2.1 indicated that the two presidents with the biggest increase in reelection fundraisers over their immediate Oval Office predecessors were Clinton and Obama. Both presidents had seen their party suffer historic midterm congressional election losses in their first term. In 1994 Republicans won control of both the House and Senate for the first time in forty years. In 2010 Democrats lost sixty-three seats in the House—the most seats lost in a midterm election since 1938—as Republicans reclaimed the majority in that chamber and picked up seats in the Senate as well.[29] Midterm election results are often viewed as a referendum on the president, and in the wake of these elections, many observers thought that the odds were stacked against either Clinton or Obama winning a second term. These midterm setbacks provided powerful motivation for both presidents to amass sufficient financial resources for their reelection bids. Additionally, two recent presidents—George W. Bush and Trump—won the Electoral College and thus the White House while coming in second in the national popular vote, and both took office with the expectation of facing another competitive election four years later.

It is against this backdrop of electoral competitiveness that we have witnessed an escalation in presidential fundraising since the 1970s. While most presidents throughout the history of the republic have been interested in winning another term in the White House, the institutional landscape in which recent presidents have sought the financial resources to support their reelection bid has evolved dramatically, and presidents have responded accordingly. What has changed?

How Public Funding Used to Lessen the Need for Reelection Fundraising

After Richard Nixon's reelection campaign received illegal corporate contributions in 1972, Congress responded by passing the Federal Election Campaign Act of 1974 (FECA), which established the foundation of the modern campaign finance landscape. The law capped individuals' political contributions to federal candidates at $1,000 per election cycle in order to prevent elected officials from being indebted to large donors. It also established a voluntary public funding program for presidential elections that offered matching funds for candidates at the nominating stage and a funding grant to party nominees for the general election. Candidates who qualified for and accepted public funding had to abide by accompanying limits on spending during the nominating phase as well as a post-convention prohibition on raising campaign committee funds to supplement the general election grant.[30] This system incentivized presidents and presidential candidates to seek donations from a large number of people during the nominating stage as a requirement to qualify for matching funds. The public funding program as a whole had the effect of limiting the amount of time that presidents spent fundraising for their reelection campaign organizations.[31]

The relatively low numbers of reelection campaign committee fundraisers headlined by Carter, Reagan, George H. W. Bush, and Clinton, indicated in light gray in Figure 2.1, were a function of this post-Watergate system. In the six presidential elections from 1976 to 1996, the campaign finance regime established by FECA limited overall reelection campaign committee fundraising and spending, as every Democratic and Republican presidential nominee over this twenty-year period chose to participate in the federal public funding program at both the nominating and general election stages. The campaign spending caps that were a condition of accepting matching funds during the nominating phase and the prohibition on post-convention campaign committee fundraising that came as a condition of accepting general election public funding served as a brake on the amount of time presidents spent raising money for their own campaign committee.

The case of Reagan's reelection bid serves to illustrate how the public funding program held down the amount of money raised and spent in presidential campaigns, and thus the time the president spent personally seeking campaign funds. The Reagan reelection campaign committee's fundraising efforts were so effective that this author found no evidence that Reagan himself headlined a fundraiser to benefit his own reelection campaign committee. Indeed, the Reagan-Bush '84 committee halted its fundraising in May 1984 because it had already raised all the money that it was allowed to spend given the caps that were a condition of taking matching funds during the nominating process. The campaign continued to receive donations after it stopped seeking them, and it ended up raising more than $1.5 million above what the law dictated the campaign could spend throughout the nominating process.[32] The public financing system was clearly designed to limit the amount of money raised and spent in presidential elections, as well as the time that presidents and candidates spend fundraising. In Reagan's case in 1984, the system worked as intended. But beginning with Clinton's bid for a second term, the time presidents spent on reelection fundraising escalated dramatically.

How Unregulated Soft Money and Public Funding's Obsolescence Changed Fundraising

The campaign finance landscape would shift in important ways during the reelection campaigns of Clinton, George W. Bush, Obama, and Trump. In the 1996 campaign, Clinton worked aggressively with his national party committee to raise large amounts of unregulated contributions, known as soft money, to help his reelection bid. Bush became the first sitting president to opt out of public funding for the nominating process during his 2004 reelection bid, and Obama became the first sitting president to decline public funding at both the nominating and general election stages when he sought a second term in 2012. These developments led to these three presidents spending far more time on fundraising than had the first three presidents elected under the post-Watergate campaign finance regime. Moreover, their efforts to coordinate and then integrate campaign and party fundraising would lead to the complicated joint fundraising committees that would become central to the reelection efforts of both Obama and Trump.

Soft money came into play starting in 1980, when national political parties were allowed to raise money in amounts not subject to federal contribution limits for use in funding state-level party-building activities such as voter registration and get-out-the-vote efforts, and to support candidates for state, but not federal, office. Campaign finance scholar Robert Mutch explains that these unregulated soft money contributions initially could not directly help federal candidates, but voter mobilization efforts for state or local candidates often indirectly benefited congressional and presidential candidates who were on the ballot as well. The amounts of soft money raised by political parties would not be known until 1992, when the FEC first required parties to disclose this information.[33]

Figure 2.1 indicates that Carter, Reagan, and George H. W. Bush did not devote substantial time to raising money for their national party committees in their third and fourth years in office. That would change with Clinton's reelection bid, when he headlined what was then a record eighty-three fundraisers for the DNC in his third and fourth years as president, in part to finance the airing of issue advertisements. These ads focused on political issues and candidates but did not directly advocate the election or defeat of a federal candidate, and thus they could be funded with soft money.[34] Although Clinton accepted public funding, which came with limits on fundraising for his reelection campaign committee, he supplemented these public funds with his extensive national party fundraising, which was a critical element of his reelection bid.

These efforts made national party organizations more important actors in presidential elections. But soft money fundraising became controversial because at a time when individuals could only contribute $1,000 per election cycle to a campaign, they could make unlimited soft money contributions to political parties. This raised Watergate-era fears about potential corruption. As one advocate of prohibiting soft money contributions put it, "When you're dealing with $250,000 and $500,000 campaign contributions you are flatly dealing with influence-buying and -selling and with political extortion."[35] Those concerns would carry the day. By the time the next sitting president, George W. Bush, began his reelection fundraising in 2003, soft money contributions to political parties had been banned by the Bipartisan Campaign Reform Act of 2002 (BCRA), popularly known as the McCain-Feingold law. As a result, all of Bush's fundraising efforts for the RNC in 2003 and 2004 would solicit lower-dollar hard money donations that were subject to the contribution limits established by campaign finance law. An unintended consequence of this law was that, as discussed below, unlimited political contributions would flow to nonparty entities instead of to political parties.

Bush in 2000 and 2004 made a campaign finance decision that would change key dynamics of presidential reelection fundraising. In 2000 Bush became the first major party presidential nominee to decline to take public funding during the nominating contest, and in 2004 he became the first sitting president to take that step. Bush's decision in 2000 was driven by the concern that public funding would not provide enough resources to compete with Steve Forbes, who had spent $37 million of his own money in his 1996 presidential bid and seemed likely to exceed that amount as he made another run for the Republican nomination in 2000. Bush was open about his reluctance to be bound by the spending caps that came with matching funds, explaining, "You've got limits that constrain a candidate. I want to be in a position to respond."[36] Bush made the same decision to decline matching funds for the nominating process when he ran for a second term in 2004, as did the eventual Democratic nominee, John Kerry. The spending cap that year for those accepting matching funds was $44.8 million; Bush raised almost $270 million in his unopposed bid for renomination, and Kerry raised close to $235 million.[37] Both candidates' decisions not to accept public funding during the nominating process allowed them to amass far greater financial resources for their campaign committee than otherwise would have been possible.

With the institutional constraint of pre-nomination spending limits removed, George W. Bush would spend record amounts of time fundraising for his reelection campaign committee, as Figure 2.1 illustrates. The decision to forgo matching funds and the spending limits that came with them led Bush to headline three times as many fundraisers for his reelection committee than had Clinton, while Clinton chose to devote more time to fundraising for the DNC than Bush would for the RNC. Bush's reelection committee fundraising goal was greater than that of any president before him, and he would need to spend record time raising committee campaign cash due to the limits on individual contributions. These donations had been raised to $2,000 per person per campaign cycle for the 2004 elections by the BCRA and were set to rise with inflation for subsequent election cycles. Every major-party nominee since 2004 has similarly declined to participate in the pre-nomination matching funds program, as the resources it provides are no longer substantial enough to run an effective nominating campaign.

In 2008 Barack Obama became the first major-party nominee since the passage of FECA not to participate in the public financing system at either the nominating or the general election stage. The spending limits that came with the public funds that year were $50.5 million for the nominating process and an additional $84.1 million for the general election. Unconstrained by these spending caps, the Obama campaign proceeded to raise $745 million.[38] Republican nominee John McCain declined matching funds at the nominating stage but accepted public financing for the general election, putting him at a severe financial disadvantage relative to Obama after the national conventions. In 2012, for the first time, neither major-party nominee participated in the public funding program at either stage of the election, as the spending limits of the program fell far short of what had become required to run an effective presidential campaign.

Without the constraints on fundraising that came with public funding, Obama headlined a record-high 223 fundraisers for his reelection campaign committee, the DNC, or both in his third and fourth years in office. In 2020 Trump became the second incumbent president to forgo public funding entirely. He took part in eighty-one fundraisers for his reelection committee, as well as for the RNC, in his third and fourth years as president—a far lower number of fundraisers than did Obama. This was due in large part to changed fundraising rules that allowed him to raise money in greater amounts via complicated joint fundraising committees than Obama had been able to do when seeking a second term in 2012. Although those dynamics were different, both Obama and Trump forewent public funding so that they could raise far more money than would have been permitted had they accepted the spending limits that accompanied public funding.

Presidents respond to the institutional rules of the campaign finance system. In the two decades from 1976 to 1996 when public funding was seen as a viable option, presidents and candidates limited their fundraising for their campaign committees, as they accepted the spending limits that accompanied public funding during both the nominating process and the general election. From 2000 to 2008, presidents and presidential candidates progressively opted out of the two-part public funding system. No major-party presidential nominee accepted public funding for either the nominating process or the general election in the 2012, 2016, or 2020 election cycles. As the costs of campaigns rose far more rapidly than did the spending caps associated with public funding, this program, which once served to limit both the amount of money raised and the time presidents and candidates spent raising it, became irrelevant for major-party nominees, who would subsequently spend much more time raising money for their campaign committees.

The proliferation and subsequent banning of soft money fundraising would also shape the ways presidents raised campaign funds. In the 1990s and early 2000s, presidents spent substantial time raising soft money donations for their national party committees, which were not subject to contribution limits. This practice continued until soft money donations to national party committees were banned by the BCRA in 2002. The law's tighter rules on contributions to national party committees meant that presidents would spend more time to raise less money. For example, CBS News White House correspondent Mark Knoller reported in July 2010 that Obama had headlined forty-nine fundraisers that had brought in more than $46 million. At the same point in George W. Bush's term eight years earlier, Bush had taken part in thirty-eight fundraising events that had yielded $145 million. Bush was able to help the RNC raise soft money donations that were not subject to contribution limits, while Obama operated in the post-BCRA setting in which parties had to bring in contributions in limited, regulated amounts. A 2010 *Wall Street Journal* article cited presidential aides who attributed Obama's more frequent fundraising to the changes that came with the passage of the BCRA: "Mr. Obama's pace is driven by fund-raising rules Mr. Bush didn't face early in his term that prevent individual donors from writing large checks to the political parties." Or as a *USA Today* headline pithily put it that same year, "Obama vs. Bush—'More Fundraisers, Less Funds.'"[39] The prohibition of soft money fundraising by political parties would lead to the empowerment of non-party groups that were not subject to the soft money ban. The increased prominence of these groups would bring even more changes to the campaign finance landscape that would influence the ways presidents choose to fundraise.

The Rise of Unregulated Super PACs and Other Nonparty Groups

Senator Mitch McConnell, a leading opponent of the BCRA, declared in 2003, "This law will not remove one dime from politics. . . . Soft money is not gone, it's just changed its address."[40] In the 2004 presidential election, the first following the passage of the BCRA, unregulated money did not vanish from the campaign scene. Instead of going to national parties, nonparty organizations, often called 527 groups after the section of the tax code under which they were organized, raised funds in unregulated amounts and then ran advertisements and conducted voter mobilization efforts designed to influence federal elections. Although one study found that spending by 527 groups in the 2004 election cycle aiming to help Democratic candidates was more than triple the amount spent to help Republicans, the single most prominent such organization that year was the anti–John Kerry group called Swift Boat Veterans for Truth. It spent more than $22 million, and its ads attacking Kerry's record of military service garnered much media attention. The 527 groups collectively spent over $550 million in the 2004 election cycle.[41] The emergence of these groups illustrates what has been called the "hydraulic theory" of campaign finance reform, which holds that money in politics is like water running downhill; if it is blocked in one place, it will seek another path.[42]

The post-BCRA era has been marked by weakened political parties and empowered outside groups not formally tied to party committees, and these changes to the campaign finance landscape have increased the pressure on presidents to fundraise for their reelection bids. Well before the Supreme Court's 2010 decision in the *Citizens United* case helped lead to the creation of nonparty groups known popularly as Super PACs, other similar organizations began to play a key role in federal elections soon after the enactment of the BCRA. The banning of soft money contributions to political parties led to the redirection of unlimited political donations to a range of less regulated nonparty groups, and presidents have responded to these changes in the campaign finance landscape.

Bush's 2004 reelection campaign adjusted course as these new dynamics emerged. The combination of the ban on soft money contributions to political parties and the new prominence of these outside groups that could receive limitless contributions incentivized the creation of joint fundraising committees that could raise larger amounts of money that would be split between campaign committees and party organizations. Operating in a new environment in which outside groups had more resources and greater influence and in which national political parties could no longer accept money that was not subject to contribution limits, the Bush-Cheney '04 campaign chose to partner with the RNC by having the president headline twenty-one fundraisers that were labeled Victory 2004 events. This fund was described in a news story as "the RNC's get-out-the-vote account," and CBS News's Mark Knoller learned from an administration official that this fund jointly benefited both the RNC and the president's reelection campaign—a precursor to the Obama Victory Fund four years later.[43]

By the time of the next presidential reelection bid in 2012, two key court decisions had further empowered outside groups to play a larger role in presidential campaigns. The cases of *Citizens United v. Federal Election Commission* and *Speechnow.org v. Federal Election Commission* were both decided in 2010. In *Citizens United*, the Supreme Court struck down a ban on corporations funding political speech by groups not tied to campaigns or parties. Justice Kennedy, writing for the court, declared, "We now conclude that independent expenditures, including those made by corporations, do not give rise to corruption or the appearance of corruption."[44] Kennedy's argument that expenditures that were made independent of campaigns and parties did not pose the risk of corrupting elected officials would help lead to a greater role for these nonparty groups.

In *Speechnow*, the DC Circuit Court of Appeals drew on the *Citizens United* case in ruling that individuals can make unlimited contributions to political groups that only make independent expenditures and do not contribute to campaigns or parties. The combined result of these decisions was the emergence of Super PACs, the informal name for groups that are legally independent of campaigns and parties and thus can accept unlimited contributions as long as they make independent expenditures and do not contribute to campaigns or parties. The FEC requires that these committees—formally called independent expenditure-only committees[45]—must disclose their donors, but other nonparty soft money groups formed under certain portions of Section 501(c) of the tax code are not required to disclose the names of their contributors. These groups, which may spend money on electoral politics as long as that is not their primary purpose, include social welfare groups organized under section 501(c)(4) of the tax code, labor unions organized under section 501(c)(5), and business groups like the Chamber of Commerce organized under section 501(c)(6). These groups, which are often referred to with shorthand references to the section of the tax code under which they are organized, are not subject to strict donor disclosure rules, contributing to a proliferation in elections of what is called dark money—funds whose source is unknown.[46]

In the 2012 presidential campaign, Super PACs and other outside groups aligned with, but legally independent of, specific candidates and political parties played a prominent role. In one leading example, Nevada billionaire Sheldon Adelson and his wife contributed approximately $90 million to Super PACs supporting certain Republican candidates in 2011 and 2012.[47] The prospect of these groups raising money in multi-million-dollar increments placed even more pressure on Obama and on the candidates vying for the Republican presidential nomination to devote more time to raising money in the relatively small increments laid out by campaign finance law. These dynamics help explain why Obama headlined a record 223 events for his reelection campaign committee, the DNC, or both, in 2011 and 2012. The legislators who led the passage of the BCRA sought to address the possibility that national parties would be corrupted by large, unregulated contributions. In doing so, the legislation unintentionally redirected these unregulated funds to other less accountable actors and increased the pressure on presidents and candidates to spend more and more time raising money in the regulated amounts prescribed by campaign finance law.

The pressure brought to bear by the specter of unlimited contributions to Super PACs led campaigns and parties to create complex joint fundraising committees in an effort to raise funds in amounts that far exceeded the limits on contributions to a candidate's campaign committee. The Obama campaign followed in the footsteps of the Bush reelection campaign's joint Victory 2004 fundraisers, but the Obama team combined their campaign and national committee fundraising efforts from the kickoff of his reelection bid in April 2011 in the form of the Obama Victory Fund. They also incorporated state parties into their fundraising efforts so that they could hold events where donors could contribute $75,800 to the Democratic campaign effort. This was far more than the amount per election cycle that they could give directly to the Obama reelection campaign, which by 2012 had risen to $2,500 for each of the nominating and general election phases, up from the cap of $2,000 per election cycle that was in place during Bush's 2004 reelection bid. At OVF events, the first $5,000 of an individual's contribution went to the Obama reelection campaign. The DNC received any additional money up to $30,800, which in 2012 was the maximum legal contribution per year by an individual to a national political party. At the events where donors gave more than $35,800, the additional money went to state parties that would support Obama's reelection bid and the campaigns of other Democrats. The highest price of admission allowed at the time under federal law was $75,800.[48]

The escalation of presidential fundraising would continue, due in part to the increasing complication of fundraising committees. These developments would be made possible by two changes in 2014 that would empower political parties once again to raise much larger sums of money and enable them to compete more with Super PACs and other nonparty groups. As a result of these legal changes, Obama's high-dollar fundraising efforts during his 2012 reelection bid would pale in comparison to the amounts of money that Trump would be allowed to raise when he was the next sitting president to seek reelection just eight years later. It is rational for presidential campaigns and political parties to respond in this way to the rising costs of campaigns and the ability of outside groups to raise contributions in multi-million-dollar increments. Such steps, however, have left us far from the post-Watergate system of campaign finance that was created in the 1970s with the intent of permitting only relatively small donations to campaigns and political parties to reduce corruption or the appearance of corruption.

How the *McCutcheon* Decision Empowered Complicated
Joint Fundraising Committees

A 2014 Supreme Court decision and a little-noticed change in campaign finance law enacted that same year that allowed national parties to raise funds in greater amounts triggered further escalation and complication of presidential reelection fundraising. These developments have received far less attention than did the *Citizens United* decision, but they have been quite consequential. Due to these changes, the strategic fundraising choices made by Obama in the 2016 election cycle that would determine his successor and by Trump as he raised funds for his own reelection bid were shaped by a legal landscape that had evolved substantially since Obama's 2012 reelection bid.

The BCRA not only established limits on contributions to campaigns, party committees, and political action committees; it also set a cap on the total amount an individual could give to these entities in a two-year election cycle. This limit was set to rise with inflation; in the 2012 election cycle, the aggregate contribution limit stood at $117,000. Of that total, only $46,200 could be donated to various candidates for federal office, while $70,800 was the aggregate cap for contributions to all party committees and political action committees.[49] Republican donor Shaun McCutcheon challenged the aggregate donation cap in court after running up against the limit. In the 2011–2012 election cycle, he contributed to sixteen candidates for federal office and to multiple party committees but contended that he was prohibited by the aggregate contribution cap from giving $1,776 to twelve other candidates and from making additional contributions to multiple noncandidate committees. He argued that he should be able to make donations to as many individual candidates and political committees as he chose, as long as each did not exceed the maximum contribution allowed to a single candidate or committee. He contended that contributions to many different entities would not have an aggregate corrupting effect. In 2014 the Supreme Court sided with him in *McCutcheon v. Federal Election Commission*, reversing the portion of the 1976 *Buckley v. Valeo* decision that had upheld aggregate contribution limits.[50]

Chief Justice Roberts, in his opinion that struck down the aggregate caps on contributions, wrote, "The Government may no more restrict how many candidates or causes a donor may support than it may tell a newspaper how many candidates it may endorse." He rejected the assertion that removing the caps would increase the risk of corruption. Justice Breyer dissented, writing, "In the absence of limits on aggregate political contributions, donors can and likely will find ways to channel millions of dollars to parties and to individual candidates, producing precisely the kind of 'corruption' or 'appearance of corruption' that previously led the Court to hold aggregate limits constitutional." Breyer went on to describe the potential for establishing joint fundraising committees that could accept checks in amounts that could exceed $1 million and then distribute those funds to various candidates and party committees.[51]

In the wake of the *McCutcheon* decision, campaigns and parties would indeed work together to create complicated joint fundraising committees that would benefit federal candidates, national parties, and state parties. In the absence of the aggregate contribution caps that had been in place for forty years, presidents would be allowed to headline fundraising events with donors who had written checks in amounts that dwarfed the amounts they had previously been able to give to campaigns and political parties under the limits imposed by the passage of the BCRA in 2002.

How Congressional Action Let Presidents Raise More Money for National Political Parties

Another change in December 2014 combined with the *McCutcheon* decision to shift the legal landscape even further and to return political parties to a greater role in campaign fundraising. Lawmakers attached a last-minute policy rider to a $1.1 trillion appropriations bill that would allow national party committees to accept contributions from individuals that were eight times larger than the previous limit. In 2014 an individual could give $32,400 each calendar year to each party's three national committee organizations. For Republicans, the committees are the RNC, the National Republican Senatorial Committee (NRSC), and the National Republican Congressional Committee (NRCC); for Democrats, the corresponding committees are the DNC, the Democratic Senatorial Campaign Committee (DSCC), and the Democratic Congressional Campaign Committee (DCCC).

The new provision would allow each party to receive donations in 2014 of $97,200 for each of seven new committee funds: one to support the party's national convention; three to fund the building or improvement of party headquarters (the national committee and the two committees focused on House and Senate elections could each establish such a fund); and an additional three funds to pay for each committee's legal expenses. If a party set up all of these committees, an individual donor could contribute up to $777,600 a year to the national party under the 2014 party fundraising limits. This limit would increase every two years, as it was indexed to rise with inflation. A *Washington Post* headline about the new rules declared, "Fundraising Expansion Slipped into Spending Deal Could Power Financial Bonanza for Parties."[52]

In the 2016 election cycle, both major national parties and their presidential nominees responded to the change in party fundraising law and the *McCutcheon* decision by creating complicated joint fundraising committees that could accept larger donations that would then be directed to various campaigns and party committees. The Democrats established a committee to which a donor could give up to a total of $358,800 in the spring of 2016. Of that total, $2,700 would go to Hillary Clinton's campaign committee for the period before the national convention, and another $2,700 would be given to the campaign for the general election.

Additionally, $33,400 would go to the DNC and $10,000 would go to each of thirty-two Democratic state parties.[53] In June 2016 that committee was expanded to include thirty-eight state parties as beneficiaries, enabling it to collect even larger donations.[54]

An invitation to a fundraiser that Obama would headline in August 2016 for the joint fundraising committee called the Hillary Victory Fund made clear the complexity of these legal entities. In small print, the invitation indicated the complicated manner in which donations to the joint fundraising committee would be divided:

> The first $2,700/$5,000 from an individual/multicandidate committee ("PAC") will be allocated to Hillary for America, designated for the primary election. The next $2,700/$5,000 from an individual/PAC will be allocated to Hillary for America, designated for the general election. For contributions made after the primary, the full amount of the contribution, up to $2,700/$5,000, will be designated to the general election. The next $33,400/$15,000 from an individual/PAC will be allocated to the Democratic National Committee. Additional amounts from an individual/PAC will be split equally among the Democratic state parties from these states up to $10,000/$5,000 per state party: AK, AR, CO, DE, FL, GA, ID, IN, IA, KS, KY, LA, ME, MA, MI, MN, MS, MO, MT, NV, NH, NJ, NM, NC, OH, OK, OR, PA, RI, SC, SD, TN, TX, UT, VA, WV, WI, and WY. A contributor may designate his or her contribution for a particular participant. The allocation formula above may change if following it would result in an excessive contribution.[55]

Republicans in May 2016 set up a complicated joint fundraising committee through which even more money would flow directly to the national party. Individual donors could contribute up to $449,400. Of this total, $5,400 would go to the Trump campaign for both the nominating and general election stages; $33,400 would go to the RNC's general account; $100,200 would go to each of three RNC committees, one for legal expenses, another for convention expenses, and a third for headquarters expenses; and $10,000 would go to each of eleven state parties. The committee was expanded in early September 2016 to benefit sixteen state parties and later that month was expanded again so that it would benefit a total of twenty-one state parties, in addition to the Trump campaign and the RNC.[56]

Although federal law places limits on the amounts that an individual can contribute to a federal campaign or a political party committee, there are no limits on the amounts that state parties can transfer to national parties, and vice versa. This legal provision means that money directed to state parties via these complicated joint fundraising committees need not stay there. Indeed, an investigation published in *Politico* in July 2016 attested that according to filings with the Federal Election Commission, "since the inception of the Hillary Victory Fund, participating state parties have received $7.7 million in transfers, but within a few days of most transfers, almost all of the cash—$6.9 million—was transferred to the DNC." Another *Politico* investigation cited the example of the Maine Democratic Party, which had received $59,800 from the Hillary Victory Fund and had subsequently transferred exactly $59,800 back to the DNC. Republicans regularly made similar transfers. Transactions like these have led critics to decry joint fundraising accounts as thinly veiled efforts to circumvent limits on contributions to the national party.[57]

How the New Legal Landscape Shaped 2020 Presidential Fundraising

It was against the backdrop of this new legal landscape that Trump began his reelection fundraising in 2017. Trump continued the escalation of his predecessors in two important respects—its record-setting early start and the large amounts of money raised at his events—but his fundraising also represented a break with past patterns of escalation. As Figure 2.1 indicates, Trump took part in only eighty-one fundraisers for his campaign committee or for the RNC in his third and fourth years in office. Trump's total was just more than one-third the number Obama had headlined and fewer than either Clinton or George W. Bush had held.

Trump's relatively low number of reelection fundraisers was due in part to the shutdown of in-person fundraising for substantial parts of 2020 in response to the COVID-19 pandemic. Indeed, Trump did not headline any in-person fundraisers from March 10 through June 10, 2020, due to pandemic-related restrictions. Looking at the three previous presidential reelection bids during that same stretch of time from March 10 through June 10 of the reelection year, in 1996 Clinton took part in twenty-five fundraisers, in 2004 George W. Bush headlined seventeen fundraisers, and in 2012 Obama participated in fifty-one fundraisers. Clearly, Trump would have attended more fundraising events if the campaign had not taken place during a pandemic.

When Trump resumed in-person fundraising efforts in June 2020, he had to do so against the backdrop of the pandemic and public health guidelines in states across the country. This complicated his ability to hold traditional in-person gatherings, though he persisted in trying to do so. Trump personally took part in only one virtual fundraiser in 2020. While that event on July 21 brought in more than $20 million, news reports indicated that Trump preferred in-person fundraising events. He again had to cancel his fundraising efforts in early October 2020 when he tested positive for COVID-19 and was hospitalized at Walter Reed National Military Medical Center. He then went two weeks without attending a fundraiser at a time when news reports indicated that his campaign's aggressive spending had left them short on cash in the closing month of the campaign.[58] Between his resumption of in-person fundraisers in June and the election in early November, Trump headlined twenty-four fundraising events.

Trump's fundraising totals certainly would have been higher had it not been for the pandemic-driven pause in and restrictions on fundraising events. But he was on track for far fewer fundraisers than Obama even before the public health situation limited his fundraising pace. What explains the additional difference? Changes to the campaign finance legal landscape in 2014, described previously, that allowed for the increasing complexity of joint fundraising committees enabled Trump to raise more money from fewer events than had Obama eight years earlier.

Two months into Trump's term as president, his campaign reorganized the Trump Victory committee so that its proceeds benefited the Trump reelection campaign and the RNC but not any of the twenty-one state parties that had been part of the complicated joint fundraising committee in the closing months of the 2016 election campaign. Even without state party beneficiaries as part of the joint fundraising committee, the 2014 campaign finance law change that authorized substantially larger donations to national party committees meant that in 2019 a donor could give up to $360,600 to the Trump Victory committee. In order to raise money in even larger increments, Trump Victory was reorganized in January 2020 to add twenty-two state parties as beneficiaries. In September 2020 it was expanded again to include forty-six state Republican parties.[59]

The proliferation of increasingly complicated joint fundraising committees in the wake of the 2014 *McCutcheon* decision and the legal change that allowed national party committees to raise money in larger increments meant that Trump in 2020 could raise money in greater amounts at fewer events than was the case when Obama sought reelection in 2012. To illustrate these dynamics, consider a day that each president spent fundraising in June of his reelection year. On June 1, 2012, Obama flew to Minnesota for a midday official presidential event at a Honeywell manufacturing plant. He then turned his attention to his reelection campaign, first headlining three fundraisers in Minneapolis before heading to Chicago for another three fundraisers that evening. Ticket prices for the six events ranged from $5,000 to $50,000 per person, with total proceeds of $7.2 million going to the Obama Victory Fund, a joint campaign committee that benefited the Obama-Biden reelection committee, the DNC, and multiple state Democratic parties.[60]

Eight years later, on June 11, 2020, Trump flew to Texas for a single fundraiser at the home of a Dallas billionaire. The cost of admission was $580,600 per couple, or $290,300 per person, and the event was estimated to raise $10 million. The fundraiser took just over an hour of Trump's time and was paired that day with an official presidential event at a Dallas church where he held a roundtable discussion on the economy and other issues.[61] Trump was able to raise more money at a single fundraising event than Obama had raised at six events eight years earlier. These changing dynamics clearly present somewhat of a tradeoff. Though less presidential time was demanded to raise $10 million in 2020, such a high-dollar event presents a greater risk of corruption or the appearance of corruption.

These newly complicated joint fundraising committees have become another element of the incumbency advantage. Sitting presidents have long enjoyed the ability to build up a substantial campaign war chest while their opponents in the other party expend their limited financial resources in an effort to win their nominating contest. But joint fundraising committees have accelerated these dynamics. In the 2020 election cycle, Trump had been fundraising jointly with the RNC for his reelection since 2017, enabling him to headline fundraisers where donors made six-figure contributions. In contrast, Democratic nominee Joe Biden did not set up a joint fundraising committee with the DNC until he became the presumptive Democratic nominee for the presidency in the spring of 2020. Until that point, contributors could only give his campaign $2,800 for the nominating contest and another $2,800 for the general election. On April 24, 2020, the Biden Victory Fund was created to benefit both the Biden campaign and the DNC. Several weeks later, on May 16, it was expanded to include twenty-six state Democratic party committees as well. On July 20, the committee's organization was changed so that it would benefit thirty-seven state parties, and on August 31, 2020, it expanded again to benefit a total of forty-six state parties, as well as the District of Columbia's Democratic party committee.[62]

A news story highlighted the increased fundraising possibilities that the new joint fundraising committees offered. "After Mr. Biden became the presumptive nominee . . . the donation limit skyrocketed—from $2,800 in the primary to more than $700,000 now, including party funds."[63] But Biden still had much ground to make up, as FEC filings through March 2020 indicated that Trump and the RNC had almost $187 million more cash on hand than did Biden and the DNC. As an April 2020 news article put it, Biden and the DNC "could raise almost $1 million every single day between now and November, and he would still barely catch up to what President Trump and the Republican Party had in the bank at the start of April—let alone what Mr. Trump will have by Election Day."[64] Biden would build a fundraising advantage over Trump by the end of the 2020 campaign, due both to his productive fundraising and to the rapid rate at which the Trump campaign spent its substantial war chest. But the extent to which Biden was far behind Trump and the RNC when he first set up his own complicated joint fundraising committee in April of that year and the amounts that Biden and the DNC raised after forming their joint committee illustrate how fundraising through a joint fundraising committee facilitates raising remarkably large amounts of money.[65]

Both Trump in 2020 and Obama in 2012 had supportive Super PACs whose efforts supplemented their reelection campaign committees and their party committees. One might think that having these groups on a president's side would reduce the need to raise money for one's campaign committee or party committee, but presidents and their political parties still feel the pressure to build up their own massive campaign treasury. Presidents and candidates like having money that they can control. Although supportive Super PACs are run by allies of the president, there are campaign finance rules that prohibit certain types of coordination between federal campaigns and Super PACs. Critics argue that those coordination rules come with many loopholes, but they do prohibit campaigns and Super PACs from jointly formulating communications strategies.[66] While Super PACs may perform many roles that campaigns find helpful, presidents and their campaign teams also choose to raise substantial amounts themselves so that they have funds that they can control and direct as they see fit.

Complicated joint fundraising committees have become a new hallmark of the campaign finance landscape. In May 2021 the DNC announced that it would relaunch the Democratic Grassroots Victory Fund, which it hailed as a partnership between the DNC and state parties across the country. The DNC touted its renewed commitment to helping Democrats at the state level, including the establishment of a Red State Fund that aimed to build up Democratic strength in states that tended to vote for Republican candidates. How would this new partnership achieve its aims? At the end of the press release, the DNC noted that the Democratic Grassroots Victory Fund is a joint fundraising committee to which an individual can contribute up to $875,000 per year.[67]

CONCLUSIONS

The campaign finance landscape has changed a great deal since Jimmy Carter headlined two reelection fundraisers in May 1980 at which donors contributed $150 to $250 to dine with the president and support his bid for another term in the White House. The post-Watergate campaign finance reforms were structured so that presidents and presidential candidates would be incentivized to draw financial resources from the public funding program and would then have less need to devote time to fundraising. The system's relatively low contribution limits were designed to prevent presidents and candidates for office from being beholden to large donors.

Decades later, a disjointed campaign finance system has emerged that bears little resemblance to the campaign finance regime that was created in 1974. The public funding program became irrelevant as presidents and candidates found it to their advantage not to be bound by the spending limits that accompanied the public funds. Presidents consequently devoted more and more time to fundraising. This escalation in the amount of time presidents spent and the point in their term when they began reelection fundraising was accompanied by the dramatic complication of fundraising committees. Campaigns and parties increasingly turned to creative legal entities that allowed them to raise money in large amounts in an effort to keep up with Super PACs and other outside groups that are not subject to contribution limits. These two trends of escalation and complication emerged as strategic responses to the shifting campaign finance landscape.

Congressional action in 2002 and 2014, as well as court cases in 2010 and 2014, would bring further consequential changes to campaign finance law. First, the banning in 2002 of unlimited soft money contributions to national party committees led to a prominent role for nonparty groups that could accept funds not restricted by contribution limits. After the so-called 527 groups became significant political actors in the 2004 election cycle, Super PACs assumed a prominent role in campaigns in the wake of the 2010 *Citizens United* and *Speechnow.org* court decisions. Then in 2014 the Supreme Court in the *McCutcheon* case invalidated the aggregate cap on federal donations by an individual, and congressional action enabled national party committees to accept contributions that would exceed $100,000 to each of multiple national party committee funds. These developments ushered in a new era of high-dollar fundraising in which Super PACs and other nonparty groups can raise money in amounts not subject to contribution limits. Campaigns and parties have responded by creating complicated joint fundraising committees as the central vehicles for donors to contribute to presidential candidates and parties in amounts that collectively dwarf what formerly had been allowed under federal law.

The escalation in reelection fundraising has affected presidential campaigns' resource allocation strategies as well. In the closing months of Obama's 2012 reelection campaign, he took time away from reaching out to voters in key battleground states to hold fundraisers in the noncompetitive states of California, Illinois, and New York. Similarly, during the final months of Trump's reelection bid, time he spent at fundraisers in the non-battleground states of California, New Jersey, New York, and Tennessee was time that he could not devote to stumping for votes in person in the critical Electoral College states that would decide the election.

Even more importantly, recent presidents have spent substantial amounts of their scarce time raising funds in their efforts to win another term in the White House, and they have started their reelection fundraising progressively earlier in their terms. While the expanded use of complicated joint fundraising committees lessened the amount of time that Trump spent on reelection fundraising, the dramatically larger contributions to these committees raise concerns about the role of wealthy donors in the US political system.

Corrupting or Strengthening Parties?

These high-dollar joint fundraising committees prompt fears about the very corruption or the appearance of corruption that the modern campaign finance system was designed to avert. During the 2016 Democratic nominating fight, Bernie Sanders's campaign manager charged, "The Hillary Victory Fund has reported receiving several individual contributions in amounts as high as $354,400 or more, which is over 130 times the $2,700 limit that applies for contributions to Secretary Clinton's campaign. . . . The Clinton campaign is bending campaign finance rules to their breaking point all so Wall Street fat cats . . . can contribute 130 times the legal limit to support her campaign."[68] Former FEC chair Trevor Potter declared that these joint fundraising committees would make "the parties more indebted to a handful of very large donors giving beyond the means—or even the imagination—of most Americans."[69]

Joint fundraising committees often distribute funds to state parties, only to have those state parties redirect the funds to the DNC or the RNC. One study found that in 2016, about 75 percent of the money received by state parties through the Hillary Victory Fund, totaling more than $84 million, was then transferred to the DNC. In July 2016 more than $7 million of the money received by the DNC originated from donors who had already given the maximum legal amount allowed to the national committee, and who then gave additional funds to state parties through the Hillary Victory Fund. Those state parties then sent that money to the DNC—a practice that was legal, but controversial—prompting headlines that declared "Millions from Maxed-Out Clinton Donors Flowed through Loophole" and "Comeback for 'Legalized Money Laundering' in Party Politics?" On the Republican side that same year, more than 90 percent of the funds directed to state parties by the Trump Victory joint fundraising committee was then sent to the RNC. The chair of the Alabama Republican Party did not lament that the money did not stay with her state party. "That was perfectly fine. We wanted to be team players to help in a presidential election year."[70] Others were less sanguine, including Fred Wertheimer, president of Democracy 21, who said, "This is a return to the old system of using the parties as vehicles to launder the buying and selling of government influence and decisions."[71]

But some political operatives and donors see the larger contributions made possible by joint fundraising committees as a healthy corrective to a system where campaigns and parties had seen their financial resources dwarfed by those of Super PACs and other outside entities. One Democratic donor declared, "I prefer to give to the party, and I think it's a good option for those who don't believe in super PACs." A Republican fundraiser concurred, declaring, "This will help stop the uncontrollable flow of non-transparent money, and it will help rebuild the parties."[72] Shawn McCutcheon, whose lawsuit led to the Supreme Court case in 2014 that struck down the aggregate cap on biennial contributions to candidates and parties and led to the proliferation of complicated joint fundraising committees, agreed. "That's a good thing in my opinion. A million in the parties is worth a billion in the super PACs. The people in the parties . . . know how to get a lot more out of their money than some of these super PACs."[73]

Prospects

A former Republican chair of the Federal Election Committee asserted that "President Trump has been a campaign finance innovator from Day 1. He's really shattered all norms. I don't think we'll ever again see a presidential candidate not raise [reelection campaign] money during the first two years of a first term any-more."[74] The chief operating officer for Trump's reelection campaign committee concurred, predicting that reelection campaigning and fundraising during the first two years in office would become the "new model" for subsequent presidents as well.[75] While advisers to Biden have told journalists that he will follow the traditional, pre-Trump timing of waiting to begin raising funds for a reelection bid until this third year in office, the precedent Trump set will likely lead a future president to begin reelection fundraising soon after being sworn into office as well.

Biden's national party committee has already reestablished a joint fundrais-ing committee that benefits the national party and state parties across the country. This entity will be able to accept contributions from individuals of up to $875,000 per year, signaling that the escalation in the amounts of money raised via compli-cated joint fundraising committees is set to continue. When it comes to attracting donations of that magnitude, a president's participation is uniquely helpful. No other figure in the American political system can match the fundraising draw of a sitting president.

The evolution of campaign finance dynamics during the forty-four years from the start of Carter's term to the end of Trump's is a tale of escalation and complication, and of consequences intended and unintended, that have led to the emergence of presidential fundraising as a frequent element of modern presiden-tial leadership. The next chapter will focus on another trend that has accompanied the escalation and complication of presidential fundraising: nationalization.

3
Nationalization

"All politics is local."

—Former Speaker of the House Tip O'Neill

"Everyone calls New York the ATM state. You come and make your withdrawals, and you leave."

—Anonymous New York Democrat, September 4, 1998

In the sixth year of his presidency, Ronald Reagan traveled extensively to raise funds for his fellow Republicans who were running for the US Senate. The class of senators elected with Reagan in 1980 had given Republicans the Senate majority for the first time since the 1954 midterm elections twenty-six years earlier. Six years later, those senators were up for reelection, and Reagan spent substantial time raising campaign cash for them and for other Republican Senate candidates in an effort to preserve his party's control of that chamber. In 1986 Reagan headlined twenty-four fundraisers for Senate candidates in sixteen states—Alabama, California, Colorado, Florida, Georgia, Illinois, Louisiana, Maryland, Missouri, North Carolina, North Dakota, Nevada, New York, Oklahoma, South Dakota, and Wisconsin. Each of these fundraisers benefited an individual senator or Senate candidate, as did an additional fundraising event in Washington, DC, to aid a Republican senator from the distant state of Alaska. In addition to these events, Reagan headlined two other DC fundraisers that jointly benefited the Republican Party's national campaign committees for the House and Senate, as well as their congressional leaders. The vast majority of his Senate fundraising efforts, however, aided individual senators and Senate candidates and took place in the states where they lived.

Almost three decades later, Barack Obama also fundraised throughout his sixth year in office to defend his party's majority in the Senate. As with Reagan, the senators on the ballot that year had won election with Obama at the top of the ticket six years earlier. As Reagan had done, Obama traveled across the country, headlining fifteen Senate fundraisers in ten states—California, Colorado, Connecticut, Illinois, Massachusetts, Maryland, New York, Texas, Virginia, and Washington—as well as an additional fundraising event in Washington, DC. But in contrast to Reagan's efforts in 1986, fourteen of Obama's sixteen fundraisers in 2014 benefited the Democratic Senatorial Campaign Committee (DSCC), the national party committee dedicated to electing Democrats to the Senate. Three of these fourteen DSCC fundraising events divided their proceeds between the national committee and a specific senator. The money raised by Obama's other two Senate fundraising events went to a Super PAC named Senate Majority PAC. Even with his party's Senate majority on the line, Obama didn't headline a single fundraiser in 2014 that solely benefited an individual Senate candidate.

The contrast between Reagan's choices about Senate fundraising beneficiaries in 1986 and Obama's in 2014 reflects the increasing nationalization of presidential fundraising. Daniel Hopkins has analyzed many of the ways in which American politics has become more nationalized in recent decades. Outcomes in gubernatorial races increasingly mirror presidential election results. Large numbers of Americans follow national political news but not the local political issues that are closer to home. The gap between turnout in presidential elections and in elections for state offices has grown over time. And increasing numbers of citizens choose to make political donations to candidates for national office as opposed to state office, and to candidates who do not represent the donor's home state.[1]

This chapter focuses on a different facet of nationalization. Presidential fundraising was once characterized by events held across the country for state parties and specific candidates who hailed from the states in which the fundraisers were held. Increasingly, recent presidents have focused their fundraising on national beneficiaries instead of specific candidates for office or state parties. As they have done so, fewer of their fundraising events have benefited candidates or party committees from the states in which they take place.

In this chapter I first present evidence that illustrates the increasing nationalization of presidential fundraising and then advance an argument about factors that have contributed to these changing dynamics. The ability of presidents to raise money in larger increments for national beneficiaries than they can for individual candidates has made nationalized fundraising a more appealing option. This is particularly the case in recent years given the rising costs of campaigns and the increased prominence of nonparty groups like Super PACs that are not subject to contribution limits. These dynamics have played out in an era in which control of the White House, the Senate, and the House of Representatives is in play in most election cycles, creating high stakes in competitive elections across the country. Additionally, a change in federal rules governing who pays for presidential fundraising travel has made hosting a presidential fundraiser more expensive for the candidate or party committee benefiting from the event, contributing to a shift toward national beneficiaries.

The nationalization of fundraising has a number of implications. For candidates running for office in states where the president is unpopular, it can be more politically convenient to offer indirect fundraising help through a national party committee rather than to have the president appear on stage with an individual candidate at a high-profile fundraising event. But these national party fundraisers are usually higher-dollar events that raise concerns about presidents and their parties becoming beholden to large donors. Additionally, these fundraisers for national beneficiaries do not offer the same chance to foster connections between presidents and individual members of their party that traditional candidate-focused fundraising events do. The result is an approach to politics that is more nationalized, centralized, and top-down.

RISING NATIONAL PARTY FUNDRAISING, DECLINING STATE PARTY FUNDRAISING

Recent presidents have devoted a greater share of their fundraising efforts to aid the Democratic or Republican National Committee, as well as the national committees dedicated to helping elect senators, House members, and governors from each party. These committees, which will be discussed throughout this chapter, are listed in Table 3.1 for ease of reference.

The nationalization of presidential fundraising is clearly conveyed by several key indicators. Figure 3.1 depicts the percentage of fundraisers that presidents held to aid national party beneficiaries from 1977 through 2020. The figure presents the percentages of a president's fundraisers that supported a national party beneficiary instead of the total number of those fundraisers. While Bill Clinton, George W. Bush, and Obama took part in many more fundraisers than did the other presidents in this study, examining the percentages of each president's national party fundraisers facilitates comparisons of each president's relative fund-

Table 3.1: Principal National Party Fundraising Committees

Republican Committees	Democratic Committees
Republican National Committee (RNC)	Democratic National Committee (DNC)
National Republican Senatorial Committee (NRSC)	Democratic Senatorial Campaign Committee (DSCC)
National Republican Congressional Committee (NRCC)	Democratic Congressional Campaign Committee (DCCC)
Republican Governors Association (RGA)	Democratic Governors Association (DGA)

Sources: https://rnc.org/, https://www.nrsc.org/, https://www.nrcc.org/, https://www.rga.org/, https://democrats.org/, https://www.dscc.org/, https://dccc.org/, https://democraticgovernors.org/.

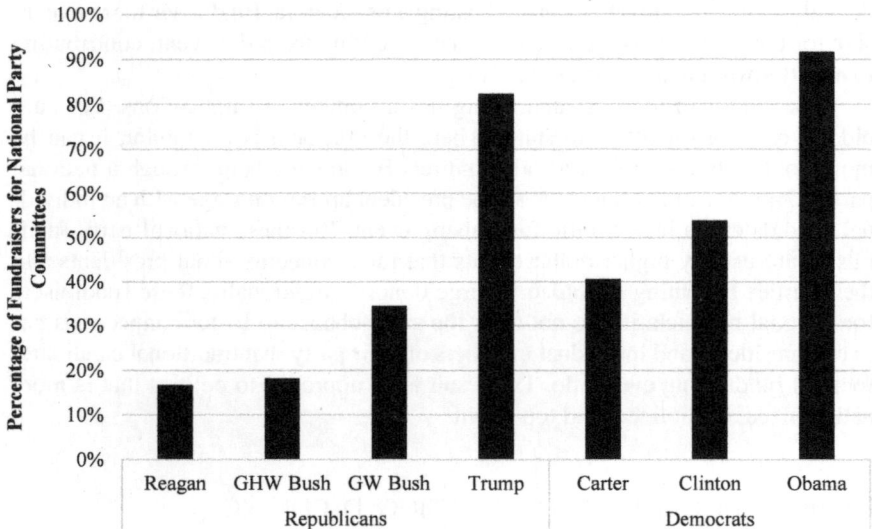

Figure 3.1: Percentage of Fundraisers for National Party Beneficiaries, by Party and President, 1977–2020
Sources: Data compiled by the author from the *Public Papers of the Presidents*, the Digests of Other White House Announcements, White House schedules and press briefings, Reagan's personal diary, and Associated Press and other news articles.

raising priorities. Each of these seven presidents was the highest profile fundraiser during the four or eight years when he was in office. Analyzing relative fundraising priorities illuminates each president's money-raising strategies in the context of the time in which he served and fundraised.

The clear trend over time is a steady rise in the percentage of fundraisers for these national beneficiaries within each party. For Republicans, the percentages of fundraisers for national party beneficiaries rose from Reagan's 16 percent to George H. W. Bush's 18 percent, to George W. Bush's 34 percent, and finally to Donald Trump's 82 percent. For Democratic presidents, the percentages of fundraisers for national beneficiaries were consistently higher than those of the Republican presidents who served immediately before or after they did. Among presidents from their party, however, Democrats saw a similar rise over time. Forty percent of Jimmy Carter's fundraisers aided national party beneficiaries, followed by 54 percent of Clinton's fundraising events and 91 percent of Obama's fundraisers that benefited the DNC, the DSCC, the Democratic Congressional Campaign Committee (DCCC), or the Democratic Governors Association (DGA).

Collectively, the DNC and the RNC were the leading national beneficiaries across these seven presidencies, as 76 percent of all national party fundraisers included either of these two principal national committees. This was consistently

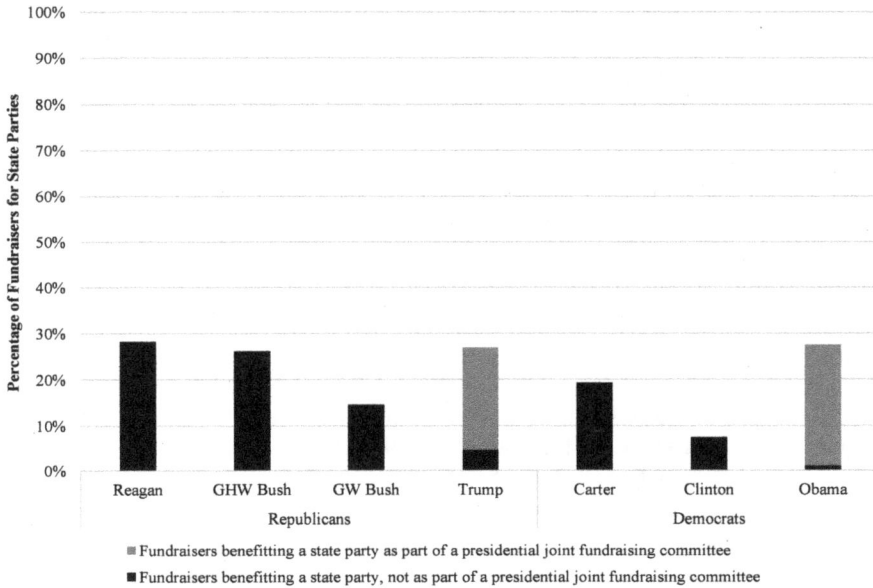

Figure 3.2: Percentage of Fundraisers for State Parties, by Party and President, 1977–2020
Sources: Data compiled by the author from the *Public Papers of the Presidents*, the Digests of Other White House Announcements, White House schedules and press briefings, Reagan's personal diary, and Associated Press and other news articles.

true over the twenty-eight years encompassing the four presidencies from Clinton to Trump, as each of these four most recent presidents dedicated at least 75 percent of his national party fundraisers to the DNC or RNC. As DNC chair Debbie Wasserman Schultz put it in 2013, "The DNC is the political arm of the president and the White House. We are the president's political voice."[2] Presidents have made funding that political voice a recurring top priority.

The rise in presidential fundraising for national party entities has been accompanied by a decline in fundraisers that have benefited state parties, as illustrated by Figure 3.2. Figures 3.1 and 3.2 use the same scale to make clear that state party fundraising at its peak was still a relatively low priority for every recent president. But over time within each party there has been a consistent decline in the percentage of fundraisers that presidents have held that benefited state parties that were not part of a presidential joint fundraising committee. For Republicans, the percentages of these state party fundraisers, depicted by the darker portions of the columns in Figure 3.2, fell from Reagan's 28 percent to George H. W. Bush's 26 percent, George W. Bush's 14 percent and Trump's 4 percent. For Democrats, those percentages dropped from Carter's 19 percent to Clinton's 7 percent and Obama's 1 percent. While Republican presidents have tended to make state party fundraising a greater priority than did contemporaneous Democrats, the trend within both parties has been a decline in focus on fundraisers that benefited state parties that were not part of a presidential joint fundraising committee.

The lighter portions of the columns in Figure 3.2 depict the percentage of each president's fundraisers that benefited a state party as part of a presidential joint fundraising committee. As discussed in chapter 2, many state parties were added to complicated joint fundraising committees during both the Obama and Trump presidencies in a way that enables donors to make ever larger contributions. State parties have been ancillary beneficiaries that have not been at the center of these joint fundraising committees. In many cases, state parties do not keep much or all of the funds that they receive via these committees. Instead, they transfer funds they receive to their party's national committee.

For example, on September 4, 2020, the Trump Victory joint fundraising committee sent $920,091 to the Florida Republican Party, $643,902 to the Arizona Republican Party, $534,674 to the Colorado Republican Party, $649,632 to the Georgia Republican Party, $701,697 to the Michigan Republican Party, and $651,469 to the Minnesota Republican Party. Each of those state parties then transferred those exact same amounts to the RNC. These transfers were legal, as federal law allows unlimited financial transfers between state and national parties. Campaign finance lawyer Brett Kappel compared this practice to money laundering. "The Supreme Court said it's legal so, you know, they don't even try to hide it. It's just a laundromat. The money goes in and goes out the same day."[3]

It is clear that these joint fundraising committee events were not held with the primary aim of benefiting state parties. While Figure 3.2 indicates that the total number of fundraisers that aided state parties did spike under Obama and Trump due to state parties being included in presidential joint fundraising committees, the darker portions of the columns in the figure show that the trend of fundraisers that were held primarily for the benefit of state parties has been consistently downward within each party over the forty-four years from Carter's presidency through Trump's.

The first five presidents in this study spent substantial amounts of time raising money for state parties. Almost one in five of Carter's fundraisers aided state parties, as he headlined twenty of these events in fifteen states plus the District of Columbia. Reagan is the president who placed the greatest relative priority on state party fundraising, with close to three in every ten of his fundraisers benefiting a state party. In his eight years in office, he headlined fifty-three fundraisers for state Republican parties in twenty-eight states. His home state party was the most frequent beneficiary, as Reagan took part in nine fundraisers on behalf of the California Republican Party. Reagan's fifty-three total state party fundraisers comprised 28 percent of all of the fundraisers he participated in as president. George H. W. Bush kept up this practice, as he took part in forty state party fundraisers in twenty-five states during his single term in the White House. Bill Clinton in eight years headlined fifty-four state party fundraisers, but his overall fundraising activity was so frequent that these state party events constituted only 7 percent of his total fundraising. And George W. Bush in his eight years in office took part in fifty fundraisers that benefited state parties, representing 15 percent of his total fundraising efforts.

Obama and Trump, however, spent very little time aiding state parties, aside from the state parties that were minor parts of their presidential joint fundraising committees. Obama headlined 132 Obama Victory Fund events that included state parties among their beneficiaries, but he only took part in five fundraisers that otherwise benefited a state party over the course of his eight years in office. In Trump's four years in office, state parties were among the beneficiaries of thirty fundraisers he headlined for the Trump Victory committee following the addition of state parties as committee beneficiaries in January 2020. Aside from those joint fundraising committee events, he participated in only five other fundraisers that benefited state parties.

While Democratic and Republican presidents fundraised more for national beneficiaries and less primarily for state parties over time, both indicators reveal party asymmetries. Democratic and Republican presidents increasingly devoted more of their fundraising efforts to national party beneficiaries and less to state parties. But Democratic presidents consistently focused more of their fundraising efforts on national parties and less on state parties than did the Republican presidents who directly succeeded or preceded them in the White House.

Prior scholarly research offers potential explanations for these party asymmetries. M. Margaret Conway, writing in the early 1980s, discussed how Democrats had centralized more power in their national party organization. In contrast, Republicans had kept more authority in the hands of state parties.[4] This difference could certainly have played into the contrast between the early presidents in this study, as Carter dedicated more of his fundraising efforts to national party beneficiaries and less to state parties than did Reagan. The increase in nationalized fundraising over time within each party then proceeded from those two different baseline levels.

Two other studies offer additional insights that could shed light on the differences between Democratic and Republican presidents' fundraising practices. Matt Grossmann and Dave Hopkins have argued that the asymmetries between the two major parties can be best understood as differences between "ideological Republicans and group interest Democrats." They contend that Republicans tend to unite around the ideological goal of decreasing the role of government, while Democrats are comprised of a broader coalition of groups that seek policies that would work to their benefit.[5] Daniel Hopkins, Eric Schickler, and David Azizi analyzed similar dynamics in their study of a century of state party platforms. They found that the issues in Republican platforms were more similar across states, while there was more variety in the issues in Democratic state party platforms. In both parties, their analysis revealed that differences across states declined over time, reflecting the nationalization of American politics.[6] Given the greater internal party cohesion among Republicans found in both of these studies, a Republican president might be more in demand at fundraising events for state parties across the country than a Democratic president who leads a more heterogeneous party, and thus might find it more appealing to fundraise more for national beneficiaries.

Additionally, Democrats have long advocated for a more prominent role for the federal government in addressing the nation's problems, while Republicans have long focused their rhetoric on their desire to reduce the power of the federal government and return authority to the states. The patterns in this study of a lower baseline of national party fundraising and a higher baseline of state party fundraising for Republicans, and the converse for Democrats, certainly fit with these rhetorical dynamics. These factors could help to explain the clear rise in fundraising for national party beneficiaries and a corresponding decline in fundraising primarily for state parties among presidents within each party over the decades since the adoption of the modern campaign finance system in the 1970s.

ATM STATES: FUNDRAISING WITH A NATIONAL OR IN-STATE FOCUS

The nationalization of presidential fundraising has an important geographic element as well. While presidents used to hold fundraisers across the country that predominantly aided beneficiaries from those states—a state party in California, a gubernatorial candidate in Illinois, or a senator in Louisiana—in recent years presidents have frequently traveled to a state to raise money for a national entity that does not have a connection to that particular state. This practice led the anonymous Democrat quoted at the beginning of this chapter to claim that New York had become a so-called ATM state. In these places, presidents and other elected or party officials visit for the purpose of raising funds and then direct that money to out-of-state beneficiaries.

In one example of these dynamics, Clinton frustrated Democratic state party leaders when he headlined two DNC fundraisers in New York City in January 1998. State party chair Judith Hope explained how national fundraising events complicated her in-state fundraising: "Virtually all of my major donors are the same as their major donors. When I'm making phone calls, and they've just been here, I hear, 'I just gave a $25,000 check to the D.N.C., and I can't give to you for a while.'" The frustration recurred later that year when Clinton returned in September to hold a DNC fundraiser at a special performance of the Broadway show *The Lion King*. The event would yield about $3.5 million and was described as "among the most profitable party fund-raisers ever," but its timing aggravated state Democratic leaders. The fundraiser took place just before the primary election that would select the Democratic challenger to incumbent Republican Senator Alfonse D'Amato. State party officials worried that donors would be less likely to give to state and local candidates after paying high ticket prices for the event with the president. The *New York Times* summed up the complaints of the Democratic state party that year with this headline: "As Clinton Eats Up Contributions, New York Party Says It's Starving." As the state party chair put it, "We are a dollar-exporting state in the Democratic Party." In response, a senior White House official admitted, "That's a common refrain everywhere."[7]

To assess the extent to which presidential fundraisers benefit politicians running for office in or party committees from the states where the events take place, each presidential fundraiser was coded for whether it aided an in-state beneficiary or not. Fundraisers that jointly benefited a candidate for office in that state as well as a national party organization, such as the March 2007 fundraiser that George W. Bush headlined for Senator Mitch McConnell and the NRSC in Louisville, Kentucky, or the October 1998 fundraiser that Clinton took part in to benefit Senate candidate Chuck Schumer and the DSCC in New York City, were coded as benefiting a candidate for office in that state. National beneficiaries include the DNC, the RNC, the DCCC, the NRCC, the DSCC, the NRSC, the DGA, and the RGA, as well as a president's reelection campaign and the campaign of the party's nominee to succeed the president. Joint fundraising committee events that supported a presidential nominee were not coded as aiding a local entity if they took place in a state where its state party was among the many beneficiaries. At these events, the state party was far from being a primary beneficiary, and in many instances the state party would later transfer the funds it received to the national party.

A fundraiser with only national beneficiaries is not tied to the place in which the funds are raised; instead, it could be held anywhere. Presidents who want to raise money for the DNC, the RNC, or any other national beneficiary are not constrained by geography. Their aides can plan a fundraiser in any place that suits their needs. A DNC or RNC fundraiser in New York could just as easily be held in Los Angeles, Dallas, Miami, Chicago, or a number of other locations.

A presidential fundraiser for a specific home-state candidate or state party is different. Those events are tied to the politics of the states in which they take place. If a president travels to Nevada or South Dakota or Minnesota to raise money for a congressional or gubernatorial candidate there, those are not events that would be likely to be held in a different part of the country. Instead, the president is traveling to that place to raise funds for a candidate or a party committee from that place.

Sixty-four percent of the presidential fundraisers headlined by the seven presidents from Carter to Trump had no local beneficiary and were instead held for the benefit of a national party committee or candidate. Washington, DC, had the most lopsided tilt toward national beneficiaries, as just four of the 486 presidential fundraisers held there were for the benefit of politicians or parties from the District of Columbia itself—one for a sitting mayor, one for a mayoral candidate, one for DC's nonvoting representative to Congress, and one for the local Democratic Party. The remaining 99 percent of fundraisers in DC benefited either national political entities or candidates or elected officials who hailed from elsewhere.

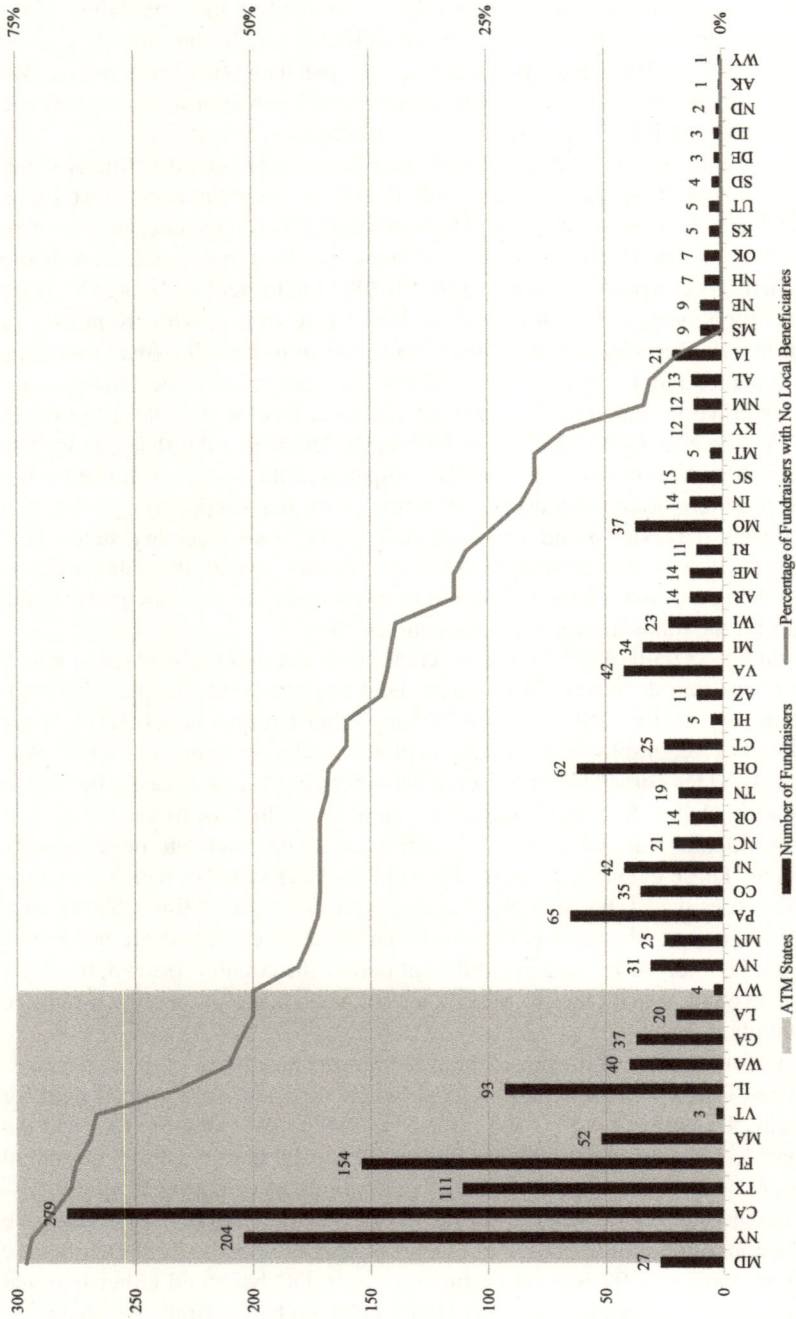

Figure 3.3: ATM States and Local Beneficiary States: Number of Fundraisers and Percentage of Fundraisers with No Local Beneficiary, 1977–2020
Sources: Data compiled by the author from the *Public Papers of the Presidents*, the Digests of Other White House Announcements, White House schedules and press briefings, Reagan's personal diary, and Associated Press and other news articles.

Figure 3.3 depicts the numbers of fundraisers held in each state and the percentage of fundraisers in those states that had no local beneficiary between 1977 and 2020. Washington, DC, is omitted because its 486 fundraisers would give the y-axis a scale that would make it difficult to distinguish the number of fundraisers in the states that hosted relatively few such events. The states are arrayed along the x-axis from those to the left, with the greatest percentages of fundraisers with no local beneficiary; to those to the right, with the smallest percentages of such events. The states to the left in the gray portion of the figure are the ATM states—those where at least 50 percent of all presidential fundraisers did not have a local beneficiary.

While 64 percent of presidential fundraisers held over this forty-four-year period did not have a local beneficiary, most of those events were concentrated in a relatively small number of states. Just twelve of the fifty states, plus Washington, DC, were ATM locations, as at least 50 percent of fundraisers held there lacked any local beneficiary: Maryland, New York, California, Texas, Florida, Massachusetts, Vermont, Illinois, Washington, Georgia, Louisiana, and West Virginia. Of the 1,398 fundraisers with no local beneficiary, 1,179, or 84 percent, were held in these twelve states and the District of Columbia. There is substantial variation among these twelve ATM states. Although Maryland was the state with the highest percentage of fundraisers with no local beneficiary, at just over 74 percent, only twenty-seven fundraisers were held there over this forty-four-year period. New York and California, with just under 74 percent and 71 percent of their fundraisers lacking a local beneficiary, respectively, hosted far more fundraisers overall. California led the way with 279 fundraisers, and only eighty of those had a local beneficiary. Some of the states on this list hosted very low numbers of total fundraisers. Vermont and West Virginia were both ATM states as well, as two of the three fundraisers held in Vermont had no local beneficiary. This was also the case for two of the four fundraisers held in West Virginia over the seven presidencies from Carter through Trump. While both states met the threshold to be ATM states, neither hosted a substantial number of presidential fundraisers.

At the other end of the spectrum, a majority of fundraisers aided in-state beneficiaries in thirty-eight states. Of these, there were twelve states where every presidential fundraiser held there helped candidates or party organizations from those states. All saw low numbers of fundraisers overall. Mississippi and Nebraska led this list with nine fundraisers apiece, followed by New Hampshire and Oklahoma with seven each, Kansas and Utah with five apiece, South Dakota with four, Delaware and Idaho with three each, North Dakota with two, and Alaska and Wyoming with just one fundraiser each. These states all have relatively low populations, and none is home to a leading metropolitan area. On the rare occasions when presidents have chosen to fundraise in these states, they have done so to help their fellow party members there.

Not depicted in Figure 3.3 are two locations that held no fundraisers for local beneficiaries—San Juan, Puerto Rico; and London, England. These two cities hosted the only fundraisers that these seven presidents attended outside of the fifty US states and the District of Columbia. In June 2011 Obama headlined a fundraiser in San Juan for the Obama Victory Fund, and in December 2019 Trump took part in a fundraiser in London for the Trump Victory joint fundraising committee. As Puerto Ricans are US citizens, and as there are many US citizens living in London as expatriates, both presidents were able to find interested donors who met the legal requirement that contributions to federal campaigns can only come from US citizens. Though each city hosted only one presidential fundraiser over the course of forty-four years, that single event with a nonlocal beneficiary made each an ATM location.

Journalists have recounted the frustrations that are common among political leaders in ATM states. In August 2010 a *Houston Chronicle* writer described what "political professionals call a 'bag drag'":

> Some state Democrats complain [that] the national party has used Texas like an ATM. The national party's constant suck of money out of the state without reinvesting in Texas has given Republicans an advantage in state elections, they say. "If they'd invest this money in Texas, we'd be a blue (Democratic) state," said long-time party consultant Glenn Smith. "They (national party leaders) come down here and drag the sack and spend the money on themselves."[8]

Similar sentiments have emanated from California. One news article described visits to the state by those seeking to win the presidency this way: "The White House candidates' path through California has become well-worn, and the itinerary generally looks like this: Fly into Silicon Valley; mingle with donors at a mansion; fly to Los Angeles; mingle with donors at a mansion; fly out to battleground state. For variety, the candidates occasionally travel south to north instead."[9]

These complaints have arisen in Illinois too. In 1994 aides to the state's Democratic gubernatorial candidate aired their frustrations in the press:

> Dawn Clark Netsch, the Democratic nominee for governor in Illinois, will be smiling at President Clinton's side Friday when he begins a party fundraising trip in Chicago but aides say she is "disgusted" by the trip. Aides said Netsch is upset about the visit, intended to raise money for the Democratic Senate [*sic*] Campaign Committee. Neither of Illinois' Senate seats is open this election, meaning any money raised in the Windy City will go out of state. Netsch, whose campaign warchest is a fraction of incumbent Republican Gov. Jim Edgar's, does not like the appeals to Illinois voters to help candidates in other states. "They are going through the same lists we are for fundraising and there's only so much money Democratic supporters can be expected to contribute," a Netsch fundraising aide told UPI.[10]

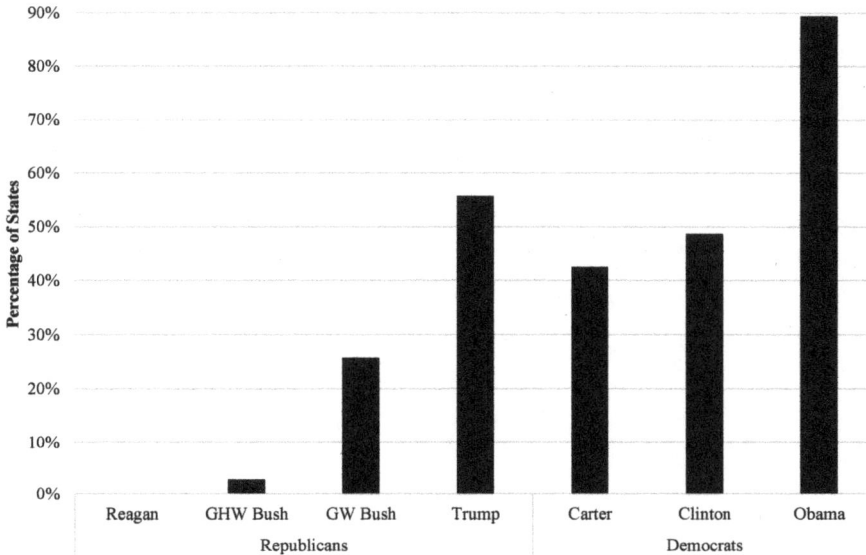

Figure 3.4: Percentage of States Where at Least Half of Presidential Fundraisers Had No Local Beneficiary, 1977–2020
Sources: Data compiled by the author from the *Public Papers of the Presidents*, the Digests of Other White House Announcements, White House schedules and press briefings, Reagan's personal diary, and Associated Press and other news articles.

In 1996 the *New York Daily News* offered another example of these dynamics. "Annoyance among House Democrats has been brewing for a month, in part, because Clinton had steamrolled the nation like a 'vacuum cleaner,' as one House leader put it, sucking up contributions and making it harder for others to raise money." This led the *Daily News* to run the following headline in its frequently used all-caps format: "WE NEED DOUGH TOO, REPS TELL PREZ."[11]

These ATM fundraising trips, or bag drags, have become increasingly common in recent years as presidential fundraising has become more nationalized. Figure 3.4 presents the percentage of states in which each president held fundraisers that were ATM states—where at least 50 percent of the fundraisers had no local beneficiary. Washington, DC, is not included, as it is not a state, though it was an ATM location for each of these seven presidents. As was the case with other indicators of nationalization, the percentage of ATM states has grown over time within each party.

Reagan had no ATM states. In every one of the thirty-eight states in which he held fundraisers, more than half of the events had local beneficiaries. Just one of the thirty-nine states in which George H. W. Bush headlined fundraisers was an ATM state, and that was Maryland, where he held only one fundraiser—a June 1992 event for the RNC that took place in a Maryland suburb just north of Wash-

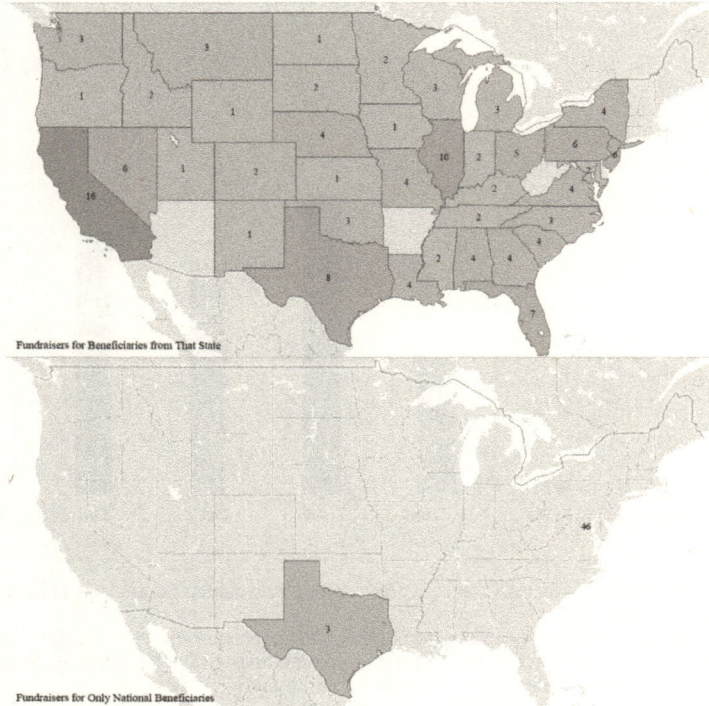

Figure 3.5: Reagan's Fundraisers for In-State and Only National Beneficiaries, 1981–1988
Sources: Data compiled by the author from the *Public Papers of the Presidents*, the Digests of Other White House Announcements, White House schedules and press briefings, Reagan's personal diary, and Associated Press and other news articles.

ington, DC. But ATM state fundraising would rise substantially over time. For George W. Bush, more than a quarter of the forty-three states in which he held fundraisers were ATM states. That percentage would rise to just over 55 percent for Trump—in fifteen of the twenty-seven states in which he held fundraisers, at least half of his events had no local beneficiary. The three Democratic presidencies displayed a similar rise over time, but with a higher initial baseline. Fourteen of the thirty-three states—more than 42 percent—in which Carter attended fundraisers were ATM states. For Clinton, almost half of the states in which he held fundraisers—seventeen of thirty-five states—were ATM states. Obama headlined fundraisers in twenty-eight states, and twenty-five of these, or 89 percent, were ATM states. The rise of the percentage of ATM states signals a clear change in the ways that presidents lead their parties. Presidents used to travel around the country to raise funds for candidates from the places they visited. They do so far less than they used to, instead traveling to raise money primarily for national beneficiaries and doing so in a relatively small number of states.

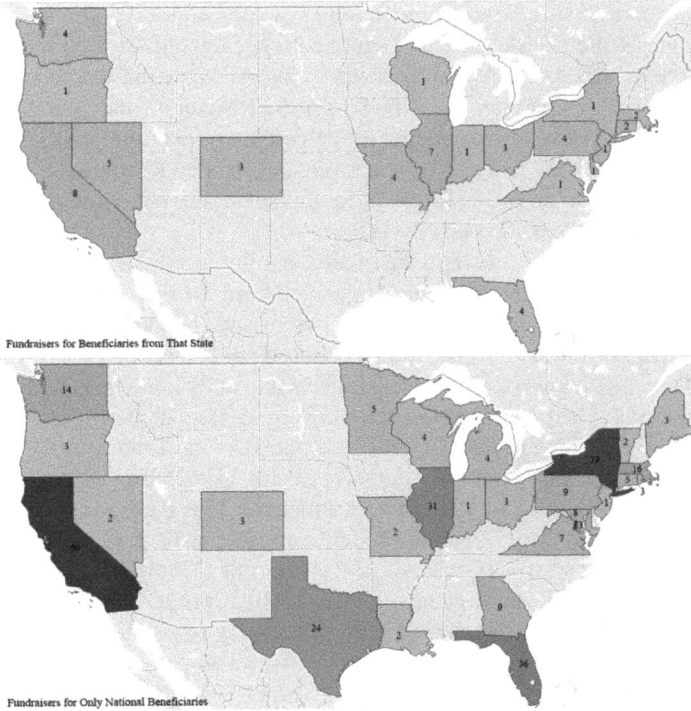

Figure 3.6: Obama' Fundraisers for In-State and Only National Beneficiaries, 2009–2016
Sources: Data compiled by the author from the *Public Papers of the Presidents*, the Digests of Other White House Announcements, White House schedules and press briefings, and Associated Press and other news articles.

THE REAGAN-OBAMA CONTRAST

Comparing the first and last two-term presidents in this study, Reagan and Obama, sheds more light on the ways in which presidential fundraising has become nationalized. Figures 3.5 and 3.6 depict the geography of fundraisers for in-state and national beneficiaries for Reagan and Obama throughout their eight respective years in office. They illustrate graphically the rising nationalization and shifting geography of presidential fundraising. In each figure, the top map presents the numbers of fundraisers that the presidents headlined in each state that included a beneficiary from that state. The bottom map portrays the numbers of fundraisers in each state that had no local beneficiary.

In Reagan's eight years as president, he participated in 139 fundraisers for in-state beneficiaries in thirty-eight states. Of the forty-nine fundraisers he headlined only for national beneficiaries, forty-six were held in Washington, DC, and the other three took place in Texas. Reagan's efforts to raise funds for in-state candidates and parties carried him to almost every region of the country. Only twelve states—the six states that comprise New England, as well as Delaware, West Virginia, Arkansas, Arizona, Hawaii, and Alaska—did not host a Reagan fundraiser for a beneficiary from those states. Reagan's fundraising solely for national beneficiaries only accounted for 26 percent of his fundraisers, and almost all of those events took place in Washington, DC. While DC was an ATM location for Reagan, since none of his forty-six fundraisers there benefited a candidate or local party from DC, he had no ATM states.

In contrast, Figure 3.6 indicates that Obama's fundraising was both more nationalized and more geographically concentrated. In his eight years in office, he took part in fifty-three fundraisers that had in-state beneficiaries. These events took place in just eighteen states and accounted for 11 percent of all of his fundraisers. The other 89 percent of his fundraisers had no in-state beneficiaries. These 445 events took place in twenty-seven states as well as in Washington, DC, and Puerto Rico. Neither the event in Puerto Rico nor one fundraiser in Hawaii is depicted on the map, which only displays events held in the continental United States. Although Obama attended fundraising events far more frequently than did Reagan, his geographical range was much narrower, as he held his 498 fundraising events in just twenty-eight states, the District of Columbia, and Puerto Rico. As Karl Rove, a top political aide to George W. Bush, put it, "There are also just so many cities capable of producing $1 million and only so many times you can hold a million dollar fundraiser in them."[12] Of the twenty-eight states in which Obama held fundraisers, twenty-five were ATM states. Only in Delaware, Missouri, and Nevada did Obama hold a majority of his fundraisers for in-state beneficiaries, and those states accounted for only fourteen of his 498 fundraising events.

The contrast between Reagan and Obama is indicative of the shift over time that has come with the nationalization of presidential fundraising. Carter, Reagan, and George H. W. Bush all held more fundraisers for in-state beneficiaries than events that exclusively benefited national beneficiaries. These dynamics reversed themselves for Clinton, George W. Bush, Obama, and Trump. All four of these latter presidents headlined more fundraisers that only aided national beneficiaries than events that supported in-state beneficiaries. The next section explores factors related to the nationalization of presidential fundraising.

WHY THE NATIONALIZATION OF PRESIDENTIAL FUNDRAISING?

Why did the forty-four years from 1977 through 2020 witness such a clear and substantial nationalization of presidential fundraising? I contend that several factors have played a key role. The elements of campaign finance law that allow presidents to raise funds in larger amounts for national beneficiaries than for individual candidates have incentivized nationalized fundraising. This is particularly the case given the rising costs of campaigns and the increased prominence of nonparty groups like Super PACs that are not subject to contribution limits. These dynamics have played out during a period in which each party believes it has a realistic chance to gain or lose substantial political power in most election cycles. Additionally, new federal requirements that beneficiaries of a presidential fundraiser must pay more of the costs for presidential travel to that event have made it less appealing for individual candidates to host a presidential fundraiser, contributing to the increase in fundraising for national beneficiaries. Nationalized fundraising also can bring political benefits, as it allows unpopular presidents to offer indirect aid through party committees to candidates who would like financial assistance but find it politically expedient to put a bit of distance between themselves and the president.

Higher Contribution Limits for National Parties

One key factor in the nationalization of presidential fundraising has been the rules allowing donors to write larger checks to national party organizations than they can to individual candidates. The maximum donations permitted to both candidates and national parties have varied over time as campaign finance laws have changed, but limits on contributions to national parties have consistently been higher than caps on donations to individual candidates throughout the modern campaign finance regime.

When the current campaign finance system was created in the 1970s, an individual could give $1,000 to a federal candidate per election cycle and $20,000 to a national party committee per year. The proliferation in the 1990s of soft money fundraising by national parties—unlimited donations that could only be used for certain purposes, as discussed in chapter 2—meant that presidents could help their parties to raise money that was not subject to contribution limits. Consequently, Clinton spent substantial amounts of time raising money for the various national Democratic Party committees. Doing so was an efficient use of his time, since what critics referred to as the soft money loophole enabled presidents to headline high-dollar fundraising events that brought in substantial amounts of money for their political party.

Following the banning of soft money contributions to national party committees by the Bipartisan Campaign Reform Act of 2002 (BCRA), presidents could no longer help their parties raise unlimited campaign funds. But parties still offered an appealing vehicle to raise funds in amounts larger than those that could be donated to specific political candidates. The BCRA initially limited contributions by individuals to candidates for federal office at $2,000 per election and to national party committees at $25,000 per year. Both amounts were set to rise with inflation.[13] In July 2008 Dana Perino, who served as White House press secretary to George W. Bush, explained the efficiency that came from fundraising for national party entities. "One of the things the president has done over time is helped to build up capacity in the committees, like the RNC and the NRCC and the NRSC, the victory committees, these congressional trusts, in ways that he can maximize the use of his time raising money for . . . several candidates all at once."[14]

The amount of money that presidents could raise for their national party committees would increase substantially due to two developments in 2014. First, the *McCutcheon v. FEC* Supreme Court decision eliminated the aggregate cap on the amount that an individual could contribute to individual candidates and to various party committees during each election cycle. Second, a law passed by Congress later that year allowed national parties to receive larger contributions to a greater number of specific party committees. Both of these developments are described in detail in chapter 2. These changes did not just open the door for joint fundraising committees involving presidential campaigns and multiple party committees. They also allowed for the creation of other complicated joint fundraising committees that would enable a president to leverage his or her fundraising prowess to raise much larger amounts of money for his party than had been possible beforehand.

In one example, Trump headlined a fundraiser on October 29, 2019, for a joint fundraising committee called Take Back the House 2020. The event that evening benefited seventy-seven different entities: the National Republican Congressional Committee, fifty-five specific candidates for the House of Representatives, the leadership political action committee of the Republican leader in the House, and twenty Republican state parties. An estimated 315 donors attended, each contributing at least $35,000 to the joint fundraising committee, which then distributed the funds among its seventy-seven beneficiaries. The event raised more than $13 million to help Republicans campaigning for House seats the following year.[15]

Presidential fundraising for national party committees and for joint fundraising committees like Take Back the House 2020 are more efficient uses of a president's time than fundraising for individual candidates. Presidents used to travel the country holding many events for individual beneficiaries, but recent presidents have done so far less frequently. Figure 3.7 depicts the decline in the percentage of non-reelection fundraisers that presidents held only for the benefit of individuals other than themselves. A president's own reelection fundraisers are excluded from the denominator, and joint fundraisers that benefit a national party committee in addition to an individual candidate are excluded from the numerator. Thus, the figure illuminates how frequently presidents fundraise exclusively for other specific individuals when they fundraise for beneficiaries apart from their own reelection campaign committee.

Within each party, there has been a decline in the percentage of a president's non-reelection fundraisers that benefited only other individuals. Among Republican presidents, these numbers fell from Reagan's 54 percent to George H. W. Bush's 51 percent, George W. Bush's 45 percent, and Trump's 19 percent. Among Democratic presidents, Carter held 34 percent of his non-reelection fundraisers

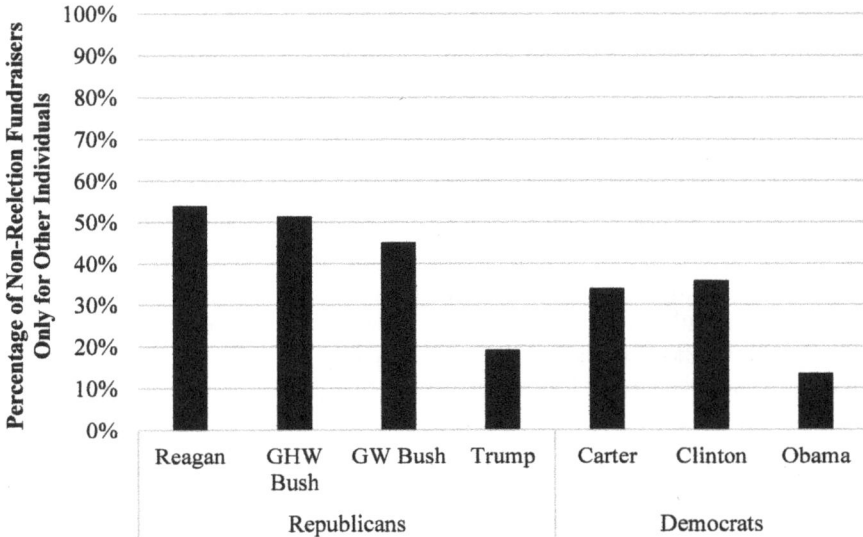

Figure 3.7: Percentage of Non-Reelection Fundraisers Only for Other Individuals, by Party and President, 1977–2020
Sources: Data compiled by the author from the *Public Papers of the Presidents*, the Digests of Other White House Announcements, White House schedules and press briefings, Reagan's personal diary, and Associated Press and other news articles.

exclusively for other individuals. Clinton's percentage was slightly higher, at 36 percent, and Obama's was much lower, at 13 percent. This decline among presidents within each party is similar to the patterns discussed earlier of decreasing relative focus on fundraisers primarily for state parties.

Holding fundraisers to benefit specific individuals used to represent a large portion of presidents' efforts to raise campaign funds for their fellow party members. When Carter embarked on a three-day fundraising swing in February 1978 in advance of midterm elections that fall, he held fundraisers for four senators: William Hathaway in Maine; Thomas McIntyre in New Hampshire; Claiborne Pell in Rhode Island; and Joe Biden in Delaware. He also headlined two state party fundraisers in Maine and Delaware. Four of the six fundraisers that Carter headlined on this trip were events held specifically to benefit fellow individual Democrats, and the other two benefited state parties, not the national party.

Trips like this one were typical decades ago. In contrast, forty years later in the midterm election year of 2018, Trump headlined six fundraisers in March. Two benefited the RNC, two were held for the Trump Victory joint fundraising committee—which directed some of its proceeds to the RNC—and one was held for the national Republican Party committee dedicated to electing House members. Just one fundraiser benefited an individual, Missouri Senate candidate Josh

Hawley, but it also aided the NRSC as part of a joint fundraising committee. All of these six fundraisers benefited national party entities, and only one also aided a specific individual candidate for office; none of these events was held exclusively for the benefit of an individual candidate.

The ability to raise funds for national party committees and joint fundraising committees in larger amounts is appealing for presidents and their fellow party members in an era marked by dramatically rising costs of campaigns and the specter of Super PACs and other nonparty groups that can raise money without the restrictions of contribution limits. Fundraising for national party entities and for joint fundraising committees that include national beneficiaries is an efficient use of a president's scarce time. While presidents used to travel frequently to a specific place to hold a fundraiser for a beneficiary from that place, that type of fundraising has become far less common.

A Change in Who Pays for Presidential Fundraising Travel

Another factor in the nationalization of presidential fundraising is a little-noticed but consequential change in 2010 to the rules governing how presidential fundraising travel is paid for that increased the costs borne by the sponsoring political organization. Taxpayers always bear much of the expense of presidential travel, even when a president hits the road for campaign-related purposes, since a president must always be on the job and have close at hand the personnel, equipment, and other resources to serve as chief executive and commander in chief at any moment. A president does not take a break from the duties of the office when he or she flies to New York, Miami, Dallas, or Los Angeles to headline a fundraiser. As Obama White House press secretary Jay Carney said in 2012, "The president is the president 24 hours a day and seven days a week, and he has to fly on Air Force One. He has to have security and communication. There are elements of his job that are always with him, regardless of whether he's in a campaign event or an official event. And costs are apportioned accordingly."[16] As discussed in more detail in chapter 6, the costs of presidential travel are substantial, but no recent administration has shared with the public the total expenses involved in planning and executing a presidential journey.

Before 2010, federal law required that when a president travels for an event determined by the White House to be campaign-related, the benefiting political party or campaign had to reimburse the government for the cost of first-class commercial airline tickets for all people on the plane who were designated as traveling for campaign-related purposes. But an ethics reform law enacted in 2007 led to new FEC regulations in 2010 that required campaigns to bear more of the costs of presidential travel. Instead of the prior practice of basing the reimbursement on the price of first-class commercial airfare rates, campaigns would have to reimburse the government for the prorated cost of what they would have spent to charter a Boeing 737 airplane for a similar journey. A 2012 news article reported that "Obama's campaign doesn't have to pay the full cost for a chartered plane, though. It pays a reduced amount based on the number of people aboard Air Force One who were traveling for political reasons. That number excludes Secret Service agents and other support staff who always travel with the president."[17]

This change had practical consequences for the campaigns and party organizations that have to pay part of the travel expenses when a presidential entourage hits the campaign trail. An Associated Press review of FEC filings from George W. Bush's 2004 reelection bid found that the Bush campaign and the RNC sent payments to the White House amounting to more than $1.3 million for what were labeled "airlift operations," a term that includes the costs of flying on the president's plane, Air Force One, as well as the presidential helicopter, Marine One. This author reviewed FEC filings detailing the amounts paid to the White House by the DNC's travel offset account during Obama's 2012 reelection campaign and found that the DNC reimbursed the White House for more than $2.9 million for "airlift operations"—more than twice the total amount reimbursed during his predecessor's reelection bid.[18] While the specifics of what the reimbursements paid for are unclear, the fact that the funds transferred in 2012 were more than double those paid during the 2004 campaign reflect at least in part the substantially greater expenses that campaigns and parties have had to bear to pay for campaign travel since 2010.

While a presidential reelection campaign, working jointly with its national party committee, is a fundraising juggernaut that can afford to pay the higher price to support presidential travel, not all fundraising beneficiaries are able to do so. In the 2020 election cycle, donors could contribute $35,500 per year to a national party committee but only $2,800 per election cycle to a candidate for federal office. A national party committee like the DNC, RNC, DSCC, or NRSC can hold a presidential fundraising event with substantially higher ticket prices, and thus those committees can bear more easily the increased costs of the president flying in to headline a fundraiser. The increase in presidents fundraising for national beneficiaries after the 2010 rule change strongly suggests that it has become too expensive for some individual campaigns to pay the increased portion of the costs that come when president travels to a fundraiser.[19]

A Benefit of Nationalization: Political Convenience

Presidents can also find it politically convenient to fundraise for national entities instead of for specific political candidates for whom direct assistance would be problematic. The example of Obama's fundraising for Senate candidates in 2014 is illustrative. The Senate electoral map that year was challenging for Democrats, who were victims of their own success six years earlier. In 2008 Democrats had won Senate races in Alaska, Arkansas, Louisiana, North Carolina, and elsewhere in what was a very good year for their party's electoral fortunes. Six years later, senators from those states had to face the voters in a very different electoral climate, which led to news headlines like "Can Democrats Hold the Senate by Running Away from Obama—and Their Own Records?" Democratic senator Joe Manchin of West Virginia declared that when it came to Democrats running in places where Obama was unpopular, "there's nothing in these states that he can do" to help Democratic candidates for office.[20]

What did Obama do in the face of these political headwinds? He helped Democratic Senate candidates indirectly. He headlined sixteen fundraisers that year that benefited Senate races. Two of those were for a Super PAC that was dedicated to helping Democratic Senate candidates. The remaining fourteen all benefited the DSCC, and of these, three had proceeds divided between the DSCC and a specific senator—one for Senator Mark Udall of Colorado, and two for old Obama friend and Illinois Senator Dick Durbin. The DSCC was permitted to accept larger contributions than individual Senate candidates could. It could then use that money to help candidates across the country wage their campaigns.

Instead of traveling to an electorally competitive state to hold a fundraiser for a home-state senator in a tough race, Obama held his sixteen Senate fundraisers in major metropolitan areas that were almost uniformly not in states with competitive Senate races that year. Obama's 2014 Senate fundraisers were held in California, Colorado, Connecticut, the District of Columbia, Illinois (2), Massachusetts (2), Maryland, New York (4), Texas, Virginia, and Washington. Of those locations, only Colorado was the site of a competitive Senate race that year, according to ratings by the Cook Political Report.[21] Obama was able to raise contributions in larger amounts for the DSCC than would have been possible for individual candidates, and he did so without having to appear alongside senators from states where the president was less popular and where his physical presence would not be helpful.

This practice did not go unnoticed by Republicans. The communications director for the NRSC in the 2014 election cycle declared, "Vulnerable Democrats like having President Obama raising money for them in New York and Los Angeles, but avoid appearing on stage with him in their home states." Not holding a fundraising event together did not spare Democratic senators from attempts by Republicans to link them to Obama. A challenger to Democratic Senator Mary Landrieu was eager to connect her to a president who was unpopular in her home state of Louisiana, declaring in a campaign video, "She's always been Barack Obama's rubber stamp." Obama's fundraisers for the DSCC indirectly aided Democrats like Landrieu without requiring her to appear with him.[22]

Colorado Senator Mark Udall was one of only two senators who was an individual beneficiary of an Obama Senate fundraiser that year. Obama had carried Colorado in both 2008 and 2012, but his national job approval rating at the time of his July 2014 fundraiser for Udall was just 42 percent, down from 52 percent immediately before Election Day in 2012. When Obama flew to Denver to give a speech on the economy and attend a fundraiser for Udall on July 9, 2014, the senator's spokesperson announced that Udall would stay in Washington to vote on Obama's nominee for secretary of the Department of Housing and Urban Development because "his responsibilities to serve Colorado in the Senate come first." That nominee would be approved by the Senate that day by a 71–26 vote. News coverage of the day included the headline "Udall Skipping Obama Fundraiser," as multiple media stories focused on Udall's apparent desire not to be seen with the president who was raising campaign funds for his reelection bid.[23]

While it was politically convenient for Obama to fundraise for national beneficiaries when he was relatively unpopular in 2014, he continued this practice in his final two years in office, even after his job approval ratings had risen substantially. In July 2016, two years after the Udall fundraiser, Gallup measured Obama's national job approval rating to be 51 percent.[24] But in 2016, when Obama headlined ten fundraisers to benefit Senate races, eight of them were for the DSCC. The other two jointly aided specific Senate candidates and state parties in Illinois and Ohio. Obama's continued prioritization of national party fundraising even after his popularity had rebounded suggests that the ability of political parties to collect contributions in greater amounts than could individual candidates, along with party committees' ability to bear their increased share of the costs of presidential fundraising travel, likely played a greater role in the nationalization of presidential fundraising than did political convenience.

CONCLUSIONS

The increasing nationalization of presidential fundraising over the course of the seven presidencies from Carter to Trump has been a strategic response to evolving campaign finance dynamics. Over time and within each political party, presidents have devoted a greater percentage of their fundraising to national party beneficiaries while dedicating a smaller percentage of their efforts to fundraisers for state parties and to events that only benefited individual candidates for other offices. The geography of presidential fundraising has become more nationalized as well. While presidential fundraising trips used to feature mostly events that aided candidates and parties in the states that presidents visited, the increase in presidential fundraising has led to the proliferation of ATM fundraising locations, where presidents fly in to raise cash for national instead of local beneficiaries.

Presidents increasingly have found it more efficient and more appealing to raise money for national political parties in amounts that are substantially larger than those that can be donated to candidates' campaigns under our evolving campaign finance laws. Since the creation of the modern campaign finance system in the 1970s, individuals have been permitted to give more to national party committees than to a particular candidate. Additionally, a series of legal provisions and changes have led presidents to devote even more of their fundraising efforts to national beneficiaries.

First, presidents worked with their parties to raise unlimited soft money donations until the 2002 Bipartisan Campaign Reform Act prohibited that practice. Candidates then partnered with parties to form joint fundraising committees that could accept larger donations and distribute them to various campaigns and party entities. These joint committees could receive even larger contributions after the Supreme Court in 2014 struck down the aggregate limit on an individual's contributions to campaigns and parties in a given election cycle, and in the wake of a new law that year that allowed national parties to set up multiple additional fundraising committees that could accept contributions of more than $100,000 per year. A change in campaign finance rules requiring the benefiting political entity to pay more of the costs of presidential fundraising travel also contributed to the trend of raising money for national beneficiaries instead of individual campaigns. These changes have taken place against a backdrop of a competitive electoral landscape, rising campaign costs, and an increased role played by Super PACs and other nonparty groups that are not bound by contribution limits.

Why do these changes matter? While higher-dollar fundraising can be a more efficient use of a president's time—enabling him or her to raise more money from fewer people at fewer events—it offers more potential for corruption or the appearance of corruption. Nationalized fundraising also represents an important change in the ways that presidents play one of their key roles—the leader of their political party. Presidential fundraising used to be largely a one-on-one endeavor, as presidents traveled around the country to raise campaign funds for specific candidates. Recent presidents have fundraised predominantly for national party entities, sometimes also jointly benefiting specific candidates, but often not, creating fewer connections to individual office holders.

Archival research at the Reagan Library turned up numerous documents that describe spirited back-and-forth exchanges about which of the senators who requested a fundraising event with Reagan would be chosen as a recipient of the president's assistance. For example, I found eight different memoranda and letters from 1981 and 1982 about whether Reagan would headline a fundraiser for Republican Senator John Heinz of Pennsylvania, heir to the global ketchup and food company of the same name. Heinz solicited White House chief of staff James Baker in a letter in March 1982. He wrote, "This will be my largest and most important fundraiser of the year. . . . When your name is HEINZ people simply don't think you need any campaign money. . . . It is a unique, major fundraising problem I will always have to confront, and I need all the help I can in overcoming it."[25]

In spite of Heinz's argument that raising campaign funds for him would be a good use of the president's scarce time, multiple Reagan aides recommended that Reagan not take part in the event. They cited Heinz's lack of a formidable opponent and his lackluster voting record in support of Reagan's legislative agenda. However, some of Heinz's Senate colleagues saw the situation differently. Thirteen Republican senators wrote a letter to Senate Majority Leader Howard Baker in early April 1982 in which they declared that if Reagan did not headline a fundraiser for Heinz, it would "only make it more difficult for the President and Senate Republicans to work together on the many important issues facing the country." Reagan himself responded with a letter to Senator Baker four days later about the potential Heinz fundraiser in which he declared, "I do reserve the right to decide how and when I will campaign in 1982." In spite of the reservations of his aides, Reagan did end up making a fundraising trip to Philadelphia for Heinz in May 1982.[26]

The exchanges between the Reagan White House and Republicans in the Senate make clear how important Reagan's fundraiser for Heinz was to the senator and to numerous Senate colleagues. In light of the heated exchanges over the course of several months about whether Reagan would or would not headline this fundraiser, the senator must have been relieved and grateful when Reagan finally acceded to his request. These interpersonal dynamics between presidents and individual senators are absent when a president forgoes fundraisers for specific Senate candidates and instead embraces a fundraising strategy that is more top-down, centralized, and nationalized.

The next chapter examines presidential priorities and strategies through a broader lens. It focuses on the extent to which presidents dedicate themselves to aiding certain parts of their party—Senate races, House contests, governors' campaigns, and more—as they fulfill the role of fundraiser in chief.

4

Priorities and Strategies

"Among [Donald Trump's] close associates, a debate is raging about whether to focus on House races that could earn the president chits with Republican lawmakers who might ultimately vote on impeachment, or to dig in to defend the party's tenuous Senate majority."

—*New York Times*, April 28, 2018

"Clinton strategy for Democratic victory in November: money, money, money."

— Associated Press, June 11, 1998

Each of the three most recent Republican presidents displayed contrasting fundraising priorities in his first midterm election cycle. When George H. W. Bush set an aggressive fundraising schedule to help his fellow Republicans in the 1990 midterm elections, more than one-third of his 108 fundraising events benefited candidates in governors' races, as he worked to give his party a greater say in the upcoming round of redistricting that would follow the 1990 census. Bush, whose party controlled neither the House nor the Senate in his first two years in office, made Senate campaigns his second priority, accounting for just over a quarter of his fundraising efforts. Events for state parties comprised just under a quarter of Bush's fundraisers that cycle, while only 13 percent benefited House races.

Twelve years later, George W. Bush would set different priorities in the 2002 midterm election cycle. With the Senate evenly divided with fifty senators from each major party in the opening months of Bush's presidency, Vice President Dick Cheney's tie-breaking vote provided Republicans with the slimmest of majorities. This gave Republicans unified control of the House, Senate, and White House for the first time since the first two years of Eisenhower's presidency forty-six years earlier. But when a Republican senator left the party in the spring of 2001 and decided to caucus with the Democrats, Republicans lost control of the chamber. Bush responded by devoting 40 percent of his seventy-five fundraisers to Senate races, with 35 percent benefiting gubernatorial contests and 21 percent allocated to defending his party's majority in the House.

Donald Trump exhibited yet another set of priorities in the 2018 midterm election cycle. Almost 30 percent of his fifty-five fundraisers in his first two years in office jointly benefited his reelection campaign committee and the Republican National Committee (RNC), and an additional 7 percent of his fundraisers benefited just the RNC. Trump was the only president in the modern campaign finance era to fundraise for his reelection campaign committee in his first two years in office, which meant less fundraising for his fellow Republicans as they prepared for the midterm elections. Most of his other fundraising efforts went to his party's efforts to defend its majorities in both chambers of Congress, with just over a quarter of his fundraisers aiding Senate races and the same proportion benefiting House contests.

These three presidents illustrate some of the divergent approaches that recent presidents have taken as they have prioritized certain parts of their parties as well as their own reelection bids as beneficiaries of their fundraising efforts. Over the forty-four years from Jimmy Carter's presidency through Trump's, presidents have devoted substantial amounts of time to their role as the electoral leader of their party. Indeed, just over 26 percent of the 2,190 fundraisers that the seven presidents from 1977 through 2020 headlined benefited the presidents' own campaign committee or the Democratic or Republican National Committees in their third or fourth year in office. The remaining 74 percent of presidential fundraisers aided their fellow party members, indicating the priority that presidents place on their role as party leader. But there has been tremendous variation within and across presidencies in the extent to which presidents have engaged in efforts to fundraise for themselves and for fellow Democrats and Republicans, as well as in the parts of their party that they have prioritized.

Presidents spend substantial time fundraising for their fellow party members to help their political allies win elections so that they can enact what they see as good public policy. When George W. Bush held his first fundraiser as president in April 2001, his press secretary, Ari Fleischer, explained why he chose to do so. "The President is going to help raise money for people who will support his agenda of improving education by voting for more accountability, he will allow people to keep more money in their pockets for tax relief and he won't go on spending sprees. That's why the President participates in these events; it's how he can get his agenda enacted into law."[1] Barack Obama sounded a similar note at a 2015 DNC fundraiser. "We've got to have what Dr. King used to call the fierce urgency of now. Because the stakes are enormous in this upcoming election. . . . Presidents are important. They can make a difference. They can help set the agenda. But Presidents without a Congress that's supportive of that agenda and cooperative and thinking about the common good is not going to get done what needs to get done."[2]

Daniel Galvin's research on presidential party building found that presidents from Eisenhower through George W. Bush who viewed their party as the minority party in the nation tended to work harder to support their party's organizational capacity. Galvin convincingly contended that presidents' tendencies to exploit or work to build their party organization depended on their perception of their party as the majority or minority party nationally, and on the strength or weakness of the existing party organization. Thus, Republican presidents over this period worked in a sustained way to build their party organizations, while Democrats did not until after Bill Clinton's first term.[3] In Galvin's argument, the 1994 midterm elections that brought Republicans their first congressional majorities in both chambers in forty years were a turning point. In this new era of competitive congressional and presidential elections, presidents of both parties would be incentivized to focus on party building, including presidential fundraising.

This conclusion aligns with the case made by Sidney Milkis, Jesse Rhodes, and Emily Charnock. They argued that presidents since Ronald Reagan have developed "an emergent style of partisan presidential leadership" in which the tension between unifying national leadership and party leadership has been increasingly heightened due in large part to greater partisan polarization. This has created a leadership challenge for presidents who seek to fulfill both roles well. In this recent era, they contended, more presidents have worked to strengthen their parties than previously had been the case.[4]

I have built on these works in my previous research on presidential efforts to expand their party's ranks in government, finding in my prior book that every president from Reagan through Obama demonstrated a significant commitment to aid in raising financial resources for their fellow party members who were running for office.[5] To explore these dynamics further, this chapter examines which parts of their diverse, big-tent parties presidents work to aid. These decisions are a question of resource allocation. Since many more fellow party members want the president's aid than he can actually help, how does he allocate his time? The choices that presidents make throughout their terms in office illuminate their strategic fundraising priorities as they fulfill their role as their party's fundraiser in chief.

DIVERGENT PRIORITIES WHEN THE PRESIDENT IS AND IS NOT ON THE BALLOT

Each presidential fundraising event attended by the seven presidents from Carter through Trump was coded for its beneficiary or beneficiaries. Presidents headlined fundraisers for their own reelection campaigns; for the Democratic and Republican National Committees; for national party committees dedicated to campaigns for the Senate, the House of Representatives, and governorships; for individual Senate, House, and gubernatorial candidates; for state parties; for their party's next presidential nominee; for candidates for other offices such as mayors and state attorneys general across the country; and, most recently, for Super PACs. Collectively, the complex patchwork of fundraising efforts paints a picture of a president's electoral priorities as he dedicates substantial amounts of time to his own campaign efforts and to electing fellow party members to office.

The forty-four-year period of this study is comprised of twenty-two election cycles: seven first midterm cycles; seven presidential reelection cycles; four second midterm cycles; and four cycles during the final two years of a two-term presidency. To understand how presidents allocate their fundraising efforts, it is helpful to divide the analysis into presidential reelection cycles and non-reelection cycles, since a president's priorities shift dramatically when his name is not on the ballot. Presidents were up for reelection during only seven of these twenty-two election cycles, or fourteen of these forty-four years. Figure 4.1 depicts the average numbers of presidential fundraisers benefiting each category of beneficiary in presidential reelection cycles and other election cycles, sorted by the declining number of fundraisers by beneficiary type during reelection cycles.

During presidential reelection cycles, the DNC and RNC were the leading beneficiaries, with an average of sixty-five fundraisers per cycle, followed closely by the president's own reelection campaign committee, which benefited from an average of fifty-nine fundraisers during a president's third and fourth years in office. It is worth noting again the substantial number of events that both Obama and Trump held jointly for their reelection campaign and the DNC or RNC respectively, and the smaller number of similar events headlined by George W. Bush. These fundraisers are double-counted in the average number of fundraisers for each of these beneficiaries. While the DNC and RNC work to elect candidates up and down the ballot, in a presidential election cycle the race for the White House is a central focus, and much of the money that presidents raised for the national committee in their third and fourth years in office would support their own efforts to win a second term.

Similarly, while an average of thirty-one presidential fundraisers per reelection cycle benefited state parties, more than two-thirds of these reelection cycle state party fundraisers came as part of the joint fundraising committees organized by the Obama and Trump campaigns. State parties were ancillary beneficiaries of these joint committees, and many of them transferred the funds they received to the national party committees, as discussed in chapter 2. Presidents held an average of just nine fundraisers per reelection cycle for state parties that were not part of presidential joint fundraising committees. This smaller number of state party–focused events is likely more indicative of presidents' efforts to provide financial resources for state parties during reelection cycles.

Unsurprisingly, presidents were far less focused on other parts of their party during their reelection cycles than in the election cycles when presidents were not on the ballot. During these seven presidential reelection cycles, presidents headlined an average of ten fundraisers for Senate races, five fundraisers for House contests, and just under three fundraisers for gubernatorial races. One reason that presidents devote few fundraisers to helping governors during reelection cycles is that the majority of governors are elected in midterm election years. For example,

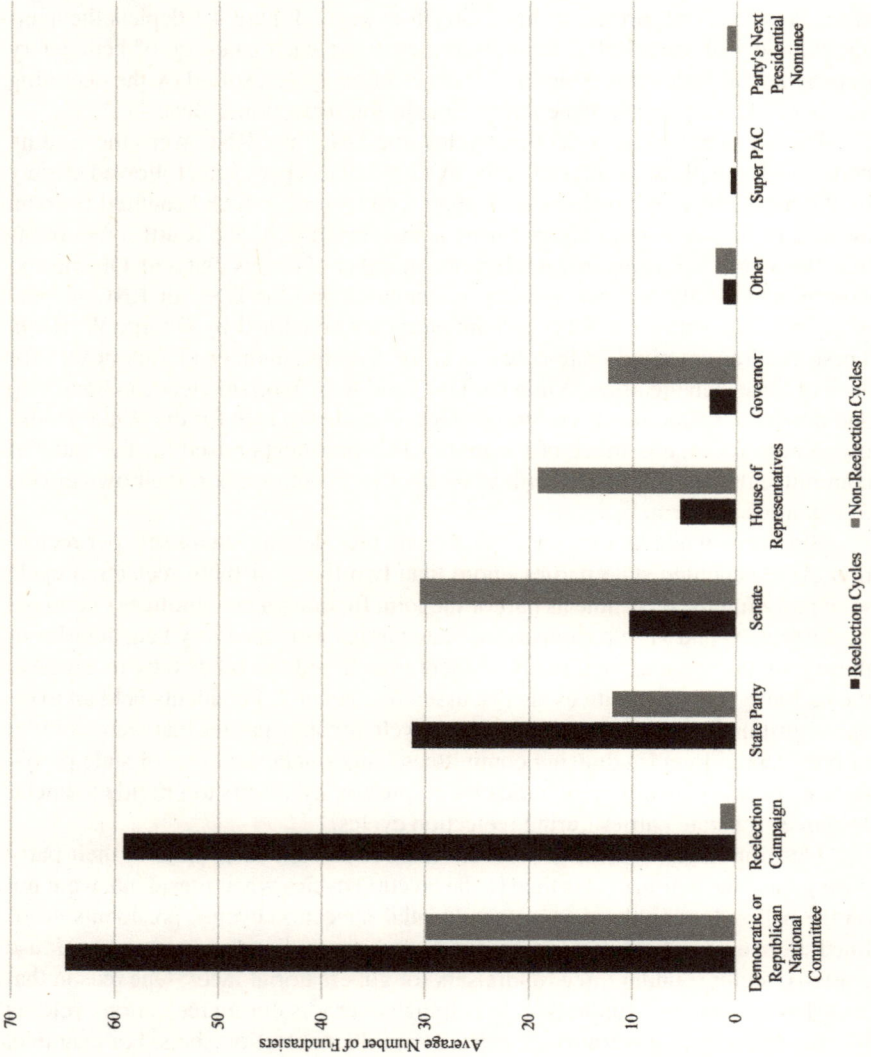

Figure 4.1: Average Number of Presidential Fundraisers by Beneficiary Category and Type of Election Cycle, 1977–2020
Note: Fundraisers that jointly aided multiple types of beneficiaries are counted in multiple categories.
Sources: Data compiled by the author from the *Public Papers of the Presidents*, the Digests of Other White House Announcements, White House schedules and press briefings, Reagan's personal diary, and Associated Press and other news articles.

in 2020 just eleven governors' seats were on the ballot.[6] However, there are plenty of other down-ballot races that a president could aid with fundraisers during a reelection cycle if he so chose, but self-interest largely drives a president's fundraising schedule in the third and fourth years in office. Presidents averaged about one fundraiser per reelection cycle for beneficiaries that fell into the category of "Other," including events for the mayor of Chicago, two county party committees, a former Virginia governor who was paying off campaign debt from two previous runs for other offices, and several political action committees. Only Trump attended Super PAC fundraisers during his reelection cycle, as he took part in three events benefiting a Super PAC that was working to secure his reelection, while a fourth event aided a Super PAC focused on helping Republicans in Senate races.

The picture painted by presidential fundraising priorities in the fifteen non-reelection cycles between 1977 and 2018 is quite different than presidential fundraising patterns when they are seeking a second term in the White House. These non-reelection cycles include seven first-term midterm elections as well as four second-term midterms and four cycles over the final two years of the two-term presidencies of Reagan, Clinton, George W. Bush, and Obama. The national committee was still a leading recipient, benefiting from an average of thirty presidential fundraisers per non-reelection cycle. Of course, presidents held very few fundraisers for their reelection committee outside of their third and fourth years in office. The exceptions are Trump's unprecedented sixteen reelection fundraisers during his first two years in office and the six second-term fundraisers that Obama attended to retire campaign debt from his 2012 reelection bid. While presidents headlined fewer state party fundraisers on average in non-reelection cycles (12) compared to reelection cycles (31), most of the latter kind of events were for joint fundraising committees where state parties were not the primary beneficiaries.

The average numbers of non-reelection cycle fundraisers dedicated to the other principal categories of recipients are all clearly greater than during reelection cycles. In these years, presidents held the most fundraisers—an average of thirty-one—to support campaigns for the Senate. An average of nineteen fundraisers per non-reelection cycle benefited House campaigns, and an average of twelve fundraising events aided governors' races. Presidents averaged two fundraisers in these cycles aiding candidates that fell in the category of "Other," including mayoral candidates, local party organizations, state attorneys general, and state legislators. Finally, an average of just one fundraiser per election cycle was held specifically for the party's next presidential nominee, though two-term presidents in their final two years in office held many fundraisers for the DNC or RNC that benefited their party's next nominee for the White House.

Only three total fundraisers were held for Super PACs in non-reelection years. Two of these events were headlined by Obama and benefited the Senate Majority PAC during the 2014 election cycle, and the third was a Trump event in his second year in office for the America First Super PAC, which supported his reelection bid. Super PAC events will likely comprise a greater portion of presidential fundraising efforts in the future, as they offer a way for presidents to help political allies raise money in unlimited amounts in support of their fellow party members or their own electoral interests.

The seven presidents from Carter through Trump collectively displayed dramatically different fundraising priorities in their third and fourth years in office than during the rest of their time as president. The next section focuses on the ways in which an increased focus on reelection fundraising has affected presidents' efforts to help their fellow party members raise campaign cash.

INCREASING REELECTION FUNDRAISING CROWDS OUT OTHER PRIORITIES

The evidence presented above makes clear that presidents devote much of their fundraising efforts in their third and fourth years in office to their reelection campaign committee and to their national party committee. This section examines how recent presidents' tendency to spend more time raising funds for their own bid for another term in the White House has come to squeeze out fundraising for other party members during a president's third and fourth years in office. The columns in Figure 4.2 provide the number of fundraisers that presidents headlined during reelection cycles for their reelection campaign and/or the DNC or RNC, as well as the numbers of fundraisers dedicated to aiding other beneficiaries. The data series in the figure depicted by a line indicates the percentage of a president's fundraisers that aided other beneficiaries during their third and fourth years in office. Examining both the numbers and the percentages gives a sense of each president's absolute and relative fundraising priorities.

The key takeaway is that the increase in reelection fundraising in recent presidencies has come at the expense of fundraising for other party members, relatively speaking. The first three presidents in this study, Carter, Reagan, and George H. W. Bush, dedicated 40 percent, 88 percent, and 61 percent, respectively, of their fundraising efforts during their third and fourth years in office to events that did not benefit either their reelection campaign or the DNC or RNC. Carter took part in twenty-five fundraisers for fellow Democrats, in addition to the thirty-seven he held for his reelection committee and the DNC in 1979 and 1980. Although Reagan held only four fundraisers for the RNC in 1983 and 1984 and none for his reelection campaign committee, he headlined an additional twenty-eight for other Republicans. In 1991 and 1992 George H. W. Bush headlined just thirty fundraisers for his reelection campaign and the RNC and took part in an additional forty-six fundraisers for fellow Republicans. All three of these presidents devoted a substantial proportion of their fundraising efforts during their reelection cycle to aiding other parts of their party.

Presidents' relative focus on fundraising for other parts of their party during

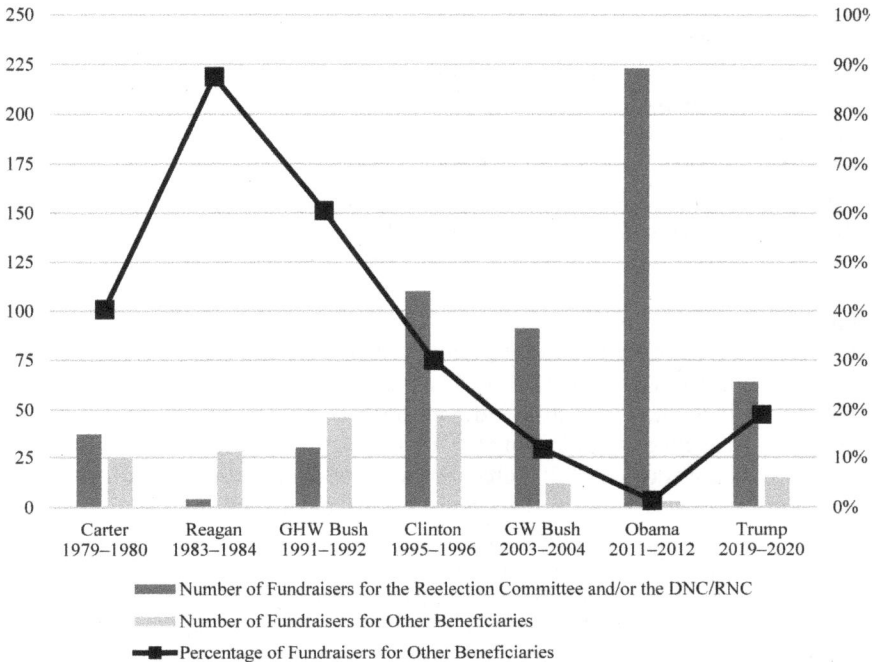

Figure 4.2: Fundraising Beneficiaries during Reelection Cycles, 1979–2020
Sources: Data compiled by the author from the *Public Papers of the Presidents*, the Digests of Other White House Announcements, White House schedules and press briefings, Reagan's personal diary, and Associated Press and other news articles.

reelection cycles has been declining since Reagan's high-water mark of 88 percent. George H. W. Bush's 61 percent of these fundraisers was followed by Clinton's 30 percent, George W. Bush's 12 percent, and Obama's 1 percent. Each of these successive presidents spent proportionally less of their time during their third and fourth years in office fundraising at events that didn't benefit their reelection campaign or their national party committee. Nineteen percent of Trump's fundraisers during his third and fourth years in office benefited these other beneficiaries, which was higher than the percentages for George W. Bush and Obama but lower than those of the other four presidents in this study.

The increased presidential focus on reelection fundraising has crowded out other party fundraising during reelection cycles, even as presidents spent more time raising money in their third and fourth years in office. Clinton held 110 fundraisers for his reelection committee and the DNC in 1995 and 1996, as well as forty-seven additional fundraisers for Democrats running for office. George W. Bush took part in ninety-one fundraisers for his reelection committee and the RNC in 2003 and 2004, and he supplemented these efforts with twelve more fundraisers that benefited Republican candidates for the Senate, the House of Representatives, and gubernatorial races.

Obama displayed the greatest relative and absolute focus on his reelection bid, with 223 fundraisers for his reelection committee and the DNC in 2011 and 2012, and only three fundraisers for other Democratic beneficiaries, all of which took place in early 2011. Once he headlined the first of his Obama Victory Fund events in April 2011, he did not take part in a single fundraiser for another beneficiary for the rest of that year or in all of 2012. While his reelection fundraising indirectly helped some down-ticket Democrats, particularly those in presidential battleground states, fellow party members in other states did not receive direct presidential fundraising help. Trump's sixty-four fundraisers in 2019 and 2020 for his reelection campaign committee and the RNC were paired with fifteen fundraising events for other Republicans. The increased demand for presidents to raise money for their own reelection bid and the national party committee has coincided with a decline in fundraising for fellow party members. All of the four most recent presidents dedicated 70 percent or more of their fundraising efforts during their third and fourth years in office to events that aided their campaign committee or their party's national committee.

When Trump became the only modern president to raise funds for his reelection campaign in his first and second years in office, some fellow Republicans worried that his early reelection fundraising would come at the expense of helping fellow Republicans in the midterm elections. In 2017 and 2018, 29 percent of Trump's fifty-five fundraising events aided the Trump Victory joint fundraising committee, which at that point in his term benefited the Trump reelection campaign and the RNC. Some party members were vocal about their concerns. Republican campaign operative Alex Conant said in March 2018, "A lot of people wish the midterms were his singular focus and he wouldn't worry about his re-election right now."[7] Former Trump aide Sam Nunberg made a similar point just weeks before the November 2018 midterm elections. In a news story headlined "As Other Republican Candidates Struggle Financially, Trump Stockpiles Cash," Nunberg said, "One of the reasons that Republicans have been outraised, particularly in the House, is because of the massive amount of money going to the president."[8] An anonymous former RNC staffer during George W. Bush's first midterm election in 2002 drew a contrast with Trump's approach in 2018: "The RNC was solely focused on electing Republicans that year, not President Bush's future election."[9]

While some Republicans were unhappy with Trump's approach, it is not surprising that a president who narrowly won the White House and who lacked long-standing ties to the Republican Party would focus more on his own reelection prospects than on those of his fellow party members. Trump's actions also represented the continuation of a pattern that evolved over multiple presidencies. A president's time is finite, and the trend over the seven presidencies from Carter through Trump is clear. As presidents have spent more time raising funds for themselves and their national party in their third and fourth years in office, their other efforts for fellow party members have become less of a focus, changing the ways that presidents perform their role as head of party when they are also seeking reelection.

THE UPHILL BATTLE FOR MAJORITIES IN THE CONGRESS

In 2005 and 2006 George W. Bush's midterm fundraising for his fellow Republicans was both unusual and typical. Races for the House of Representatives were his top focus, benefiting from thirty-two of his eighty-nine fundraisers as he tried to preserve the majority that Republicans had held since the 1994 midterm elections. Contests for the Senate were his second-highest priority, as he headlined twenty-four fundraisers to help his party hold the Senate majority that they had won in the 2002 midterm elections four years earlier. Bush's focus on the Senate was typical of other presidents. Indeed, fundraisers for Senate beneficiaries were among a president's top two priorities in fifteen of twenty-two election cycles in this study, including thirteen of fifteen non-reelection cycles, when presidents focus more on fellow party members. But Bush's efforts for House races were quite unusual, as presidents often made fundraising for House races far less of a priority. Fundraisers for House beneficiaries were among a president's top two priorities in just two of these twenty-two election cycles.

To shed more light on presidential fundraising priorities and strategies, the next several sections focus on efforts to help in congressional races. First, it is important to know that the standing of the president's party in Congress tends to deteriorate over the course of a presidency. Because of this, presidents are more likely to find themselves defending congressional majorities early in their term and pursuing them later, though, as Table 4.1 illustrates, this is not universally the

Table 4.1: Chambers of Congress Controlled by the President's Party, 1977–2020

	Years 1&2	Years 3&4	Years 5&6	Years 7&8
Carter	House & Senate	House & Senate		
Reagan	Senate	Senate	Senate	Neither
GHW Bush	Neither	Neither		
Clinton	House & Senate	Neither	Neither	Neither
GW Bush	House*	House & Senate	House & Senate	Neither
Obama	House & Senate	Senate	Senate	Neither
Trump	House & Senate	Senate		

* This table indicates that George W. Bush's party did not control the Senate during his first midterm election cycle, as that was the situation during the majority of his first two years in office as a result of a senator's decision to leave the Republican Party in mid-2001, giving Democrats control of the chamber.
Sources: "Party Divisions of the House of Representatives (1789 to Present)," http://history.house.gov/Institution/Party-Divisions/Party-Divisions/; "Party Division in the Senate, 1789-Present," http://www.senate.gov/history/partydiv.htm.

case. Just two of these seven presidents faced dynamics of congressional party control that did not change throughout their presidency—Carter and George H. W. Bush, who each served only one term. Carter's Democrats maintained control of both chambers throughout his four years, though their large majorities shrank in both the House and Senate as Carter's term progressed. And the first President Bush faced opposition party control of both chambers throughout his term and saw his party's seat share decline slightly in each chamber after the midterm elections.

Four presidents saw their party's majority control of Congress erode as their time in office progressed: Reagan, Clinton, Obama, and Trump. Reagan came into office with a new Republican Senate majority, the first since the 1954 midterm elections, and he would work to preserve his party's Senate standing throughout his term. Republicans maintained their Senate majority in the 1982 and 1984 elections and then surrendered control of that chamber following the 1986 midterms. Reagan faced a Democratic House throughout his entire presidency. Clinton had Democratic majorities in both chambers during his first two years in office. Then Republicans won control of both the House and the Senate in 1994 for the first time in forty years. They maintained their majorities throughout Clinton's final six years in the White House. Obama came into office with his party in control of both the House and the Senate, only to lose the majority in the House in 2010 and then in the Senate in 2014. Trump started his presidency with Republicans in control of both the House and the Senate, but Democrats retook the majority in the House in the 2018 midterms. Republicans lost the Senate in 2020 alongside Trump's unsuccessful bid for a second term, making him the first president since Herbert Hoover to preside over his party's loss of the House, the Senate, and the White House in just four years.

Just one of these seven presidents saw his party's control of Congress improve before it declined. George W. Bush's fellow Republicans had a clear majority in the House after the 2000 elections and controlled a 50–50 Senate thanks to Vice President Cheney's tie-breaking vote. But Senator Jim Jeffords of Vermont announced in May 2001 that he would leave the Republican Party two weeks later and become an independent who caucused with the Democrats, giving them control of the Senate for the rest of 2001 and 2002. Bush's first two years in office are depicted in Table 4.1 as having Republican control of the House but not the Senate, as that was the situation for the majority of Bush's first midterm election cycle and the backdrop against which most of his fundraising occurred. Republicans won back the Senate in 2002, this time with a clear majority, and held control of both chambers for four years before the Democrats reclaimed majorities in both the House and Senate in 2006.[10]

Stepping back, the landscapes of threat and opportunity that presidents fundraising for their congressional copartisans confront are frequently marked by worsening fortunes throughout the course of a presidency. Each of the four two-term presidents began their time in the White House with control of at least one chamber of Congress; by the final two years of their term, each faced a House and

Senate controlled by the opposite party. Two of the three one-term presidents did not see their party's majority status change in either chamber of Congress, but each saw his party lose seats in both chambers in midterm elections. Each of the three Democratic presidents started with control of both chambers of Congress, due in part to the long-term Democratic dominance of Congress that marked most of the latter half of the twentieth century. Each Republican president except Trump spent much or all of his first two years confronting at least one chamber of Congress controlled by the opposite party. Three of the four two-term presidents in this study—Reagan, George W. Bush, and Obama—lost party control of one or both chambers of Congress in their second term. The other two-term president, Clinton, had already seen his party lose control of both chambers in his first term. These trends put most presidents in the position of defending majorities early in their terms and pursuing them later.

Presidents and their allies are well aware of the uphill battle they face in trying to defend or win majorities in Congress. In 2010 Senator Bob Menendez, who was chairing the Democratic Senatorial Campaign Committee (DSCC), praised Obama's efforts as he assessed the political landscape. "The president has done just about anything we've asked him to do. Very clearly the president knows history as well as I do, and the history of midterms means the president's party loses seats." It is worth noting, however, that historical midterm seat losses have been far more consistent in the House than in Senate contests, where the president's party sometime fares moderately better depending on which Senate seats are up for reelection in a given year. In 2014 Senator Dick Durbin gave a similar assessment: "Here's the reality—he knows it, we know it—and that is that off-year elections are historically not kind to incumbent presidents." In the 2018 midterm election cycle, Trump adviser Bill Stepien declared, "History tells us it will be challenging. How challenging, time will tell." In the face of often long odds, presidents devote their time to fundraising in Senate and House races. Why? As Republican operative Scott Jennings said during Trump's midterm election cycle, "I think there's a realization that there's at least a 50 percent chance one or both chambers could fall. In less than one year, this first term could be, for all intents and purposes, over if the Democrats take control of either chamber."[11] These are the stakes that presidents and their aides consider as they decide how to allocate the president's fundraising efforts.

FREQUENTLY PRIORITIZING THE SENATE

Fundraisers for Senate races were often among a president's top priorities. Overall, 530 presidential fundraisers from 1977 through 2020, or just over 24 percent, aided Senate races. Table 4.2 depicts that Senate races were consistently among a president's top fundraising priorities. Of the twenty-two election cycles over this forty-four-year period, Senate fundraisers were a president's highest priority

Table 4.2: Top Beneficiaries of Presidential Fundraisers, by Election Cycle, 1977–2020

President & Election Cycle	Top Priority	Second Priority	Third Priority
Carter			
Years 1&2	Senate	Governors	State Parties
Years 3&4	DNC	State Parties	House
Reagan			
Years 1&2	State Parties	Senate	Governors
Years 3&4	Senate	State Parties	House & RNC (tie)
Years 5&6	Senate	Governors	State Parties
Years 7&8	Senate	State Parties	House
GHW Bush			
Years 1&2	Governors	Senate	State Parties
Years 3&4	State Parties	Reelection	Senate
Clinton			
Years 1&2	Senate	Governors	DNC
Years 3&4	DNC	Senate	Reelection
Years 5&6	DNC	Senate	House
Years 7&8	DNC	Senate	House
GW Bush			
Years 1&2	Senate	Governors	House
Years 3&4	Reelection	RNC	Senate
Years 5&6	House	Senate	RNC
Years 7&8	RNC	House	State Parties
Obama			
Years 1&2	DNC	Senate	House
Years 3&4	DNC	Reelection	State Parties
Years 5&6	DNC	Senate	House
Years 7&8	DNC	Senate	State Parties
Trump			
Years 1&2	RNC	Reelection	House& Senate (tie)
Years 3&4	Reelection & RNC (tie)	State Parties	Super PACs

Sources: Data compiled by the author from the *Public Papers of the Presidents*, the Digests of Other White House Announcements, White House schedules and press briefings, Reagan's personal diary, and Associated Press and other news articles.

in six election cycles and were the second-highest priority in an additional nine cycles. Senate fundraisers received less attention in presidential reelection cycles, when most presidents devoted much of their focus to their own bids for a second term. But the Senate was a president's first or second priority in thirteen of the fifteen cycles when presidents weren't seeking reelection.

This sustained focus on the Senate across presidencies makes strategic sense given the importance of that chamber to the president's agenda, the competitive nature of many Senate races, and the relatively frequent changes in party control in the Senate in recent decades. The Senate's role in approving nominations and treaties gives a president clear motivations to try to improve or maintain his party's standing in the chamber. Clinton summed up the critical consequences of Senate elections when he touted Democratic candidate Debbie Stabenow at a Michigan fundraiser in September 2000:

Nobody in America now appreciates the importance of every single Senate seat as much as I do. They confirm judges. They can hold up bills. They can hold up judges, including two from Michigan that should have been confirmed a long time ago. In the Senate, except for the budget, 41 Senators, not a majority—41—can stop anything from happening. . . . She can win, and she will win if you will fight for her. And do not be discouraged. Do not give up. Fight. This is worth fighting for. It's worth fighting for.[12]

Senate races are often competitive, since many attract well-funded candidates with a record of electoral success. Additionally, the gerrymandering of district lines that yields so many noncompetitive seats in the House does not apply to Senate elections, which must be run statewide.[13] And in a body of 100 senators where the margin dividing the parties is often just a handful of seats, influencing a small number of key races can go a long way toward determining which party will win a Senate majority. Between the start of Carter's presidency and the end of Trump's term, party control of the Senate changed eight times—seven times following elections in 1980, 1986, 1994, 2002, 2006, 2014, and 2020, and once following Senator Jim Jeffords's departure from the Republican Party in the spring of 2001. In short, presidents have a number of good reasons to prioritize fundraising for Senate races.

Figure 4.3 depicts both the number of Senate fundraisers that each president headlined and the percentage of presidential fundraisers during each election cycle that benefited Senate races. The data are grouped by election cycle, with every other election cycle shaded to facilitate comparisons of strategies and priorities at similar points in a president's term. Analyzing both the numbers and percentages of Senate fundraisers illuminates a president's absolute and relative fundraising priorities. The contrast between Reagan and Clinton illustrates why both measures are informative. In Clinton's seventh and eighth years in office, he participated in eighty-nine fundraisers that benefited Senate races, which was the highest total by far in an election cycle by any of these seven presidents. But Clinton was such an aggressive fundraiser that he took part in 283 fundraisers overall in 1999 and 2000. His eighty-nine Senate fundraisers comprised 31 percent of his fundraising efforts during that election cycle. Clinton aide Bruce Reed explained Clinton's proclivity for fundraising this way: "In fact, one of the striking things about him was that he's the only politician I've ever seen who loved everything about politics, all the jobs that a politician has to do. He liked fundraising, he got a kick out of talking to people about how they made the money they were giving him."[14]

In contrast, thirty-six of Reagan's sixty-three fundraisers in his fifth and sixth years in office were focused on the Senate. Reagan's absolute commitment to Senate fundraising was far lower than Clinton's, who devoted more time to fundraising than did any other modern president. But Reagan's efforts took place in an earlier period when presidents spent less time raising campaign cash. Reagan's relative commitment to the Senate in those two years, when 57 percent of his

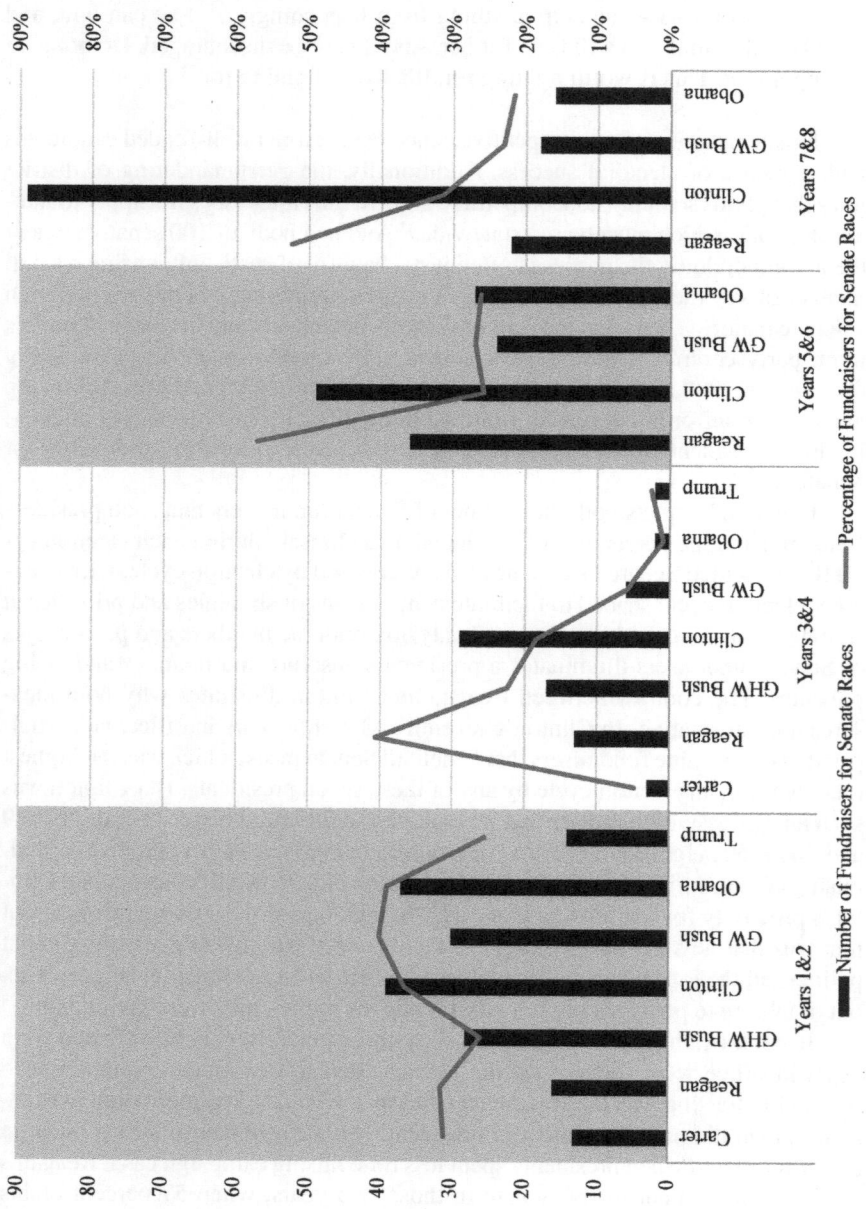

Figure 4.3: Number and Percentage of Presidential Fundraisers for Senate Races, 1977–2020

Note: Shading provides visual differentiation of various election cycles.

Sources: Data compiled by the author from the *Public Papers of the Presidents*, the *Digests of Other White House Announcements*, White House schedules and press briefings, Reagan's personal diary, and Associated Press and other news articles.

fundraisers aided Senate races, was the highest of any president during any election cycle in this study. While one could just focus on a president's absolute level of fundraising, it is also helpful to examine each president's relative priorities. Although Reagan did not embrace the role of fundraiser in chief to the same extent that many of his successors did, he was his party's biggest fundraising draw for the eight years he was in office, and measures of his relative priorities shed light on his fundraising strategies in the context of the politics of the day.

Given how often presidents headline Senate fundraisers, it is instructive to consider the relatively few election cycles when raising money for Senate races was not a high presidential priority. Each of the seven presidents from Carter through Trump headlined their lowest number of Senate fundraisers during their reelection cycle. For six of the seven presidents, the reelection cycle also represented the smallest percentage of fundraisers devoted to the Senate, with Reagan the lone exception. In absolute numbers, Clinton held the most Senate fundraisers during a reelection cycle, with twenty-nine, and George H. W. Bush headlined seventeen Senate fundraisers in his third and fourth years in office. Both of those presidents still placed both a greater absolute and relative priority on the Senate in all of their other election cycles. It is worth noting that those were the only two presidents whose parties were seeking a Senate majority during a reelection cycle. For the other five presidents, their party was defending its majority control of the Senate as they sought reelection, and all spent less time than Clinton or Bush fundraising for Senate races in their third and fourth years in office. Reagan, who did not headline fundraisers for his own reelection campaign committee, made the Senate his second-highest priority during his reelection cycle, as close to half of his thirty-two fundraisers aided Senate races. But as demonstrated earlier, presidents in recent years have tended to focus on their own reelection campaign, the DNC and RNC and, to a lesser extent, state parties in their third and fourth years in office. These efforts increasingly have taken priority in reelection cycles over fundraising for other parts of the party, including events for Senate races.

There are few other cases of presidents not prioritizing Senate fundraisers. Indeed, the Senate was among a president's top two priorities in all but two non-reelection cycles. The exceptions were George W. Bush's final two years and Trump's first two years. In 2007 and 2008, 23 percent of Bush's seventy-eight fundraisers benefited the Senate, making it his fourth-highest beneficiary category behind the RNC, the House of Representatives, and state parties. Bush and his party were seeking a Senate majority, as the Democrats had won control of the chamber in the 2006 midterms. Saddled with an average Gallup poll job approval rating of just 32 percent over his final two years in office, Bush did not make raising money for Senate races a top priority. In Trump's first two years in office, the Senate was his third-ranking beneficiary, as 26 percent of his fifty-five fundraisers aided Senate races. His unprecedented early reelection fundraising made the RNC and his reelection campaign committee his top priorities in his first two years in office, leaving his efforts to defend his party's Senate majority in third place.

Aside from these exceptions, the Senate was consistently among a president's top two fundraising priorities during non-reelection cycles. In the first two years in office, every president except Trump made the Senate either his top or second relative fundraising priority, as between 26 percent and 40 percent of their fundraising events benefited Senate races. A White House aide to Reagan explained their desire to defend the Republican Senate majority in 1982: "Our top priority is to maintain the Senate because that gives us at least one house [of Congress] where we can move forward with our legislative program."[15] Similarly, five of the seven presidents were defending their party's Senate majority in their first two years, including the two presidents who held the most Senate fundraisers for their party in advance of the midterm elections, Clinton and Obama. Only the two Bushes were seeking a Senate majority. George W. Bush had seen a 50–50 Senate, which had been controlled by his party via his vice president's tiebreaking vote, turn into a 49–51 Senate minority in the spring of 2001 when a Republican senator left the party and decided to caucus with the Democrats. Bush responded by allocating 40 percent of his fundraisers that cycle to Senate races. When he embarked on a fundraising trip in March 2002 to aid candidates in three key Senate races, Bush declared, "The Senate races are very important to me. I want the Republicans to take control of the Senate."[16] Bush's overall fundraising totals would likely have been higher had it not been for his four-month hiatus from raising campaign funds after the terrorist attacks on September 11, 2001. But when he did dedicate himself to fundraising during his first two years as president, his top priority was his party's successful effort to reclaim a Senate majority.

Of the four two-term presidents, Reagan placed the most relative emphasis on the Senate. In July 1986 Reagan's White House political director, Mitch Daniels, summed up the president's priorities: "Obviously, we're fixed on the Senate races—nothing's more important."[17] The numbers back up Daniels's claim. Reagan devoted 57 percent of fundraisers to Senate races in his fifth and sixth years in office when he was defending his party's majority in the chamber. In his final two years, just over half of his fundraisers aided Senate contests at a time when he was trying to help his party reclaim the majority it lost in 1986. No other president in this study dedicated more than half of his fundraising efforts to Senate races in any other election cycle.

In absolute terms, Clinton, who spent all of his second term seeking a Senate majority, aided Senate races most often. His forty-nine fundraisers in his fifth and sixth years in office and eighty-nine fundraisers in his final two years exceeded any other president's total in any election cycle between 1977 and 2020. Clinton had unusual incentives to fundraise for Senate races in both of his second term election cycles. In 1998 allegations and revelations about Clinton's extra-marital relationship with a former White House intern meant that he was fundraising for senators and candidates who could be jurors in his eventual Senate impeachment trial early the next year. In 1999 and 2000 Clinton's record eighty-nine Senate fundraisers were due in part to forty events aiding the unprecedented run of his wife, First Lady Hillary Rodham Clinton, for the Senate in New York. But even without those events, Clinton took part in more Senate fundraisers in his last two years than did any other recent president in a single election cycle.

Reagan, Clinton, George W. Bush, and Obama all made Senate fundraisers a relatively high priority in both election cycles of their second term. Three of those four presidents—Reagan, Bush, and Obama—were defending a Senate majority in their fifth and sixth years in office. None did so successfully, and all four two-term presidents were helping their party to seek a Senate majority in their final two years in office. The Senate was consistently a top priority for recent presidents, whether seeking or defending a majority, in almost every election cycle when presidents were not focused on their own reelection fundraising.

On Offense and Defense for the Senate

Presidents who want to boost their party's prospects in Senate races have to decide whether the best use of their scarce time is to fundraise for incumbents, for challengers to incumbents of the other party, for candidates seeking open seats, for national party committees focused on Senate races, or for a Super PAC. This section examines the extent to which presidents have employed offensive or defensive strategies when fundraising for individual Senate candidates. When presidents raise campaign cash for a Senate incumbent of their own party, that is a clear example of defense, as the president is helping his party to retain a seat it already holds. When presidents fundraise for a candidate who is challenging an incumbent from the other party, that is a clear instance of offense. When presidents raise funds for candidates seeking open Senate seats, they are on defense if the seat was previously held by a member of their party, and on offense if it was previously held by a senator from the other party.

Every presidential fundraiser for a specific Senate candidate was coded to account for whether the beneficiary was an incumbent senator, a challenger, or a candidate for an open seat, as well as which party previously held the open seat. Occasionally, these dynamics for a particular Senate race would vary over the course of an election cycle. For example, in 2009 Obama raised money for Senator Arlen Specter, who had just switched parties and was running as the incumbent for reelection to the seat he had held for almost three decades. After Specter was defeated by Joe Sestak in the Democratic primary in 2010, Obama fundraised for Sestak, who was then a nonincumbent seeking what had become an open seat.

In an even more unusual example, when Ronald Reagan held a fundraiser for James Broyhill on June 4, 1986, the candidate was running for an open seat to succeed the retiring senator, John East. After East died by suicide later that month, the Republican governor of North Carolina appointed Broyhill to fill the vacancy, so when Reagan headlined another fundraiser for him on October 8, 1986, Broyhill was then the incumbent seeking to be elected to a seat he already held.[18] Even

Table 4.3: Defensive and Offensive Fundraisers for Senate Races, 1977–2020

President and Election Cycle	Defensive Fundraisers		Offensive Fundraisers		Neither
	For a Senate Incumbent	For an Open Seat Held by the President's Party	For a Nonincumbent Challenging an Incumbent	For an Open Seat Held by the Other Party	For the DSCC or NRSC, but Not for Individual
Carter					
Years 1&2	6	0	5	1	1
Years 3&4	2	**0**	0	0	1
Reagan					
Years 1&2	5	2	7	1	1
Years 3&4	**7**	0	0	0	6
Years 5&6	**20**	4	3	6	3
Years 7&8	9	0	6	3	4
GHW Bush					
Years 1&2	**10**	2	11	0	5
Years 3&4	**9**	0	2	1	5
Clinton					
Years 1&2	**18**	3	7	3	9
Years 3&4	**7**	5	3	3	11
Years 5&6	**17**	2	5	1	24
Years 7&8	14	**40**	9	0	26
GW Bush					
Years 1&2	9	**7**	11	0	3
Years 3&4	**2**	1	1	0	2
Years 5&6	**13**	2	2	2	5
Years 7&8	**10**	2	1	0	5
Obama					
Years 1&2	**20**	7	0	2	8
Years 3&4	**1**	0	0	0	1
Years 5&6	**3**	0	0	0	22
Years 7&8	1	1	2	0	12
Trump					
Years 1&2	3	3	6	0	2
Years 3&4	**1**	0	0	0	0
Total	187	81	81	23	156

Note: Numbers in bold indicate when defensive fundraisers outnumbered offensive fundraisers or vice versa in a given election cycle. One fundraiser had both incumbent and nonincumbent beneficiaries and is counted in both columns. Three fundraisers that benefited Super PACs focused on Senate races are not included.

Sources: Data compiled by the author from the *Public Papers of the Presidents*, the Digests of Other White House Announcements, White House schedules and press briefings, Reagan's personal diary, and Associated Press and other news articles.

though both fundraisers were for the same beneficiary in the same year, the first had different incumbent and open seat status than the second.

Table 4.3 depicts whether a president took part in more defensive or offensive fundraisers in a given election cycle. To do so, it conveys how many Senate fundraisers presidents headlined benefiting Senate incumbents, candidates challenging a Senate incumbent of the other party, and candidates seeking an open seat. The open seat contests are divided into whether the seat was formerly held by a member of the president's party or of the other party. The numbers of defensive or offensive fundraisers are shaded to indicate when defensive fundraisers outnumbered offensive fundraisers or vice versa in a given election cycle.

The table also presents the number of fundraisers that benefited one of the two national party Senate committees, the Democratic Senatorial Campaign Committee (DSCC) or the National Republican Senatorial Committee (NRSC), but not an individual Senate candidate. It is not possible to declare these events to be offensive or defensive in nature, as we cannot discern to which races the national party committees directed the money raised at these specific fundraising events. When a fundraiser jointly benefited an individual candidate and the DSCC or NRSC, it is included in the column appropriate to that candidate's status. For example, Obama headlined six fundraisers in his first two years that jointly benefited Senator Barbara Boxer of California and the DSCC; those fundraisers are included in the column that details aid to Senate incumbents.

Defensive fundraisers have been much more common than offensive ones. These seven presidents collectively headlined 270 fundraisers for Senate incumbents and for candidates seeking open seats previously held by the president's party (hereafter called same-party open seats for the sake of brevity). In contrast, they took part in just 102 fundraisers for candidates either challenging an incumbent from the other party or seeking an open seat that had been vacated by a member of the other party (hereafter called opposite-party open seats). Defensive fundraisers outnumbered offensive fundraisers in seventeen of these twenty-two election cycles, while offensive events were more frequent in only one election cycle, Reagan's first two years in office. In just four cycles, presidents headlined an equal number of offensive and defensive fundraisers. Senate incumbents comprised the single-largest category of beneficiary for these seven presidents, with 187 fundraisers, more than double the seventy-nine fundraisers for candidates challenging incumbents. Of the 106 open-seat fundraisers, defensive events predominated. Eighty-three aided candidates running for same-party open seats, and only twenty-three benefited candidates seeking to capture an opposite-party open seat.

The nationalization of presidential fundraising has complicated the ability to assess a president's fundraising efforts as offensive or defensive. In five election cycles in this study, a president held double-digit fundraisers that benefited one of the national party's Senate campaign committees without also aiding an individual candidate. Clinton's reelection cycle marked the first instance of this. While Clinton's fundraisers for specific candidates in his third and fourth years in office clearly favored incumbents and same-party open seats, the large number of DSCC fundraisers precludes us from declaring definitively that Clinton's strategy that cycle was a defensive one.

In which years did presidents' Senate fundraising most clearly indicate that they were playing defense? Defensive fundraisers outnumbered offensive fundraisers by ten or more events in seven different election cycles, and in most of those cases, the political environment was a tough one for the president and his party. In four of these cycles, presidents were defending their party's majority. In his fifth and sixth years, Reagan headlined twenty-four defensive fundraisers for incumbents and for same-party open seat races. That far outpaced his nine offensive fundraisers for challengers and for opposite-party open seats. Reagan was trying to help the senators who had won election when he did in 1980 in an unsuccessful effort to preserve his party's Senate majority. As is often the case with Senate elections, Republicans were victims of their own success six years earlier. Of the thirty-four Senate seats up for election that cycle, twenty-two were held by Republicans. Clinton's first two years were another clear example of defense. Of the thirty-three Senate seats up for election that year, twenty were held by Democrats, and Clinton headlined twenty-three defensive and eight offensive fundraisers.[19] Clinton's Gallup poll job approval rating in 1994 averaged 46 percent, which helped to set the stage for his party's loss of their Senate majority in spite of Clinton's efforts to solicit campaign funds.[20]

George W. Bush in his fifth and sixth years in office held more than three times as many defensive fundraisers as offensive ones. Bush's Gallup poll job approval rating in 2006 averaged 38 percent, which contributed to the difficult electoral environment for Senate Republicans.[21] Despite Bush's efforts, Democrats took control of the Senate in the 2006 midterm elections. Obama in his first two years in office was the only one of these four presidents with such a dramatic tilt toward defensive fundraisers whose party did not lose their majority. His Gallup poll job approval rating in 2010 averaged 47 percent, and he didn't hold a single fundraiser for a candidate challenging a Republican incumbent.[22] He held twenty-seven defensive fundraisers and only two offensive ones, both for opposite-party open seats. Though his party would lose six Senate seats, Democrats managed to hold on to a reduced majority.[23] Each of these four presidents displayed a clear defensive fundraising strategy as they faced substantial political headwinds.

Presidents held at least ten more defensive than offensive fundraisers in three election cycles when their party was seeking, not defending, a majority in the Senate. In 2008 George W. Bush's Gallup poll job approval rating averaged 30 percent in a year when Republicans had to defend twenty-two of the thirty-three Senate seats that were up for election.[24] Bush took part in twelve defensive fundraisers and only one offensive fundraiser as he tried to limit Republican losses in a challenging election cycle when they were already in the minority in the Senate. Clinton's fifth and sixth years in office also saw a defensive focus on incumbents, as he held nineteen defensive and just six offensive fundraisers. But in these two years, Clinton also headlined twenty-four fundraisers for the DSCC as he tried to help Democrats win back the Senate. While his fundraisers for individuals were lopsidedly defensive, his extensive fundraising for his party's national Senate campaign committee makes it impossible to know if his overall focus was defensive or not.

Finally, in Clinton's last two years in office, his fifty-four defensive Senate fundraisers were far more numerous than his nine offensive money-raising events. Those fifty-four defensive fundraisers included forty in a race for an open seat held by his party. All forty of those fundraisers benefited a single candidate, Hillary Rodham Clinton, who was seeking to win the seat of retiring Democratic senator Daniel Patrick Moynihan. Though Clinton's fundraising for his wife was a defensive effort to retain a seat held by his party, the unique circumstances surrounding the candidacy of the only First Lady to seek a Senate seat put the president's efforts for his wife in a category of their own.

Recent presidents have consistently made Senate fundraising a top strategic priority, and defensive fundraisers in Senate races have been far more common than offensive ones. In most election cycles, presidents have chosen to hold more defensive fundraisers for incumbents and same-party open seat races than for challengers and for opposite-party open seat contests. However, the rise of nationalized fundraising has made it more difficult to determine whether a president employed an offensive or defensive fundraising strategy in a given election cycle, as funds raised for the DSCC or NRSC can subsequently be directed to whichever races the national party chooses.

RARELY PRIORITIZING THE HOUSE

The seven presidents from Carter to Trump frequently prioritized fundraising for Senate campaigns, but presidential fundraising for House of Representatives contests was much rarer. Table 4.2 makes clear that House races were among a president's top two priorities in just two of the twenty-two election cycles in this study, while Senate races were a president's first or second priority in fifteen of twenty-two cycles. In total, these seven presidents headlined 326 fundraisers that benefited House races over the course of forty-four years, far fewer than the 530 Senate fundraisers over the same time period.

Figure 4.4 depicts both the numbers and percentages of presidential fundraisers for House races. It has the same scale as Figure 4.3 to facilitate visual comparisons of House and Senate fundraising. House races were a president's top relative priority just once, in the first two years of George W. Bush's second term when 36 percent of his eighty-nine fundraising events benefited contests for the House. Republicans were facing an uphill climb that election cycle as they tried unsuccessfully to maintain the House majority that they had held since the 1994 midterm elections. In Bush's seventh and eighth years in office, House races were his second-highest relative priority behind the RNC, as 28 percent of his seventy-eight fundraisers aided House campaigns. House races benefited from more than 25 percent of a president's fundraisers in a given cycle just four times—in both cycles of George W. Bush's second term, in Clinton's final two years, and in Trump's first two years. In contrast, Senate races were beneficiaries of more than

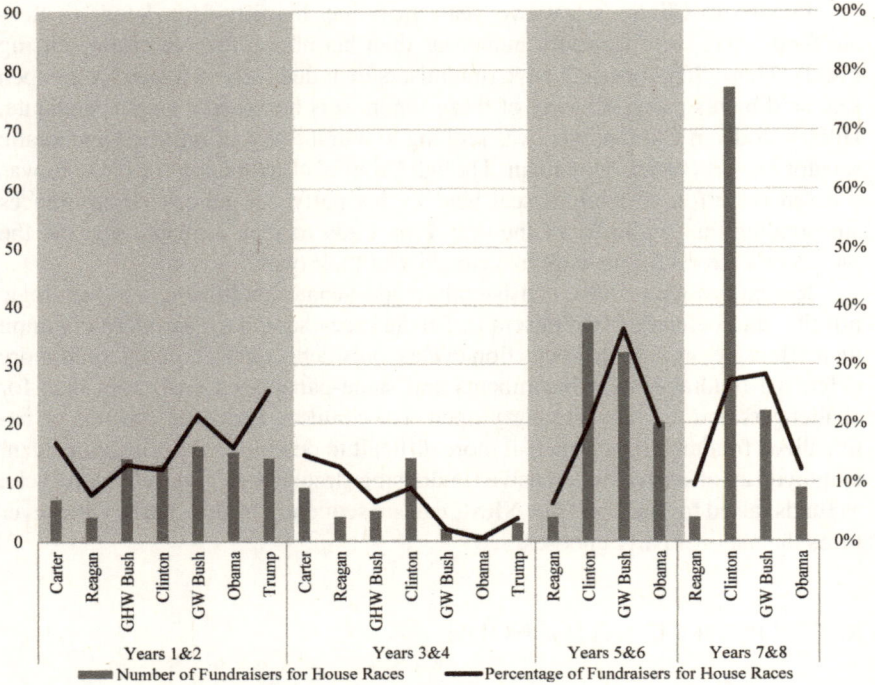

Figure 4.4: Number and Percentage of Presidential Fundraisers for House Races, 1977–2020
Note: Shading provides visual differentiation of various election cycles.
Sources: Data compiled by the author from the *Public Papers of the Presidents*, the Digests of Other White House Announcements, White House schedules and press briefings, Reagan's personal diary, and Associated Press and other news articles.

25 percent of a president's fundraisers in fourteen of these twenty-two election cycles. In six cycles, the percentage of fundraisers for Senate races exceeded the high-water mark of 36 percent of a president's fundraisers for House races, which was set by George W. Bush in 2007 and 2008. In short, House races have been far less of a relative fundraising priority for presidents than Senate races.

In absolute terms, House races also received relatively little presidential fundraising attention. There were only five election cycles in this study when a president headlined twenty or more fundraisers for House contests—far fewer than the eleven cycles with twenty or more Senate fundraisers. All took place in a president's second term. The absolute leader in fundraising for House races was Clinton in his final two years as president. His seventy-seven House fundraisers were more than double that of any other president's highest election cycle total. But Clinton attended so many fundraisers in his seventh and eighth years in office—a record 283 events—that his seventy-seven House fundraisers were only

27 percent of his total effort. House races represented his third-highest priority that cycle, behind Senate contests and the DNC.

Clinton also laid claim to the second-highest number of fundraisers for House races, with thirty-seven in his fifth and sixth years in office. But since he took part in 190 fundraisers overall that cycle, House fundraisers represented only 20 percent of his total effort and were again his third-highest relative priority, behind his 100 fundraisers for the DNC and forty-nine events for Senate races. In both cycles of his second term, Clinton's Democrats were in the minority in the House. Clinton had particular incentive to help them win back a majority in 1998 as potential impeachment proceedings loomed. Clinton headlined multiple House fundraisers that autumn alongside Democratic House leader Dick Gephardt, who was likely to become Speaker of the House if his party retook the chamber. An October 1998 news story headlined "Clinton Raising Cash as Congress Moves toward Impeachment Inquiry" described a joint appearance by Clinton and Gephardt at a House fundraising event. Gephardt told supporters, "Vote for the Republicans and vote for two more years of investigating everybody and everything." An anonymous Democrat fleshed out what Gephardt had implied. "Speaker Gephardt would change the complexion on Capitol Hill," making Clinton's impeachment far less likely. While Democrats would defy historical trends and pick up five seats in the House in that fall's midterm elections, those gains would not be enough to reclaim the majority, make Gephardt the speaker, and forestall impeachment.[25]

Presidents took part in twenty or more fundraisers for House races in just three other election cycles. George W. Bush attended the third- and fourth-greatest numbers of House fundraisers, as discussed above, with thirty-two events to raise money for House races in his fifth and sixth years in office as he fought to preserve his party's majority. Bush then held twenty-two House fundraisers in his final two years, as Republicans tried to win back the majority they had lost in 2006. And Obama headlined twenty House fundraisers in his fifth and sixth years in office as he helped to finance his party's unsuccessful effort to win back the majority Democrats had lost in Obama's first midterm election. In the five election cycles in which a president participated in twenty or more fundraisers for House races, all were in a president's second term. In four of the five cycles, the president was trying to win back a House majority, and only once, in George W. Bush's second midterm election, was a president with twenty or more House fundraisers defending his party's House majority.

In spite of the important role that the House plays in a president's legislative agenda, it has been a relatively low priority in almost every election cycle. Presidents regularly lend some aid to House races, but they devote less time to fundraising for them than they do for other parts of their party. One factor is likely the size of the margins of majority control in the House as compared to the Senate. In the twenty-two election cycles in this study, the average margin of House control was twenty-nine seats above the 218 required for a majority in the chamber, whereas the average margin of Senate control was just under five seats above the midpoint value of fifty seats in the chamber. In only three cycles—1998, 2000, and 2002—was the margin of House control in the single digits. And in each of those cycles, presidents did focus more on the House. Clinton's fundraising for House races in the 1998 and 2000 cycles exceeded that of any other president in any election cycle during this study. And George W. Bush held more fundraisers for House races in the 2002 election cycle than did any other first-term president during this period. With greater numbers of seats required to achieve or lose majority control in the House, presidents likely see less payoff from aiding a candidate for one of 435 seats in the House than from aiding a candidate for one of the 100 seats in the Senate, where much smaller shifts in the number of seats held can determine majority control of the chamber.

Another likely factor in presidents not fundraising as much for House races is rooted in campaign finance rules. As discussed in chapter 3, when a president travels for a fundraiser, the benefiting campaign or party organization is required by federal law to pay a portion of the travel expenses. Those costs are and were substantial, even before the changes in 2010 that required the fundraising beneficiary to pay an even greater share of the costs of fundraising travel. Joan Baggett, who directed the White House Political Affairs Office in Clinton's first term, described the situation before those changes this way: "Typically, the President, just because of the expense, went in for statewide candidates. You would have, just as Bush did this past election . . . an official event that you were traveling to in the state, so a lot of the costs were covered by that. Then there were additional costs that the campaign had to pay for. So it was expensive to have the President come."[26] Those significant expenses meant that better-financed statewide campaigns or party committees were more likely to be able to support some of the costs of a president coming to town for a fundraiser. Despite the House of Representative's key role in the success or failure of a president's legislative agenda, presidents rarely prioritized fundraising for House races. Almost all of the relatively few exceptions to this relative lack of presidential fundraising help came in a president's second term.

On Offense and Defense for the House

While presidents have spent far less time fundraising for the House than for the Senate, their efforts for individual House candidates have one clear element in common with their strategies for Senate fundraising—defensive fundraisers far outnumbered offensive fundraisers. Presidential fundraisers are defensive when they raise money for a House incumbent of their own party or for a candidate seeking an open seat being vacated by a fellow party member. In contrast, presidents are on offense when they fundraise for a challenger to an incumbent of the other party or for a candidate seeking an open seat previously held by the other party. Table 4.4 depicts the numbers of offensive and defensive fundraisers for

Table 4.4: Defensive and Offensive Fundraisers for House Races, 1977–2020

President and Election Cycle	Defensive Fundraisers		Offensive Fundraisers		Neither
	For a House Incumbent	For an Open Seat Held by the President's Party	For a Nonincumbent Challenging an Incumbent	For an Open Seat Held by the Other Party	For the DCCC or NRCC, but Not for Individual
Carter					
Years 1&2	**3**	**0**	0	1	3
Years 3&4	**5**	**0**	1	0	3
Reagan					
Years 1&2	2	0	1	1	1
Years 3&4	**2**	**0**	0	0	2
Years 5&6	**2**	**0**	0	0	2
Years 7&8	**1**	**0**	0	0	3
GHW Bush					
Years 1&2	**6**	**2**	0	2	4
Years 3&4	**1**	**1**	0	0	3
Clinton					
Years 1&2	**8**	**0**	0	0	5
Years 3&4	**3**	**2**	0	0	9
Years 5&6	**8**	**1**	0	0	28
Years 7&8	**45**	**0**	10	1	21
GW Bush					
Years 1&2	**9**	**1**	1	1	2
Years 3&4	0	0	0	0	2
Years 5&6	**18**	**6**	3	0	4
Years 7&8	**4**	**3**	5	0	10
Obama					
Years 1&2	**4**	**0**	0	1	10
Years 3&4	0	0	0	0	1
Years 5&6	0	0	0	0	20
Years 7&8	0	0	0	0	9
Trump					
Years 1&2	**5**	**3**	0	1	6
Years 3&4	**1**	**0**	1	0	2
Total	127	19	22	8	150

Note: Nnumbers in bold indicate when defensive fundraisers outnumbered offensive fundraisers.
Sources: Data compiled by the author from the Public Papers of the Presidents, the Digests of Other White House Announcements, White House schedules and press briefings, Reagan's personal diary, and Associated Press and other news articles.

individual House candidates that each president held in the twenty-two election cycles in this study. The numbers of defensive or offensive fundraisers are shaded to indicate when defensive fundraisers outnumbered offensive fundraisers or vice versa in a particular election cycle. The table also includes the number of fundraisers that benefited one of the two national party House committees, the Democratic Congressional Campaign Committee (DCCC) or the National Republican Congressional Committee (NRCC), but not an individual House candidate.

Presidential fundraising for individual House races has been overwhelmingly defensive. Defensive fundraisers outnumbered offensive fundraisers in sixteen of these twenty-two election cycles. Defensive and offensive fundraisers were tied in two cycles—Reagan's first two years and Trump's reelection cycle—and in the other four election cycles presidents did not hold any fundraisers that benefited individual House candidates. Overall, seven presidents collectively took part in 146 defensive House fundraisers, along with just thirty offensive House fundraisers. When presidents aided individual House candidates, they spent the most time fundraising for incumbents, with 127 events. Challengers to House incumbents received just over one-sixth of that level of attention, with just twenty-two presidential fundraisers. Of the twenty-seven fundraisers for open seats, nineteen had been previously held by the president's party and thus were defensive, and just eight had been held by the other party. The number of fundraisers for House incumbents far outnumbered the combined fundraisers for open seats and challengers to incumbents of the other party in almost every election cycle when presidents fundraised for individual candidates. In short, presidential fundraising for individual House candidates has been predominantly defensive, focusing most on aiding incumbents.

Presidents held at least ten more defensive than offensive House fundraisers in just two election cycles—Clinton's final two years in office and George W. Bush's fifth and sixth years. Clinton again stands out for his fundraising efforts. He took part in forty-five fundraisers for House incumbents in 1999 and 2000, a total more than double the next-highest election cycle total and five times more than the third-greatest number of fundraisers for House incumbents. While Clinton's forty-five defensive fundraisers that cycle quadrupled his eleven offensive fundraisers, his ten fundraisers for candidates challenging incumbents of the other party were also more than double the next-highest entry by any president on that side of the ledger. Clinton was in a class of his own when it came to committing his time to fundraising. His defensive and offensive efforts for House races in his final two years came at a time when his party was just five seats shy of reclaiming the majority in the chamber that it had lost in the 1994 midterm elections.[27] Democrats did not retake the majority in 2000, but Clinton's efforts helped provide the financial resources to contest House races across the country. Bush's focus on defensive House fundraisers in his fifth and sixth years in office came at a time when his party was defending its majority. His defensive focus was understandable given his relative unpopularity at the time and the accurate predictions that Republicans would lose their House majority in the 2006 midterm elections. While these were the only two election cycles when a president headlined at least ten more defensive than offensive fundraisers, the trend overall is clear. There was not a single cycle where offensive House fundraisers outnumbered defensive ones, reflecting a clear defensive and incumbent-focused fundraising strategy for president after president when they raised money for individual House members.

As was the case with Senate fundraisers, the nationalization of House fundraising has made it difficult to assess whether a president's strategy was offensive or defensive in certain election cycles. Overall, presidents spent even more time fundraising for their national party's congressional campaign committees, the DCCC and the NRCC, with 150 events, than they did for incumbents, who benefited from 127 fundraisers. As these national fundraising events became more frequent over time, presidents spent even less time aiding individual House members. In the ten election cycles from 1977 through 1996, presidents collectively took part in thirty-five fundraisers that benefited the DCCC or NRCC but not an individual candidate, an average of just 3.5 per cycle. In the subsequent twelve election cycles from 1997 through 2020, presidents headlined 115 such fundraisers, an average of almost ten per cycle. Obama did not headline a single fundraiser for an individual House member in his final six years in office. Instead, he took part in thirty different events for the DCCC. Fundraisers for the DCCC and NRCC cannot be categorized as offensive or defensive, as we do not know to which competitive races the national party committees directed the funds they raised.

Rivalries abound between House members and senators. In the case of presidential fundraising, the contest is not close. House members receive far less fundraising aid than do their Senate colleagues. The fundraisers that presidents do hold for individual House members overwhelmingly help incumbents, though in recent years nationalized fundraising increasingly has crowded out fundraising for individual House members.

OCCASIONALLY PRIORITIZING GOVERNORS

Fundraising for governors' races presents a different strategic imperative than does fundraising for the House or Senate, where winning and maintaining a majority of seats in each chamber is vital to the president's legislative agenda. While a president and his party would prefer to have more governors' seats in their column, whether or not a president's party holds a majority of these offices does not affect a president's agenda in the same way that majority dynamics in the Congress do. Governors are particularly important in the decennial redrawing of legislative districts that follows every census. In many of the forty-three states with more than one congressional seat (that number will increase to forty-four states in 2023 once Montana is awarded a second member of Congress as a result of the decennial post-census reapportionment process), governors can approve or veto the newly redrawn congressional district maps that establish the electoral landscape for House elections for the next decade.

An additional benefit of having governors of the president's party was illuminated by the state-by-state variation in the implementation of the Affordable Care Act. Many Democratic governors worked to roll out the law with the aim of helping it succeed, including some in more conservative states like Kentucky, but many Republican governors wanted little to nothing to do with the law's implementation. Additionally, an Electoral College battleground state with a friendly governor is often seen as an important resource in a presidential reelection cam-

paign, suggesting another potential benefit for presidents that can flow from helping their fellow party members win gubernatorial elections. A former director of
the Democratic Governors Association (DGA) made the case in 2013 that Obama
should focus his attention on governors' races. "Anyone who cares about a pro-
gressive agenda—and that includes our president—ought to be paying very close
attention to what's happening in the states. If I were him, I would be doing everything I can to raise money for the DGA and help elect Democratic governors,
because these are the people who are going to protect his legacy."[28]

In the aggregate, governors' races benefited from fewer presidential fundraisers—just 204 over forty-four years, as compared with 530 for Senate contests
and 326 for House races. Most governors' races take place in midterm election
cycles, when thirty-six states elect their governors. Just two states, New Jersey
and Virginia, choose their governors in the year following a presidential election,
and three other states, Kentucky, Louisiana, and Mississippi, elect their governors in the third year of a president's term. Eleven states choose their governors
during a presidential election year. There are fifty-two total state gubernatorial
elections over a four-year span because two states, New Hampshire and Vermont,
elect their governors every two years.[29] Presidents who wish to raise funds for
governors' contests have many chances to do so in midterm election years, but
they have far fewer candidates to support in other years. Indeed, collectively the
seven presidents in this study headlined 164 gubernatorial fundraisers in midterm
election cycles, compared with just forty in presidential election cycles.

Figure 4.5 illustrates the absolute and relative commitments that presidents
made to fundraising for gubernatorial elections. The figure uses the same scale as
the previous figures for the Senate and the House of Representatives to facilitate
comparisons. The first two years of a president's first and second terms drew the
most fundraising for governors, which makes sense given that thirty-six gubernatorial contests take place during midterm election cycles. Presidential election
cycles, when only eleven governors' seats are on the ballot, received much less
attention. During a president's own reelection cycle, no president took part in
more than five gubernatorial fundraisers, and the greatest relative commitment to
governors' races was Reagan's 6 percent in 1983 and 1984. The final two years of
a two-term president's time in office witnessed only slightly greater presidential
attention. The high-water mark was Clinton's thirteen gubernatorial fundraisers
in his seventh and eighth years in office, which represented less than 5 percent of
his extensive fundraising efforts that cycle. It's clear that presidents spend little
time aiding gubernatorial contexts during their third, fourth, seventh, and eighth
years in office.

Table 4.2 reveals that governors' races were a president's top relative priority
in only one election cycle and received the second-greatest amount of attention
in an additional four cycles. These contests were regularly a lower priority than
Senate races. But presidents had more cycles in which they made governors a top
priority than was the case for House races. The only cycle in which governors'

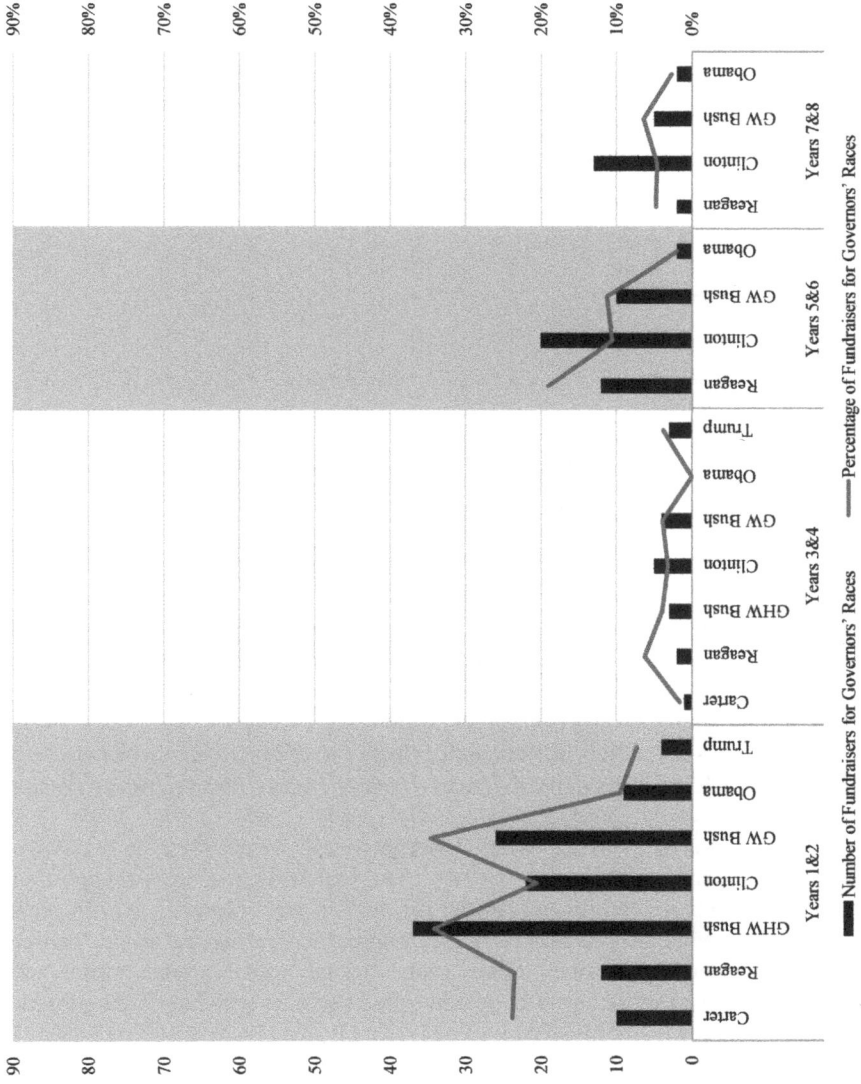

Figure 4.5: Number and Percentage of Presidential Fundraisers for Governors' Races, 1977–2020

Note: Shading provides visual differentiation of various election cycles.

Sources: Data compiled by the author from the *Public Papers of the Presidents*, the Digests of Other White House Announcements, White House schedules and press briefings, Reagan's personal diary, and Associated Press and other news articles.

Table 4.5: Defensive and Offensive Fundraisers for Governors' Races in Presidential Election Cycles, 1979–2020

President Election Cycle	Defensive Fundraisers		Offensive Fundraisers		Neither
	For an Incumbent Governor	For an Open Seat Held by the President's Party	For a Nonincumbent Challenging an Incumbent	For an Open Seat Held by the Other Party	For the DGA or RGA, but Not for Individual
Carter					
Years 3&4	1	0	0	0	0
Reagan					
Years 3&4	0	0	0	2	0
Years 7&8	0	0	0	0	2
GHW Bush					
Years 3&4	1	0	0	2	0
Clinton					
Years 3&4	3	0	0	0	2
Years 7&8	4	2	3	2	2
GW Bush					
Years 3&4	0	0	1	2	1
Years 7&8	0	1	0	1	3
Obama					
Years 3&4	0	0	0	0	0
Years 7&8	1	0	0	0	1
Trump					
Years 3&4	1	0	0	0	2
Total	11	3	4	9	13

Note: Numbers in bold indicate when defensive fundraisers outnumbered offensive fundraisers or vice versa.
Sources: Data compiled by the author from the *Public Papers of the Presidents*, the Digests of Other White House Announcements, White House schedules and press briefings, Reagan's personal diary, and Associated Press and other news articles.

races were a president's top priority was during George H. W. Bush's first two years in office, when just more than one in every three fundraisers aided a gubernatorial contest. Redistricting is a key part of that story, as Bush, a former chair of the Republican National Committee, fundraised extensively for gubernatorial candidates and state parties in 1989 and 1990 as part of an effort to win state-level races that would give his party a greater say in the upcoming redrawing of congressional districts.

The director of the Republican Governors Association, Michele Davis, described her party's focus in early 1990: "The real battleground is reapportionment. That's where we hope to put the majority of our resources to help break the hold the Democrats have on the U.S. Congress."[30] During that cycle, California was expected to gain seven House seats after the upcoming reapportionment process. Because Democrats already controlled the state legislature, winning the governor's race was the only way to get Republicans a seat at the redistricting table. White House political director Ed Rogers explained, "It is the motherlode of congressional seats," and he declared that Republican nominee Pete Wilson's campaign was Bush's "number one target."[31] Bush went on to headline seven fundraisers that election cycle for Wilson—the second-greatest number that any recent president held for any other individual beneficiary in a given election cycle, trailing only Clinton's fundraising for his wife's Senate campaign in his final two years in office.

While George H. W. Bush made governors' contests his top fundraising priority in the 1990 cycle, other presidents campaigning on the eve of a round of redistricting did not follow suit. Of the five such election cycles between 1977 and 2020, three took place during presidential election years—1980, 2000, and 2020—and two fell during a president's first midterm election—1990 and 2010. When Carter and Trump sought a second term in 1980 and 2020, they headlined just one and three fundraisers, respectively, for gubernatorial candidates. In 1999 and 2000, only thirteen of Clinton's 283 fundraisers benefited governors' races. Although just three states chose their governors in 1999 and eleven more did so in 2000, one still might have expected Clinton to fundraise more for gubernatorial candidates given the impact those races could have on the redistricting process that would take place the following year. In 2009 and 2010 only nine of Obama's ninety-five fundraisers benefited governors' contests. That represented his fourth-highest priority that cycle, behind the DNC, Senate races, and House campaigns.

Obama would later come to regret not having put more effort into trying to shape state-level races in 2010 that could have led to a better redistricting outcome for his party. In the closing weeks of his presidency, Obama told an interviewer that in 2010:

> We were just at the beginnings of a recovery. And the, you know, whoever is president at that point is gonna get hit and his party's gonna get hit. That then means that suddenly you've got a redistricting in which a lot of state legislatures are now Republican. They draw lines that give a huge structural advantage in subsequent elections. So some of this was circumstances. But what I think that what is also true is that partly because my docket was really full here, so I couldn't be both chief organizer of the Democratic Party and function as Commander-in-Chief and President of the United States.[32]

In early 2017 Obama announced that in his postpresidency he would work with a newly formed group dedicated to winning state-level offices that could affect the redistricting process.[33] He likely wished that in 2010 he had followed the example of George H. W. Bush, the only recent president to make governors a leading priority during the election cycle preceding a round of redistricting.

Governors were the beneficiaries of more than 20 percent of a president's fundraisers in four other election cycles. All took place during first midterm election cycles—in the first two years of the presidencies of Carter, Reagan, Clinton, and George W. Bush. Perhaps not coincidentally, all four had served as governors

Table 4.6: Defensive and Offensive Fundraisers for Governors' Races in Midterm Election Cycles, 1977–2018

President Election Cycle	Defensive Fundraisers		Offensive Fundraisers		Neither
	For an Incumbent Governor	For an Open Seat Held by the President's Party	For a Nonincumbent Challenging an Incumbent	For an Open Seat Held by the Other Party	For the DGA or RGA, but Not for Individual
Carter					
Years 1&2	**4**	**3**	2	1	0
Reagan					
Years 1&2	**8**	**3**	0	1	0
Years 5&6	1	0	4	**5**	2
GHW Bush					
Years 1&2	**13**	**10**	1	10	3
Clinton					
Years 1&2	**9**	3	5	2	3
Years 5&6	1	1	**9**	**6**	3
GW Bush					
Years 1&2	**9**	**6**	9	1	1
Years 5&6	1	**4**	4	0	1
Obama					
Years 1&2	**5**	**3**	0	0	1
Years 5&6	**1**	0	0	0	1
Trump					
Years 1&2	**2**	**1**	0	0	1
Total	54	34	34	26	16

Note: Numbers in bold indicate when defensive fundraisers outnumbered offensive fundraisers and vice versa.
Sources: Data compiled by the author from the *Public Papers of the Presidents*, the Digests of Other White House Announcements, White House schedules and press briefings, Reagan's personal diary, and Associated Press and other news articles.

before winning the presidency. The two presidents who had previously served neither as governor nor as party chair, Obama and Trump, made governors' races a low fundraising priority in each of their election cycles. Reagan continued his focus on governors' races in his second midterm election cycle, when his twelve gubernatorial fundraisers made them his second-highest priority after the Senate. His top White House aide for political affairs declared in 1986 that Reagan's top short-term focus that cycle was Senate races, but added, "In terms of the next five to ten years, it could be that what is most important is what happens in the gubernatorial races," alluding to the redistricting process that Reagan's successor would work hard to influence during the 1990 midterm election cycle.[34] Overall, while presidents took part in fewer fundraisers for governors' races than for House or Senate contests, gubernatorial elections were an occasional top priority for recent presidents.

On Offense and Defense in Governors' Races

When presidents fundraise for individual gubernatorial candidates, they must decide whether to aid incumbent governors, challengers to incumbents from the other party, or candidates running for open seats. Tables 4.5 and 4.6 show that dynamics of offensive and defensive fundraising for specific candidates were different for governors' races in midterm and presidential election cycles. The numbers of defensive or offensive fundraisers are shaded to indicate when defensive fundraisers outnumbered or were outnumbered by offensive fundraisers in a certain election cycle. During presidential election cycles, defensive fundraisers were more common in five cycles, offensive in three, and totals for both categories were tied in the other three election cycles. But since far fewer governors are on the ballot in presidential election cycles, and since presidents' attention is often focused on the presidential race and the national party in these cycles, the overall number of fundraisers for gubernatorial candidates in these election cycles tends to be relatively low. In the three election cycles in which offensive fundraisers outnumbered defensive ones, presidents headlined just two, two, and three offensive fundraisers, respectively, illustrating the consistently low levels of fundraising effort devoted to gubernatorial races during presidential election cycles.

Midterm election cycles are where most of the action is when it comes to governors' elections, as more than 80 percent of presidential fundraisers for gubernatorial races took place during midterm cycles. Table 4.6 indicates that defensive fundraisers outnumbered offensive ones in nine of eleven midterm election cycles. The only cycles in which offense outnumbered defense were in Reagan's and Clinton's fifth and sixth years in office. In those cycles, offensive fundraisers outpaced defensive ones by a wide margin—nine to one in Reagan's case, and fifteen to two for Clinton. In each case, the strategy was driven by the electoral landscape that cycle. In 1986 twenty-seven of the thirty-six governors' seats up for election were held by Democrats, and Reagan's party held only one-quarter of the seats that were on the ballot. Similarly, in 1998 twenty-four of the thirty-six gubernatorial contests were seats held by Republicans, as Clinton's fellow Democrats held only one-third of the governors' seats that were up for election that year.[35] For both Reagan and Clinton, the other party's previous electoral successes created a situation where presidential fundraising would be offensive in nature.

Incumbents made up a smaller share of beneficiaries for governors' races than for Senate or House races. While 72 percent of all presidential fundraisers for individual House candidates benefited incumbents and 50 percent aided Senate incumbents, only 37 percent of gubernatorial fundraisers helped incumbents. The difference is likely due to the lack of term limits for members of Congress. As of this writing in early 2022, there are term limits of some sort for governors in thirty-six states.[36] When term-limited governors are prohibited from running again, open-seat races result. The seventy-two fundraisers for open-seat governors' races exceed the sixty-five for incumbents, as well as the thirty-eight for candidates challenging an incumbent governor of the other party. But when open-seat races are divided according to which party previously held the seat, defensive fundraisers still regularly outnumbered offensive fundraisers.

Presidential fundraising for governors has not become as nationalized as fundraising has for other parts of a president's party. Collectively, the seven presidents from Carter to Trump only took part in twenty-nine fundraisers that benefited the Democratic or Republican Governors Association and that did not also benefit an individual gubernatorial candidate. That total pales in comparison with the 156 fundraisers held for the DSCC or the NRSC but not for an individual Senate candidate, as well as in comparison with the 150 fundraisers held for the DCCC or the NRCC but not for an individual House candidate. In recent years, presidents have held fewer fundraisers for individual gubernatorial candidates, but they have not correspondingly increased the number of fundraisers they held for the DGA or the RGA. This is odd, given that the DGA and RGA are state-focused entities that are not subject to the federal contribution limits that apply to federal candidates and the national party organizations focused on the federal government.[37] Presidents have aggressively worked with their federally focused national party entities to raise funds, but they have not done so to aid governors' races to nearly the same extent. In recent decades, control of the House, Senate, and White House have changed hands numerous times. Perhaps the uncertain balance of power at the federal level has drawn presidents' fundraising attention at the expense of fundraising for governors' races.

Overall, presidents have placed less emphasis on fundraising for gubernatorial contests than for Senate and House races. Presidents did make governors' races a rare top priority during occasional midterm election cycles, when most gubernatorial elections take place. Indeed, while presidents held more fundraisers for House races than gubernatorial contests in the aggregate, governors' contests were a top-two priority in more specific election cycles than House races were. The four presidents who were former governors—Carter, Reagan, Clinton, and George W. Bush—as well as the lone former national party chair—George H. W. Bush—placed the most emphasis on governors' contests in their first midterm election cycle. The first President Bush made governors his leading beneficiary in the 1990 cycle, which immediately preceded congressional redistricting. Interestingly, four other presidents did not prioritize governors' races in 1980, 2000, 2010, and 2020 as redistricting loomed. Gubernatorial fundraising was less focused on incumbents, likely due to term limits on governors in many states. Overall, presidents still tended to employ defensive fundraising strategies, holding more events for candidates seeking open seats that were being vacated by their party, as well as for incumbents. Gubernatorial fundraising did not experience the same dramatic nationalization that was evident in fundraising for other party members. Indeed, as presidents came to focus more on nationalized fundraising for federal offices, they held fewer fundraisers for governors' races.

OTHER PRIORITIES

What other parts of the party do presidents prioritize in addition to their own reelection campaigns, the Senate, the House, and governors' races? Chapter 3 already examined the rise in fundraising for national party committees and the accompanying decline in fundraising for state parties that were not part of a presidential reelection-focused joint fundraising committee. While this chapter will not revisit that analysis, it is important to note that the DNC and the RNC raise large amounts of money that they can either spend themselves on electoral efforts or transfer to other parts of the party.

In October 2014, less than a month before midterm elections, party officials shared that the DNC would transfer up to $3 million apiece to the DSCC and the DCCC. The DNC was Obama's leading fundraising beneficiary by far that election cycle, as it was aided by 57 percent of his money-raising events. The *Washington Post* reported that "party officials credit much of the DNC's financial health to President Obama. While he's been absent from the campaign trail, he's been raising millions of dollars for Democratic candidates and campaign committees this year." Similarly, the RNC was Trump's leading fundraising beneficiary in his first two years in office. In July 2018 the RNC approved a plan to send $4 million to both the NRSC and the NRCC. Trump's then-campaign manager, Brad Parscale, credited the president for the financial assistance. "The president authorized this support for the GOP committees and candidates because he is committed to supporting the NRSC, NRCC and congressional candidates who will work with him as we make America great again." *Politico* headlined its story about the transfers "Trump Intervenes to Save the House."[38] In both 2014 and 2018, presidential fundraising made the DNC and the RNC central players in their parties' strategies in the midterm elections.

Figure 4.1 indicates that there are three other categories of beneficiaries that presidents aid with their fundraising: the party's next presidential nominee, Super PACs, and a catch-all category labeled "Other." While none has been a leading recipient of a president's fundraising help, each merits a brief discussion. Only the four two-term presidents in this study—Reagan, Clinton, George W. Bush, and Obama—had the opportunity to fundraise as a sitting president for their party's next nominee for the White House. Collectively, they did not do so often, as the four presidents headlined only fourteen fundraisers that directly benefited their potential successor in the White House. But Figure 4.6 shows that most of the two-term presidents did engage in substantial fundraising for the DNC or RNC in their final two years in office, a time when national party committees are largely focused on aiding their presidential nominee. The Bush and Obama fundraisers that jointly benefited their party's next nominee and their national party committee are counted in both appropriate columns in the figure.

Reagan was the lone exception. He took part in only forty-two fundraisers in his final two years in office. None benefited Republican nominee George H. W.

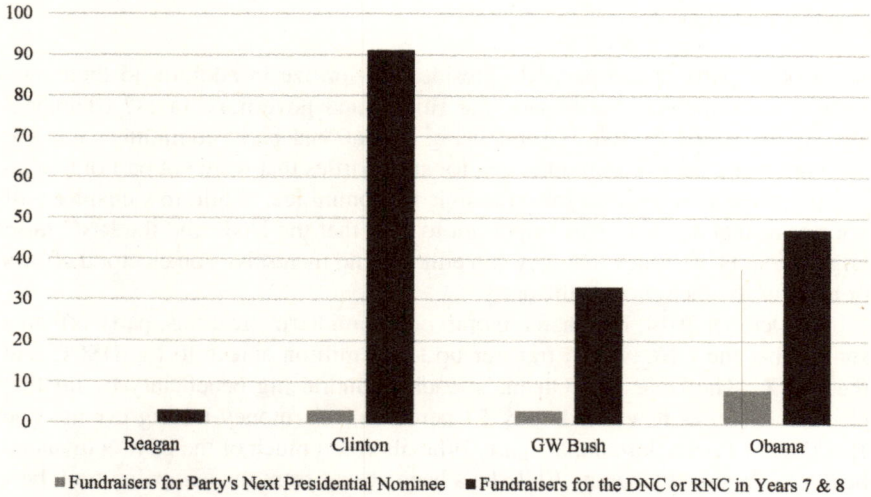

Figure 4.6: Presidential Fundraisers for Their Party's Next Presidential Nominee and DNC/RNC in Their Seventh and Eighth Years in Office
Sources: Data compiled by the author from the *Public Papers of the Presidents*, the Digests of Other White House Announcements, White House schedules and press briefings, Reagan's personal diary, and Associated Press and other news articles.

Bush directly, and just three aided the RNC. The other three two-term presidents would fundraise more extensively in their final two years in office. While Clinton headlined only three fundraisers for Democratic nominee Al Gore in 2000, his ninety-one fundraisers for the DNC in his final two years in office certainly helped Gore's campaign. In June 2000 White House deputy press secretary Jake Siewert explained that Clinton "feels fund-raising took too much of his time in '96. He wants Gore to be able to collect votes instead of money."[39] Similarly, in 2008 George W. Bush participated in just three fundraisers that jointly benefited GOP nominee John McCain and the RNC, and he headlined an additional thirty events that aided the RNC in his final two years. Obama headlined eight Hillary Victory Fund events that directly aided Hillary Clinton's 2016 campaign and the DNC, and he took part in thirty-nine more fundraisers in his last two years that benefited the DNC. Presidents must often strike a balance when trying to support a presidential nominee who wants to stand on his or her own. When McCain came to the White House in March 2008 to receive the endorsement of the unpopular president, Bush acknowledged those dynamics:

> If my showing up and endorsing him helps him, or if I'm against him and it helps him—either way, I want him to win. You know, look, this is an age-old question that you—every President has had to answer, and there's an appropriate amount of campaigning for me to do. But they're not going to be

voting for me. . . . But I'm going to find ample time to help, and I can help raising money.[40]

Clinton, Bush, and Obama provided limited direct fundraising help for their party's next presidential nominee, but they each spent much more time raising money for their party's national committee in their final two years as president.

The seven presidents from Carter to Trump collectively took part in thirty-nine fundraisers that fell in the category of "Other." These included seven events for mayoral candidates, another seven for traditional political action committees, five events whose beneficiaries were unclear, three for county party committees, two for state legislative contests, two for former officeholders who were not running for another office, two for candidates for state attorney general, one for a lieutenant governor candidate, one for a local committee supporting a national party convention, and one for a candidate for borough president of Staten Island in New York City. Although presidents did not spend much time on these events, understanding that these types of beneficiaries occasionally receive support rounds out the picture of presidential fundraising priorities.

While most fundraising events for these kinds of beneficiaries draw little attention, an Obama fundraiser in April 2013 was an exception to the rule. When Obama helped raise money in northern California for state attorney general Kamala Harris, he praised her by asserting, "She is brilliant and she is dedicated and she is tough, and she is exactly what you'd want in anybody who is administering the law, and making sure that everybody is getting a fair shake." Obama continued, saying, "She also happens to be, by far, the best looking attorney general in the country." When media coverage focused on this remark, Obama called the future vice president to apologize. The next day, the White House press secretary said, "They are old friends and good friends and he did not want in any way to diminish the attorney general's professional accomplishments and her capabilities."[41] The flurry of media attention for a fundraiser like this was a rare occurrence, however.

Finally, Super PACs have become an occasional presidential priority that could expand in the future. After Obama initially criticized their role in US elections, he took part in two Super PAC fundraisers during the 2014 election cycle. Both benefited the Senate Majority PAC. Trump decried Super PACs during the 2016 campaign. But once he became president, he attended one Super PAC fundraiser focused on Republican Senate candidates, as well as four more for America First Action, a Super PAC that supported his reelection bid. Additionally, both Obama and Trump attended small numbers of events organized by Super PACs that were declared not to be fundraising events. While there was no price of admission at these donor maintenance events, one can certainly imagine that the Super PACs hoped that an intimate event with a president would lead the past donors in attendance to support the group again in the near future. Donor maintenance events like these are discussed further in the appendix.

Although some have contended that presidents attending Super PAC fundraisers raises concerns about corruption or the appearance of corruption, the Federal Election Commission has determined that presidents and other candidates for federal office can attend Super PAC fundraisers as long as they themselves do not ask attendees to make any contribution greater than the amount that individuals are allowed to donate by law to a regulated political committee.[42] As a practical matter, presidents generally do not ask for money at fundraising events. Instead, that work is done ahead of time by staff, and presidents come to the event to serve as the headline speaker. Given that reality, the FEC's ruling limiting the amount of money a president can solicit at a fundraiser does not amount to much of a restriction in practice. While the numbers of Super PAC fundraisers have been small so far, it would not be surprising to see presidents take part in more of these events in the future, as campaign costs and the pressure to fundraise are both likely to continue to increase.

CONCLUSIONS

Over the forty-four years from 1977 through 2020, seven presidents devoted substantial amounts of their scarcest resource, their time, to fundraise for themselves and for their fellow party members. Presidents raise campaign funds as a means to an end, as they seek to create a more favorable political landscape that will enable them and their allies to achieve their policy goals. The research here shows that the beneficiaries of presidential fundraising are quite different in presidential reelection and non-reelection cycles, with the former characterized by a focus on the president's reelection campaign and the DNC or RNC. Over time, an increased focus on reelection fundraising has crowded out raising money for other parts of the party. This initially took place during a president's third and fourth years in office, but Trump's decision to begin to fundraise for his own reelection bid less than six months into his presidency corresponded with a decrease in fundraising for fellow party members during his first two years in office as well.

Analysis of non-reelection cycles sheds light on various strategies and dynamics of party leadership. In these cycles, Senate races have been these presidents' top priority in the aggregate, followed by House campaigns, governors' races, and state parties. But there has been a good deal of variation in the strategies that presidents employ as they embrace the role of fundraiser in chief. Much presidential fundraising is focused on the Congress, and the president's party's standing in both the House and Senate tends to deteriorate over the course of his time in office. This often means that presidents defend congressional majorities early in their presidency, and later in their term they often fundraise in the hope that their party will reclaim a lost majority.

The Senate was a consistent top-two priority in thirteen of fifteen non-reelection cycles. The House was a far rarer area of focus, ranking among a president's top-two priorities in just two election cycles. Governors' contests benefited from fewer fundraisers overall but were a leading priority more often than were House races. As detailed in previous chapters, through the years presidents have spent increasing amounts of time fundraising for the DNC and the RNC and less time raising money for state parties that were not part of a presidential election-focused joint fundraising committee. Presidents have spent relatively small amounts of time fundraising for assorted other beneficiaries. Among these rare beneficiaries, Super PACs represent a potential growth area when it comes to presidential money-raising strategies.

Fundraising for individual Senate and House candidates has been predominantly defensive, as presidents have consistently spent more time raising funds for incumbents and for open seats vacated by their fellow party members than for challengers to incumbents of the other party and open seats previously held by the opposing party. Presidents placed less of an emphasis on fundraising for incumbent governors, perhaps because of term limits in many states that lead to more open-seat contests. The rise of fundraising in recent years for the national party committees focused on the House and Senate has complicated the ability to assess whether a fundraising strategy in a given cycle was offensive or defensive. There was not a similar rise in fundraising for the national party committees focused on governors' races, reflecting an increased presidential focus on fundraisers for federal offices in the recent era of uncertain congressional majorities and fierce party competition.

The efforts of presidents to fundraise for their fellow party members are consistent with the arguments in the research of Galvin, as well as of Milkis, Rhodes, and Charnock. Galvin argued that the loss of the Democrats' long-standing congressional majorities in 1994 ushered in a new era of competitive national parties in which presidents of both parties would be incentivized to provide resources to their fellow party members. And Milkis, Rhodes, and Charnock contended that presidents since Reagan have emphasized partisan leadership as they worked to strengthen their parties in an environment marked by increased polarization. In the forty-four year period from the start of Carter's presidency to the end of Trump's term, seven presidents embraced a wide range of strategies as they responded to the political demands of their time and assumed the role of fundraiser in chief. Each dedicated his valuable time to try to help win elections in an ongoing quest to bring the nation closer to his particular version of a more perfect union.

The following chapter examines a different element of presidential fundraising—the extent to which presidents headline fundraising events that are either open to the news media or are held behind closed doors with no press access allowed.

5

Fundraising behind Closed Doors

"Everybody wants the money that the president is capable of raising but would just as soon not be seen with the president when he is raising it."

—Stephen Hess, aide to Dwight Eisenhower and Richard Nixon, talking about Bill Clinton, October 4, 1994

"Presidents often find it necessary to maneuver in secrecy."

—Fred Greenstein, *The Hidden-Hand Presidency: Eisenhower as Leader*, 1982

An observer of the final two years of George W. Bush's presidency would be forgiven for concluding that he did not actively embrace his role as the electoral leader of his party at a time when his popularity had plummeted, his party had lost control of both chambers of Congress, and much national attention was focused on who would succeed him in the Oval Office. Indeed, according to the record of his speeches in the *Public Papers of the Presidents of the United States* and on his White House website, Bush headlined only twelve fundraisers for his fellow Republicans in 2007 and 2008. But this public record tells only a fraction of the story. A review of other sources reveals that Bush took part in an additional sixty-six fundraisers that were closed to the press in his final two years in office, working assiduously to aid his fellow party members behind the scenes in ways that were more shielded from the glare of the media spotlight.

Bush was engaging in a form of what Fred Greenstein, in his study of Eisenhower's presidency, labeled hidden-hand leadership. Most presidents take their role as the leader of their political party quite seriously and often spend substantial amounts of time working to elect their fellow party members to office. But these efforts can conflict with the president's role as the national head of state—who is supposed to be, at least in some circumstances, above party. Indeed, the demands that the president serve as a unifying national leader as well as the divisive head of a political party, in the words of Greenstein, "seem almost designed to collide."[1] This conflict is, as Thomas Cronin and Michael Genovese have argued, one of the central paradoxes of the office of the presidency.[2] Julia Azari, Lara Brown, and

Zim Nwokora captured this challenge in the title of their edited volume, *The Presidential Leadership Dilemma: Between the Constitution and a Political Party*. Their book highlights how difficult it can be for a president to juggle these competing imperatives with respect to presidential mandates, reelection strategies, specific policy issues, and other elements of presidential leadership.[3]

Greenstein contended that Eisenhower's solution to this leadership dilemma was to play up publicly his unifying national role while working covertly behind the scenes in a hidden-hand manner to deal with the divisive demands of party leadership. In Greenstein's assessment, this allowed Eisenhower to operate effectively as a political leader while still portraying himself publicly as a president who could unite the nation at large. A number of recent presidents have employed a hidden-hand strategy when it comes to one increasingly frequent and sometimes controversial form of party leadership—presidential fundraising.

Fundraising has both benefits and costs for presidents and for the beneficiaries of their efforts. The benefits are relatively straightforward. The president is the single most effective fundraiser on the American political scene. As campaign costs have risen in recent decades, his aid is in greater demand to help co-partisans wage successful campaigns for office. Presidential fundraising can provide critical resources that allow candidates and party organizations to wage competitive campaigns for elected office. But presidential fundraising for fellow party members and for a president's own reelection campaign is not without costs as well. While any president likes to be seen as the leader of ordinary, hard-working Americans, spending time at fundraisers invites criticism that a president is out of touch and catering to wealthy elites. A 1993 *Washington Post* headline declared that "Behind Closed Doors, Clinton Mixes with Democratic Fat Cats" at fundraisers. In early 2002 a *Washington Post* editorial argued that Bush's commitment to fundraise extensively for his fellow Republicans "underscores yet again the corrosive grip of the money chase on national politics."[4]

Another common vein of criticism is that the president is neglecting his official duties in order to fundraise. In March 2002 Democratic National Committee chair Terry McAuliffe criticized George W. Bush for fundraising six months after the attacks on September 11, 2001, asking, "Is his priority to be the commander in chief or the fund-raiser in chief?"[5] Almost a decade later Karl Rove, who had helped to coordinate the fundraising efforts of George W. Bush while in the White House, wrote a 2011 *Wall Street Journal* op-ed titled "The President Who Hates to Govern," in which he charged Barack Obama with focusing too much on campaigning in general and fundraising in particular.[6] Such a critique is usually situational, as each party accuses the other party's presidents of fundraising at the expense of doing their job but are silent when a president of their own party is the one spending substantial time raising campaign funds.

There are additional costs associated with unpopular presidents' fundraising efforts. Fellow party members want and need the financial resources a president can attract, but many are reluctant to be identified publicly with a president who does not enjoy broad public approval. In 2006 Bush traveled to Ohio to fundraise for Senator Mike DeWine's reelection bid. When asked about the visit, DeWine said, "I appreciate the president coming in. He raised a lot of money. It's always good to be with the president." When a reporter asked if Bush could "do him any good," DeWine did not directly answer the question and instead repeated, "It's always good to be with the president." Congressman Chris Shays of Connecticut cited the benefits of Bush's fundraising aid that same year. "He is helping us to raise money and get out the vote and that is very helpful." But he also discussed the political challenges of being closely associated with the president. "You know and I know that my opponent is running as if President Bush is up for reelection, and he obviously isn't." Democrats like Senator Chuck Schumer of New York were eager to tie Republican candidates to Bush that year and highlight their political dilemma, declaring, "There's a four-letter word Republican candidates are not using: B-U-S-H."[7]

A hidden-hand leadership strategy that embraces closed-press fundraising is one way to reap the benefits of presidential fundraising while mitigating some of these costs. A fundraiser that is closed to the press might be noted in a news article and could trigger the occasional critique from the press or from the other party for its lack of transparency, such as this 2013 *Politico* headline: "Obama Attends Secretive Fundraiser." But closed-press events provide no quotations from the president's speech there and no photographs of him meeting with political donors. This research has found that closed-press fundraising events garner far less media attention than do fundraisers that are open to the media. Indeed, that 2013 *Politico* story about Obama's closed-press fundraiser was a mere 114 words long. For the sake of comparison, this paragraph is 238 words long. Without access to the event, there wasn't much for the reporter to write about it. The secrecy means that fellow party members who might be unwilling to campaign publicly with an unpopular president can accept the proceeds from a closed-press fundraiser without risking images of the candidate with the president that could be used in opponents' campaign advertisements. Headlines like this one from 1994 capture the dilemma that presidents and candidates often confront: "Democrats Like Those Big Bucks, but Wary of Clinton Record." Closed-press fundraising is a hidden-hand strategy that can address this political problem for presidents and their fellow party members.[8]

DETERMINING WHICH FUNDRAISERS WERE OPEN- OR CLOSED-PRESS

Multiple approaches were used to document the many presidential fundraisers that were closed to the press or did not involve a speech by the president and thus were not included in the *Public Papers of the Presidents of the United States*. I first conducted LexisNexis searches of Associated Press articles that contained each president's name within twenty-five words of the word "fundraiser" or one of its variants and checked the thousands of resulting news stories against my data set of presidential fundraisers. To find additional closed-press fundraisers that these searches might not have captured, I reviewed the Digests of Other White House Announcements that are issued by the White House press office. Additionally, I examined the minute-by-minute White House schedules for the entire presidencies of Jimmy Carter, Ronald Reagan, and Bill Clinton, and for the years of George H. W. Bush's term that were available online. I also reviewed the public White House schedules that were available for George W. Bush, Barack Obama, and Donald Trump, as well as Reagan's personal diary, which often mentions the fundraisers Reagan attended on a given day. Information from these sources was frequently cross-referenced with additional news stories and with the discussions of the president's activities by White House press secretaries in their regular sessions with the press corps. Each of these efforts revealed yet more closed-press fundraisers not found in other sources.

Each of the 2,190 presidential fundraisers from 1977 through 2020 was coded for whether or not it appeared in the *Public Papers*. The detailed review of a wide variety of presidential records that led to this study made it clear that almost all fundraisers that did not appear in the *Public Papers* were closed to the press. I did find a handful of examples when the media were allowed into a fundraiser at which the president did not make a speech, and thus there was no entry in the *Public Papers* for what was an open-press fundraiser. These instances appear to have been rare. When possible, I have checked presidential schedules to see if they indicate whether the press were allowed into a given fundraiser. Thus, whether a fundraiser appeared in the *Public Papers* is a very good, if not perfect, indicator of whether a fundraiser was open to the press or not. This approach was the best way to get at these dynamics when creating a data set going back in time over multiple decades, since the actual information on press coverage was not available for many of these events. While it is impossible to guarantee that these efforts have yielded every closed-press presidential fundraiser, the resulting data set is the most comprehensive record available of presidential efforts to fundraise both with the media present and behind closed doors.

It is worth noting that an open-press fundraiser is often open for only part of the event. It is a common practice for the media to be allowed to cover the president's remarks at the beginning of a fundraiser, and then to be ushered from the room so that the president can hold a confidential question-and-answer session with the donors. Although the press do not get to report on everything that went on at most fundraisers, allowing the media in for part of the event leads to more news coverage of the fundraiser. Conversely, fundraisers that are completely closed to the press result in less of a public spotlight shining on the president's hidden-hand party leadership efforts. Mark Knoller of CBS News tracked press access to recent presidential events and labeled them either open-press, partially open, or closed-press. Because the research for this book involved constructing a data set going back almost half a century, there was no feasible way to determine for many events that took place decades ago whether members of the media who were allowed to cover a fundraiser were permitted to stay for the entire event or were ushered out at some point. Thus, in this study each presidential fundraiser was coded as either closed-press or open-press, and open-press events were those at which the media were afforded access to part of or all of the event.

THE CONTOURS OF CLOSED-PRESS FUNDRAISING

The seven presidents from Carter through Trump varied substantially in the extent to which fundraising events were open to the media. Figure 5.1 displays the percentage of closed-press fundraisers by term headlined by each of these presidents. In total, 762 of the 2,190 presidential fundraisers over these seven presidencies, or 35 percent, were closed to the press. Several dynamics are immediately evident. First, a majority of fundraisers were open-press in eight of these eleven presidential terms. The only exceptions occurred during Clinton's first term, when 60 percent of his fundraisers were closed to the press; George W. Bush's second term, when 64 percent of his events were similarly held away from media scru-

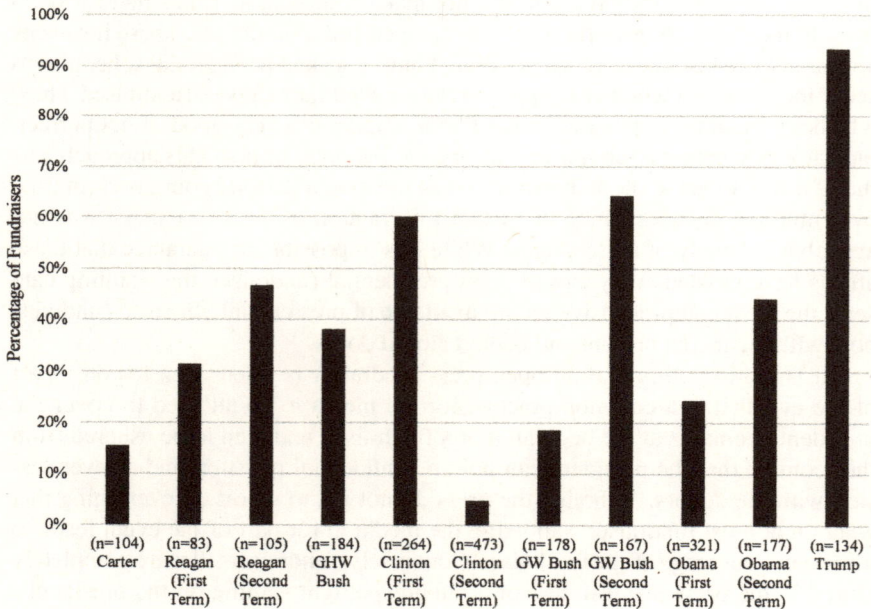

Figure 5.1: Percentage of Fundraisers Closed to the Press, by Term, 1977–2020
Sources: Data compiled by the author from the *Public Papers of the Presidents*, the Digests of Other White House Announcements, White House schedules and press briefings, Reagan's personal diary, and Associated Press and other news articles.

tiny; and Trump's single term, when 93 percent of his fundraisers were closed to the press. Trump was so used to his fundraisers being closed to the media that at one of his rare open-press fundraisers—an April 2019 gala to benefit the National Republican Congressional Committee—he mused in his speech to donors, "It's always somebody going to leak this whole damn speech to the media." As he spoke, cameras recorded his remarks for airing on C-SPAN.[9]

Four terms in this study fell in the middle range of closed press events: Reagan's first term (31 percent); George H. W. Bush's only term (38 percent); Obama's second term (44 percent); and Reagan's second term (47 percent). The lowest percentage of fundraisers that were closed to the press occurred during Clinton's second term, when only 5 percent of his events were not open to the media. Carter's only term was the second most open, with only 15 percent of his events closed to the press, followed by George W. Bush's first term, at 19 percent, and Obama's first term, at 24 percent. The contrasts between the first and second terms of Clinton and George W. Bush are dramatic and important, and they are explored in further detail below. Of the four two-term presidents in this study, three held a greater percentage of closed-press fundraisers in their second term, when they themselves would no longer have to face the voters. The lone exception was Clinton, whose first-term closed fundraiser rate of 60 percent dropped to just 5 percent in his second term.

These percentages must be understood in the context of the rise over time in the amount of presidential fundraising. As the numbers in Figure 5.1 above each president's name indicate, the increase in overall fundraising has not been linear, and Bill Clinton's record-setting second-term efforts can overshadow the fundraising of his fellow presidents. But most recent presidents have spent substantially more time raising money than did those earlier in the FECA era. Indeed, while only 24 percent of Obama's first-term fundraisers were closed to the press, he took part in a total of 321 fundraisers during those four years. Obama's 78 closed-press first-term fundraisers were more numerous than the total of open-press fundraisers for each term of Reagan's presidency, and almost equal to Carter's number of open-press fundraisers. The absolute number of Obama's closed-press events is substantial, but the percentage is relatively low given his overall level of fundraising activity. Obama's 321 first-term fundraisers are more than the first-term totals of any other president in this study, and they trail only Bill Clinton's second-term efforts.

WHEN UNPOPULAR PRESIDENTS RAISE MONEY

The ebb and flow of presidential popularity play a key role in many elements of presidential leadership. In any election cycle, a president's unpopularity can be a tide against which his fellow party members must swim. Fewer candidates want to campaign publicly with a president who does not enjoy widespread public

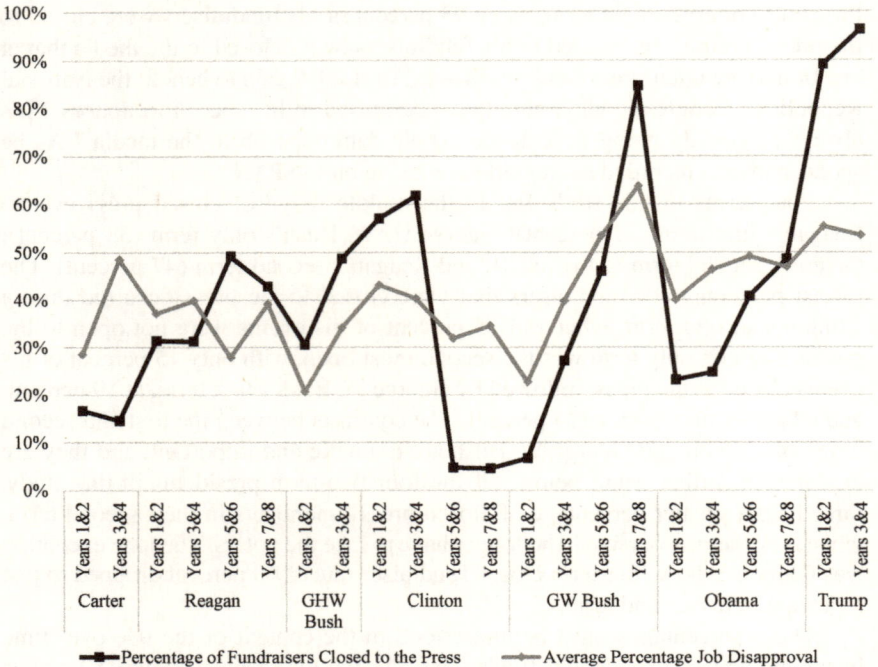

Figure 5.2: Percentage of Closed Press Fundraisers and Average Presidential Job Disapproval, by Election Cycle, 1977–2020
Sources: Fundraising data compiled by the author from the *Public Papers of the Presidents*, the Digests of Other White House Announcements, White House schedules and press briefings, Reagan's personal diary, and Associated Press and other news articles. Job disapproval data compiled from Gallup poll results at the American Presidency Project, available at https://www.presidency.ucsb.edu/statistics/data/presidential-job-approval.

approval. While an unpopular president is not in high demand as a public campaigner, even a president with low poll numbers is a top attraction for donors and can still serve as an important resource for many of his fellow party members' campaigns. A Democratic strategist captured these dynamics in 2010 when asked whether Obama should campaign for embattled Democratic candidates. He replied, "It is much more important for him to talk about his economic policies and what he's trying to get accomplished—and to solicit support from the electorate nationwide—than it is for him to campaign for congressional and senatorial candidates at this point. Of course, we wouldn't mind him showing up at a fundraiser now and then."[10]

Figure 5.2 presents data on both closed-press fundraisers and the public's opinion of the president's handling of his job. The data series marked by squares indicates the percentage of presidential fundraisers in a given election cycle that were closed to the press. The data series marked by diamonds shows the average percentage of the public that disapproved of the way the president was handling his job in that election cycle, as registered in Gallup polls. As Gallup has asked this question with great frequency, 3,800 polls were averaged by the election cycle in which they were conducted to generate the data displayed over the forty-four years covered by this study.

The correlation coefficient for these two sets of data is .64, indicating a relatively strong association between average job disapproval and the percentage of closed-press fundraisers in a given election cycle. The data show that presidents who are unpopular tend to have more fundraisers that are closed to the media. As examination of Figure 5.2 suggests, the association is even stronger for the latter five presidents. For Carter and Reagan, the correlation between job disapproval and percentage of closed-press fundraisers was both lower and negative, with a correlation coefficient of –.39. But for George H. W. Bush, Clinton, George W. Bush, Obama, and Trump, the correlation coefficient was .73.

The dynamics of George W. Bush's two terms as president provide perhaps the clearest demonstration of the relationship between presidential popularity and open- and closed-press fundraising. In Bush's first term, just 19 percent of his fundraisers were closed to the press, whereas 64 percent of his second-term fundraisers were closed. When Bush was fundraising for fellow Republicans in his first two years as president, just 7 percent of his fundraisers were closed to the press. His popularity soared in the wake of the terrorist attacks on September 11, 2001, and, on average, only 23 percent of the public disapproved of his handling of his job as president in his first two years in office. In his third and fourth years, 27 percent of his fundraisers were closed-press and his average job disapproval rating rose to 40 percent. As increasing numbers of Americans registered their disapproval of the job he was doing as president, his proportion of closed-press fundraisers increased as well. In his final two years in office, when the average disapproval of his performance in office was 64 percent, he held 85 percent of his fundraisers closed-press. Indeed, the correlation coefficient between Bush's percent of closed fundraisers and the percent disapproving of his job as president by year is .95, indicating a strikingly strong association.

In 2008, Bush's eighth and final year in office, David Wasserman of the Cook Political Report discussed the president's status as a public liability for his campaigning co-partisans, declaring, "In 2006 there were a few districts where he was very helpful. I don't think there's a district now where he can help."[11] But while Bush was not in demand in public, his aid as a hidden-hand fundraiser was still widely sought. Republican pollster David Winston summed up the conundrum confronting Republican office-seekers that year. "For the candidates, there are pluses that Bush brings and difficulties. The plus is that he can raise money. The difficulty is that he brings his job approval with him, and people are going to have to figure out how to effectively balance that out as they look at their own situation."[12]

Many Republican candidates concluded that they did want Bush's financial support. In July 2008 press secretary Dana Perino asserted that there were many more requests for the president's fundraising assistance than could fit in his busy schedule, declaring, "There's more demand than supply can meet." When asked about the president's many closed-press fundraisers, Perino responded, "He'll be out on the road doing some, but remember he's not on the ballot. Senator John McCain aspires to be the leader of this party and we intend to make sure that the light can fully shine on him, as it should, as he heads into the last 90 days before the election."[13]

Democrats worked to tie Bush to Republican candidates even when he aided them behind closed doors. An Associated Press story with the headline "Democrats Accuse GOP of Hiding President Bush's N.J. Visit" described how these dynamics played out in two New Jersey House races. When two Republican House candidates did not publicly announce an upcoming visit by Bush to the state to raise campaign funds for them, a Democratic press aide declared, "This has become the game plan for Bush loyalists in New Jersey who want to take the money the president can bring in without getting caught on film. But Chris Myers and Leonard Lance are Bush Republicans and they have the campaign cash to prove it."[14] Bush headlined almost as many fundraisers in his second term, when he was deeply unpopular, as he did during his first term, when he enjoyed record public support. But in his second term, Bush let the light shine on McCain and his fellow Republicans by helping them in a hidden-hand manner with a substantial number of closed-press fundraisers. Clearly, presidential popularity played a role in these dynamics.

Another example of the relationship between presidential popularity and fundraising behind closed doors is that of Clinton's first term. As the 1994 midterms approached, his approval ratings had fallen substantially, and relatively few Democrats wanted him to campaign publicly with them. In a Gallup poll taken just after his inauguration, 58 percent of the public approved of the job Clinton was doing as president. By early June of 1993, that number had plunged to just 37 percent. While his approval rating would climb back to 54 percent in early 1994, it would decline again over the following months, bottoming out for the year at 39 percent in September, just two months before the midterm elections.[15]

The connection between public opinion dynamics and the demand for Clinton as a public campaigner was on display when Clinton traveled to Michigan on October 11, 1994, where he spoke to employees of the Ford Motor Company in Dearborn, Michigan, and made the case for both Democratic policies and candidates in the upcoming elections. One news account indicated that while 4,000 Ford workers had been given the morning off because of his visit, only 600 attended the speech, and not one of the state Democratic candidates for office stood on stage with the president. Representative Bob Carr, who was running for an open Senate seat, did sit in the audience for the speech, and said to reporters, "This is not a campaign event, this is a Ford event." He explained his seat in the audience instead of on stage, saying, "I did not invite the president. I was told he was coming." Given that presidents are usually flanked by their party's candidates for office at such an event one month before Election Day, the trip led to this series of headlines: "Democratic Candidates Steer Clear of Clinton"; "President Campaigns without Candidates"; "Clinton Lauds His Policies, but Listeners Are Sparse"; and "Clinton Boosts Party—Or Does He?"[16]

But Clinton's public appearance in Michigan without Carr at his side only tells part of the story. Two days later Clinton headlined a fundraiser for Carr at a hotel in Washington, DC, just blocks from the White House. When asked whether the event would be closed to the press, White House press secretary Dee Myers answered, "We hope so," prompting a reporter to chime in with, "Bob Carr hopes so."[17] Being seen publicly with Clinton was not necessarily an asset for many of his party's candidates that fall. As the Democratic nominee for governor of Wyoming that year said of Clinton, "Why be cute about it? Of course he's a liability."[18] The October fundraiser for Carr was indeed closed to the press, as were sixty-one of Clinton's 107 fundraisers in 1993 and 1994.

These dynamics played out repeatedly for unpopular presidents. In only nine of the forty-four years of this study did the majority of the American people disapprove of the job the president was doing, based on the averages of Gallup poll results in those years: 1992, 2006, 2007, 2008, 2014, 2017, 2018, 2019, and 2020. The annual percentages of closed-press fundraisers during these nine years of presidential unpopularity ranged from 47 percent—George W. Bush in 2006—to 100 percent—Trump in 2020. Trump, whose average annual job disapproval numbers ranged from 53 percent to 56 percent throughout his four years in office, kept at least 88 percent of his fundraisers closed to the press in each year in office. Collectively, the four presidents who served during these nine years—George H. W. Bush, George W. Bush, Obama, and Trump—held 286 of 404 of their fundraisers during these years of unpopularity, or 71 percent, behind closed doors with no media access allowed. As Republican strategist Stuart Stevens put it in 2014, "The Democrats are treating Mr. Obama like an embarrassing wealthy relative—they don't want to be seen with him, but please, please send money."[19]

Relatively unpopular presidents often confront a complicated political calculus when seeking to aid their fellow party members. Nevertheless, presidents have aggressively embraced the role as party fundraiser in chief over the course of recent decades. In the face of low job approval ratings, these presidents have worked to help their fellow party members by raising funds, often without allowing the media to witness them doing so. Even a relatively unpopular president can provide essential financial support as the hidden-hand electoral leader of his political party.

THE PRESSURE FOR FUNDRAISING TRANSPARENCY

Another important factor to consider when analyzing these dynamics is the pressure for greater fundraising transparency. Over the seven presidencies from Carter through Trump, White House press secretaries had to field repeated inquiries from the press corps about the extent of closed-press presidential fundraising. While it would be very difficult to develop an objective measure of the pressure for transparency that accurately captures these dynamics over a forty-four-year period, there are points at which certain administrations did appear to hold fewer closed-press fundraisers in response to these dynamics.

The first such instance took place during Bill Clinton's presidency. In the fall of his first year in office, news stories critical of Clinton's closed-press fundraisers drew the attention of the White House. As one article described, "Clinton attended a $1,500-a-plate, black-tie fund-raising dinner for the Democratic Senatorial Campaign Committee in California last week. Reporters, photographers and camera crews were blocked from covering it, lest the president be seen mingling with the high-powered lobbyists he lit into during last year's presidential campaign." Clinton's communications director promised more media access, leading to this October 1993 headline: "Clinton to Drop Secrecy from Fund-raising Events."[20] In spite of this pledge, 56 percent of Clinton's fundraisers during the following year were closed to the media, followed by 51 percent and 65 percent of fundraisers that were closed-press in his third and fourth years in office.

In 1996, in the midst of Clinton's reelection campaign, White House aides attributed the closed-press fundraisers to issues associated with holding these events in private homes. Fundraisers in large venues like the National Building Museum in Washington, DC, have plenty of room to accommodate the media, but smaller events that are often held in private homes do not. Anonymous White House officials from the Clinton administration made the case that "opening all fund-raisers would pose logistical problems. Many events are small, intimate meals with perhaps 20 or 30 donors who have chipped in tens of thousands of dollars each. Allowing a phalanx of cameras and lights into such gatherings would change their dynamics."[21] This approach to fundraisers in private homes would be emulated by Clinton's successors, though his administration would relent on this point during his second term.

Only when controversy erupted at the end of 1996 about the fundraising practices of Clinton and Vice President Al Gore did the administration substantially change the amount of access the press had to the president's fundraising events. In the wake of allegations that Gore had made fundraising calls from the White House in violation of campaign finance law, controversy over illegal contributions from non-US citizens, and charges that donors had been rewarded with special access to the president—including White House sleepovers in the Lincoln Bedroom—the White House made the vast majority of Clinton's subsequent fundraisers open to the press.[22] Just under 5 percent of his second-term fundraisers were closed-press, and in 1997, when the controversy received the most public attention, seventy-five of his seventy-six fundraisers were open to the press.

Perhaps the most dramatic example of Clinton's new spirit of fundraising transparency was on display during a weekend-long fundraising retreat in 1997 at an exclusive resort in Florida, which was described in the press as a "first-of-its-kind weekend fundraiser for a president," with at least a $50,000 contribution required in order to attend. While previous big donor events had been quite likely to be closed to the press, a newspaper story reported that "Democrats opened the event to press coverage in an effort to deflect criticism from them and onto Republicans, who held a close-door retreat in Palm Beach last February with congressional leaders." Allowing the media into the event led to headlines like this one in the *Atlanta Journal and Constitution*: "Speak Softly, Carry a Golf Club and Raise Money; Hoarse Clinton Enjoys a Holiday with the Rich." This is just the sort of negative press coverage that might have incentivized more closed-door fundraising at other times in the Clinton presidency. But the imperative to be transparent outweighed any desire to hold this event away from the glare of the media spotlight.[23]

In the early years of George W. Bush's presidency, he followed Clinton's second-term practice and allowed the media into the vast majority of his fundraisers, holding no closed-press fundraisers in 2001, followed by 7 percent and 8 percent of his fundraisers that were closed-press in his second and third years in office. Bush had criticized the reelection fundraising practices of Clinton and Gore when he was campaigning for the White House. When Clinton aides in 2000 accused candidate Bush of using language that was similar to the president's, a Bush adviser replied, "Let me assure the president, with all due respect, he is not our model for speechmaking, fund-raising, or conduct in office."[24] Early in his term, the Bush team opened its presidential fundraisers to the press, in part to draw a contrast with Clinton's first-term practices.

But in the reelection year of 2004, 44 percent of Bush's fundraisers were closed to the media, followed by 40 percent in 2005, 47 percent in 2006, 75 percent in 2007, and 91 percent in 2008, Bush's final year in office. The political calculus changed substantially in Bush's second term, when he worked to raise campaign funds for his fellow Republicans at a time when his approval ratings had declined substantially. In 2006 White House press secretary Tony Snow fielded repeated media questions about access to Bush's fundraising events. Unlike Clinton in his second term, Bush's team did not change their approach in the face of media pressure. Instead, they demonstrated that excluding the press from a fundraiser in a private home is a bipartisan practice.

Snow was asked in September 2006 if George W. Bush had five closed-press fundraisers on his schedule during one week that month because "candidates maybe have not been entirely eager to be seen with him." Snow replied, "No, we're having them because they're in private homes. . . . Typically, you try to make sure that if you're having an event in somebody's private home, that it remains private. That's been a standard not only in this administration, but prior." In response, the journalist pointed out that Clinton had changed course after receiving criticism, saying, "Well, actually, in the previous administration they started this way and there were a lot of protests from the media—and from Republicans, as a matter of fact—and they allowed a feed to come out to reporters and they allowed a print reporter to be in." Snow responded with one word: "Understood."

The reporter followed up by asking, "So are you all considering that at all?" Snow responded succinctly again: "No." "Why not?" asked the reporter. Snow replied, "As I said, because, frankly, we're just not in the business of revisiting this. The President is certainly going to be plenty accessible to you guys and he's going to be accessible to the public and you know what his positions are. And we're going to continue to express them." Finally, a reporter asked, "But is this the way for Republican candidates who perhaps might not want to be pictured publicly with the President to avail themselves of his fundraising prowess while not being seen with him?" Snow closed the conversation by saying, "You're going to have ask them. That's not my reading, but feel free to ask them."[25]

In 2008, when Bush would keep more than 90 percent of his fundraisers closed to the press, his next press secretary, Dana Perino, faced repeated questions about why the events weren't open to the media. Her consistent response was that their practice was to keep fundraisers in private homes closed to the press. In May 2008 a Bush fundraiser to benefit John McCain's presidential campaign was moved from a convention center, where it would have been open-press, to a private residence, where the media would not be allowed access. Perino explained, "Our practice has been for fundraisers that the president does, if they're at a venue like a hotel, that they are open to press. The McCain campaign has a practice that's different, and that is that all of their fundraisers, regardless of location, are closed to the press. And so to accommodate the practices, they decided to move it to a private residence today." Obama, who would face McCain in the November election that year, responded by criticizing McCain for "holding a fundraiser with George Bush behind closed doors in Arizona. No cameras. No reporters. And we all know why. Senator McCain doesn't want to be seen, hat in hand, with the president whose failed policies he promises to continue for another four years." The Bush team chose to hold a remarkably high percentage of its fundraisers in Bush's final year as president behind closed doors in private homes, in spite of the media's repeated questions about press access.[26]

When Obama became president, he had to decide whether to adopt or abandon the practice of closed-press fundraising that he had criticized as a candidate. Decisions about whether to allow members of the press to cover fundraising events would be made in the context of Obama's oft-repeated pledge to run "the most transparent administration in history."[27] While many journalists disputed this claim, administration officials defended it with respect to fundraising. In 2010 White House press secretary Robert Gibbs had a spirited exchange with Mark Knoller of CBS News, who asked, "Do you think the spirit of political openness ought to embrace the President when he does closed-door fundraisers?. . . . In the spirit of openness, if he's addressing big money donors, shouldn't that be open to coverage?" In response, Gibbs defended the president's fundraising practices and declared, "I'd put our openness, Mark, against anybody's."[28] In a 2014 news story on closed-press fundraisers titled "Barack Obama Locks Out the Press—Again," a White House press aide rebutted the charges of secrecy, saying, "I would only ask that you judge us by our record and the record of our predecessors. Without a doubt, I think we've done more to achieve the president's commitment to transparency than any previous administration."[29]

The clash of Obama's transparency pledge with the reality of frequent closed-press fundraisers led to critical media coverage that sometimes did not attempt to hide journalists' disdain. A 2014 *Politico* story focused on limited press access to fundraisers and lamented:

> Despite constant complaints from the press corps and promises from White House officials, access to the president continues to be limited. The constantly repeated line that they're running the "most transparent administration in history" tends to prompt snickers. Halfway through Obama's West Coast swing, it's tipping toward outrage. . . . How many people Obama met with was a secret. How much they paid to get in was a secret. Finding out who the people were? Forget it. Even a general account of what the president said to them? Not from this White House.[30]

Obama's aides, like those to Clinton and George W. Bush, made the case that holding fundraisers in private homes made it difficult to allow media coverage. Obama press secretary Robert Gibbs explained in 2010, "Some people have private homes that we don't—we just—you can't bring that many people into."[31] But Mark Knoller of CBS News noted that same year that private homes didn't account for all decisions to exclude the media from fundraisers. "Often, the excuse is that the event is being held in a private residence and there's no room for the press. But sometimes closed fundraisers are held in a hotel ballroom and the only reason for barring reporters is the whim of the White House or the political committee or candidate involved." In 2012 Obama's next press secretary, Jay Carney, offered a different reason for keeping the media out of Obama's fundraisers. "We open fundraising remarks on a regular basis. If he's not making remarks and he's just visiting with folks, then they tend to be closed press."[32]

By 2014 the Obama administration had yielded and allowed a limited number of reporters into some but not all fundraisers in private homes. When members of the media covering a presidential trip to the West Coast asked about Obama's participation in closed-press fundraisers for Super PACs that supported Democratic candidates, deputy press secretary Eric Schultz tried to avoid the specific question. Instead he asked the media to give the administration credit for allowing some reporters into fundraisers at private residences:

> Without a doubt, I think we've done more to achieve the President's commitment to transparency than any other previous administration—that includes, by the way, opening up fundraising events at private homes to the print pool,

people like yourself. So we feel good that you were able to cover events to-day and yesterday on this trip. That's a change that we implemented to give reporters more access than they've had before, and that's a change we feel good about.[33]

But members of the media asking questions that day were not interested in acknowledging that the administration had opened up some previously closed fundraisers. Instead, one reporter followed up by asking, "It just seems, Eric, that the President, one of his objections to the super PACs to begin with was their secretive nature, and isn't he just fostering that by participating in them and not providing any sunshine into them?" Schultz shut down the line of questioning by responding, "I would refer you to the outside groups for the policies that they've adopted for how they disclose information."[34]

Later in 2014 White House press secretary Josh Earnest gave a more direct answer when asked why reporters who were allowed the cover Obama's remarks at a fundraiser were ushered out before the president's question-and-answer session with the contributors:

The fact of someone observing something necessarily changes what is actu-ally being observed. And I think that's at play in a dynamic like this when you have a relatively small group of individuals who are seeking to have a conversation with the president of the United States. So, what we have done is we have structured this in a way that tries to balance your understandable interest in the pitch that the president makes to donors with the ability of do-nors to have a frank and candid conversation with the president of the United States in a relatively private setting.[35]

When a reporter pointed out that Earnest's explanation would apply to any presidential event that the media covered, Earnest responded:

It does, which is why we try to balance them. I think that if you're in a setting where the president is speaking as he did in Maryland over the weekend to 8,000 people it would be hard for me to make the case that letting 12 addi-tional people observe that speech would necessarily change the interaction. But I think the dynamic is different when we're talking about a smaller group of individuals, a couple of dozen, that increasing the number of people who are participating in that session does necessarily change the interaction.[36]

Earnest was asked if the real reason for limiting press access was an expecta-tion of privacy on the part of the donors. He responded, "I don't think that there is an implied expectation of privacy. I think what is implied is a little intimacy and the opportunity to have a frank and candid conversation that is different than one that's observed by journalists."[37]

Two years later Earnest again defended the partial access to fundraisers granted to journalists and compared it favorably to the practices of prior presidents. He declared, "That kind of transparency goes beyond what just about every other President in the modern era has allowed." Earnest acknowledged that reporters would "be angling for more and you should. I don't anticipate a change in our policy across the board, but, look, we'll see what happens. Maybe there will be a time when we just decide to open it up just for fun." "Just for fun?" a reporter asked. "Just for fun," Earnest responded.[38]

In spite of Earnest's claims, the Obama administration's fundraising was neither the most nor the least transparent when compared to other recent presidents in relative terms. Indeed, his 31 percent of fundraisers that were closed to the press made him the third most transparent president when it came to press access to fundraisers, following Carter's 12 percent and Clinton's 24 percent. Obama's mark was more transparent than George H. W. Bush's 38 percent, Reagan's 40 percent, George W. Bush's 41 percent, and Trump's 93 percent of fundraisers that were closed to the press. But in absolute terms, Obama's 156 closed-press fundraising events trailed only Clinton's 180 such events. Overall, Obama took part in so many fundraising events that his substantial number of closed-press fundraisers only comprised 31 percent of all his fundraising events.

It is also worth noting that decisions on whether Obama's fundraisers should be open or closed to the press were made in light of the president's promise of unprecedented transparency. There was a great deal of attention paid to this pledge in the modern era of nonstop electronic communication, as reporters frequently wrote web posts and used Twitter to highlight what they saw as the administration's shortcomings when it came to transparency. It is certainly plausible, though unverifiable, that Obama might have held even more closed-press fundraising events had it not been for such a prominent transparency pledge. Obama's promises of transparency likely invited more scrutiny of press access to his fundraising events. I found numerous extended interactions between journalists and various White House press secretaries discussing whether the media would be given more access to Obama's fundraisers. Over his eight years in office, the press were granted access to 69 percent of those events.

In contrast, Trump granted press access to only 7 percent of his fundraising events. I searched the Trump White House website and found only two instances recorded there of his press secretaries being asked about media access to fundraisers, and those discussions were brief. When asked if there would be any press access to Trump's first presidential fundraiser in March 2017, Sarah Sanders responded, "I don't think so, as of now. I think the standard policy has usually been not to have press at fundraisers, but I'll check and let you guys know." Three months later, after the press had not been allowed into Trump's first reelection fundraiser in June 2017, she was asked if the media would be allowed access to future fundraisers. She replied, "Certainly on the table for future events." Trump's press office held far fewer briefings than did predecessors from previous administrations, allowing for fewer chances to ask these questions.[39] Members of the press did ask numerous questions about many other controversies during the Trump era. But while Trump would exclude the press from 93 percent of his presidential fundraisers, media access to these events was not a frequent topic at White House press briefings.

The pressure for greater media access to presidential fundraisers has played out in different ways across multiple administrations. Clinton's team was pushed to be more transparent and chose to grant much more media access in Clinton's second term than in his first. George W. Bush's presidency was marked by widespread media access to fundraisers during his early years in office, followed by far less access in his second term, when he was much less popular. Media requests for greater access did not yield the same results as they did in the Clinton administration. Obama's aides jousted with the press frequently about the extent to which his fundraisers were open to the media. Although they declared over and over that they were much more transparent than many of their predecessors, the evidence in this chapter shows that to be only partially accurate. Finally, Trump allowed the least media access by far to his fundraising events, but his press aides faced few questions about this as the media focused on the many other controversies during his time in office. While the pressure for greater transparency has at times moved administrations to change their policies about press access to fundraisers, sometimes the desire to fundraise in a hidden-hand manner takes precedence over demands for greater openness to the media.

CONCLUSIONS

Presidents are expected to lead on many fronts, and their fellow party members frequently seek their help raising campaign funds. The ways in which they juggle their duties as a unifying national leader and as the divisive head of a political party shed light on the ways in which they view their role as president. Closed-press fundraising offers the opportunity for presidents to fundraise for themselves and to play the role of party leader in a manner that is reminiscent of Greenstein's study of Eisenhower's hidden-hand leadership. Greenstein made the case that some political leadership is most effective if it takes place away from the public eye. This chapter reveals that most recent presidents have held substantial numbers of closed-press fundraisers. Some of these patterns of activity have been correlated with dynamics of presidential popularity, particularly in the case of George W. Bush. Members of the media often seek more press access to fundraising events, and at times presidents have responded to pressure for more transparency with more openness while at other times they and their aides have not heeded these appeals. Hidden-hand closed-press fundraising has tended to draw less press scrutiny than fundraising efforts that granted access to the media. This has allowed unpopular presidents to raise funds for their fellow party members with fewer political costs, and for presidents and donors who prefer privacy to hold fundraising events away from media scrutiny.

Christi Parsons, the president of the White House Correspondents' Association in 2014, laid out why the press believe they should have access to fundraising events: "We think these fundraisers ought to be open to at least some scrutiny, because the president's participation in them is fundamentally public in nature. Denying access to him in that setting undermines the public's ability to independently monitor and see what its government is doing. It's of special concern as these events and the donors they attract become more influential in the political process."[40] Intimate events with small numbers of high-dollar donors that are held in private homes are the fundraisers that are most likely to be closed-press. Parsons's argument implies that these events are the ones where it is most important to have press access so that the public can know what goes on behind the closed doors of a high-dollar presidential fundraiser. It is natural to wonder just what a president says to donors who paid $580,600 per couple for an hourlong session with the nation's chief executive, as was the case for Trump on multiple occasions in 2020.[41] Some political leaders in both parties have claimed for decades that Washington insiders are beholden to special interests. Parsons argues that closed-door, high-dollar fundraisers like these can fuel these suspicions in ways that are problematic for our system of democratic government. Melanie Sloan, executive director of the organization Citizens for Responsibility and Ethics in Washington, summed up a key concern raised by closed-press fundraisers: "What do they tell their big donors that they don't tell the rest of us?"[42]

Rufus Gifford, a former national finance director for Obama, made the case that opening fundraisers to the media can serve presidents and candidates well. He referred to several instances of recorded comments at closed-press fundraisers that were leaked and caused political controversy. In 2008 Obama talked at a closed-press fundraiser in San Francisco about rural Pennsylvania voters who "cling to guns or religion or antipathy to people who aren't like them." In 2012 Republican presidential nominee Mitt Romney said at a closed-press fundraiser that he would never win the votes of "47 percent" of Americans who "are dependent upon government, who believe that they are victims, who believe the government has a responsibility to care for them, who believe that they are entitled to health care, to food, to housing, to you name it." Gifford contended that comments like these feed the "concern that candidates say things behind closed doors to financial supporters that they wouldn't say on the stump. That's why having media in the room is a good thing."[43]

As of early 2022 all of Joe Biden's initial presidential fundraisers have been open-press events. Early in the 2020 presidential campaign, Biden opened many of his fundraising events to the media. An anonymous Biden donor explained his reasoning, saying, "He wants to make sure that everybody understands what he says in public isn't any different than what he says in private. He understands: too many phones, too many recordings."[44] Biden, like his predecessors in the Oval

Office, likely will be tugged by competing incentives as he decides whether to allow the media to cover his future presidential fundraising efforts or to keep them closed from press scrutiny. As rising campaign costs, limitations on campaign contributions, the emergence of Super PACs, and a competitive electoral landscape all place pressure on candidates and elected officials to spend substantial amounts of time raising money, the president will continue to be in high demand as party fundraiser in chief, both in full view of the press and behind closed doors.

6

Controversies and Prospects

"I suffer from the same original sin of all politicians, which is we've got to raise money."

—Barack Obama, August 17, 2007

"Somebody gives them money—not anything wrong—just psychologically when they go to that person, they're going to do it. They owe them."

—Donald Trump on the instinct to reciprocate a donation, January 17, 2016

In the spring of 1972, Richard Nixon's reelection campaign took in more than $11 million in contributions that it hoped to keep secret. After a lawsuit forced the campaign to disclose donor information, the public learned that it had received contributions from two individuals of $1 million and $2 million apiece, in addition to multiple illegal $100,000 donations from corporations. This money was then used to fund the illegal operations that comprised the more well-known parts of what came to be called the Watergate scandal. Nixon White House counsel John Dean later declared, "A lot of us believe Watergate might never have happened without all that money sloshing around." In response, Congress amended the Federal Election Campaign Act. The updated law created the foundation of the modern campaign finance system, which mandated limits on contributions to campaigns, political parties, and political action committees, while also requiring disclosure of both donations and campaign expenditures. When Gerald Ford signed the bill into law in October 1974, he issued a statement declaring, "The unpleasant truth is that big money influence has come to play an unseeming role in our electoral process."[1]

Almost a half-century later, the American campaign finance system has evolved substantially, but it is still marked by many of the issues that concerned the reformers of the 1970s. Fred Wertheimer, a longtime advocate of tighter campaign finance regulations, asked in 2014, "What was at the core of the Watergate campaign finance scandals? Corporate money, secret money, unlimited contributions from individuals. What do we have today? Corporate money, secret money, unlimited contributions from individuals." Senator John McCain concurred, declaring, "We are full circle to the days prior to Watergate. There are not people walking around the streets of Washington, DC with briefcases full of money, but we are very close to that."[2]

Presidential fundraising sits at the intersection of campaigning and governing, and it is a commonly used tool of modern presidential leadership. Presidents use fundraising as a means to an end as they work to improve their own electoral prospects and fulfill their role as party leader. This book sheds light on these dynamics by drawing upon a unique data set that tracks the time that presidents have devoted to fundraising since the beginning of the current campaign finance regime in the 1970s. Although the current campaign finance system was designed to reduce the potential for corruption or the appearance of corruption, the evidence presented in this book indicates that these controversies have reemerged again and again throughout the near-half-century since 1974.

Over the forty-four years during the presidencies of Jimmy Carter, Ronald Reagan, George H. W. Bush, Bill Clinton, George W. Bush, Barack Obama, and Donald Trump, presidential fundraising has been characterized by both escalation and complication. Public funding for presidential elections became irrelevant as campaign costs rose and presidents consequently dedicated more and more time to fundraising and began their reelection fundraising progressively earlier. Presidents and their parties spent much time raising unlimited soft money contributions to political parties until this practice was banned in 2002. Unregulated and unlimited money then flowed to a range of newly empowered nonparty organizations that are not subject to contribution limits. The rules of the system shifted again due to both congressional action and judicial rulings. Super PACs emerged, and presidents and their fellow party members responded to new rules and an evolving campaign finance landscape by increasingly turning to complicated joint fundraising committees that allow them to legally circumvent contribution limits. What has resulted is an illogical and disjointed campaign finance system that is now far removed from the imperatives that Congress responded to when it created a new campaign finance regime in 1974, and that no one would have designed from the ground up. In the current campaign finance system, there is abundant appearance of corruption.

Fundraising has also become increasingly nationalized and high-dollar, as presidents have more frequently chosen to raise campaign funds in larger amounts for national political entities while devoting less of their efforts to fundraising for individual candidates and for state parties that are not part of a presidential joint fundraising committee. Presidents have employed a range of fundraising strategies, and their priorities in reelection cycles are far different than when their name is not on the ballot. The increase in reelection fundraising has increasingly crowded out fundraising for other party members in a president's third and fourth years. With Trump's unprecedented decision to raise money for his reelection bid in his first two years in office, reelection fundraising took precedence over party fundraising in a first midterm cycle as well for the first time.

When presidents are not focused on their own reelection, they consistently prioritize raising campaign cash for Senate races. House contests are far less frequent recipients of the president's fundraising aid, and they have only been an occasional top priority for second-term presidents. Governors' races, most of which take place during midterm election cycles, were a top priority in the first two years in office for a number of presidents but have faded in importance during Obama's and Trump's terms. Presidents tend to focus more on helping incumbents and defending open seats their party previously held in Senate and House races, though the nationalization of presidential fundraising in recent presidencies has meant fewer events for individual candidates. The same nationalization has not taken place in governors' contests, which have received less presidential attention. Presidents have also engaged frequently in hidden-hand closed-press fundraising, and these dynamics have at times fluctuated with a president's unpopularity and with media pressure for transparency.

Presidents are strategic, goal-oriented actors who respond to the incentives created by the rules of the system in which they operate. Campaign costs have risen in an era marked by competitive elections for the White House, the Senate, the House of Representatives, governors' seats, and more. While presidents and their parties must raise money in the amounts prescribed by contribution limits, they must compete with nonparty groups like Super PACs that are not bound by limits on the amounts of money they can take in. These dynamics create pressure on political actors to spend substantial amounts of time raising money, and the president's fundraising aid is in great demand. Presidents' time is a scarce resource, and the decisions they make when they allocate their time to fundraising can reveal a great deal about presidential priorities.

CONTROVERSIES

Presidential fundraising can help provide presidents and their fellow party members with the resources they need to wage competitive campaigns. Early fundraising can scare off potential challengers, facilitate future fundraising success, and pave an easier path to electoral victory. A president who spends his time raising funds for his party's candidates hopes to end up with more elected allies who will help him enact his policy agenda. Fundraising does not win votes, but it does provide critical resources so that candidates are well positioned to work to win more votes. From a president's perspective, a successful fundraising effort can lead first to campaign success and then to more effective governance that improves the state of our union. But presidential fundraising can spark many controversies as well.

The Appearance of Corruption Abounds

The Supreme Court cited the desire to reduce corruption or the appearance of corruption when it upheld the constitutionality of limits on contributions to federal candidates in the 1976 *Buckley v. Valeo* decision. Individual donors were limited to contributing only $1,000 per election cycle to a federal candidate at the time the law was passed. This amount was increased to $2,000 and was set to rise with inflation as part of the Bipartisan Campaign Reform Act of 2002 (BCRA). By the 2020 cycle, the limit had risen to $2,800 per election cycle. In setting these limits, Congress aimed to make candidates for office reliant on a large number of relatively small donors. If a candidate for president, the Senate, or the House had to raise millions of dollars in increments in the low thousands, that candidate would need many financial backers and thus would not be overly reliant on any individual donor. This would reduce the potential of corruption.

Successive efforts to limit money in politics have led political actors to find various ways to work around those limits. In the 1990s and early 2000s, political parties raised so-called soft money in unlimited amounts, which raised concerns about corruption. When the BCRA banned soft money contributions to political parties that work to influence federal elections, nonparty groups that could receive unlimited contributions became more prominent. These groups played important roles in elections before the Supreme Court's 2010 decision in the *Citizens United* case, but that ruling helped lead to even more activity from these groups, the most prominent of which are known as Super PACs.

The current campaign finance landscape is a far cry from the dynamics envisioned by campaign finance reformers. The two presidents who sought reelection in the Super PAC era, Obama and Trump, both had supportive Super PACs that backed their reelection bids. Obama did not headline any fundraisers for the Super PAC that supported him, but Trump did on several occasions. Both Obama and Trump took part in fundraising events for Super PACs that supported their party's Senate candidates. The Federal Election Commission has held that presidents and other federal office holders and candidates can take part in Super PAC fundraisers as long as they themselves do not ask attendees to make any contribution greater than the amount that individuals are allowed to donate by law to a political committee that is subject to contribution limits.[3] This restriction does not do much to limit presidents' activities, as presidents themselves generally do not ask invited guests at fundraisers to contribute a certain amount of money. Instead, that ask is made by staff in advance of the fundraising event. Even if a president doesn't attend a Super PAC event himself, presidents often can easily learn which individuals have written seven- or eight-figure checks to a supportive Super PAC.

In response to the prominence of Super PACs and other nominally independent groups, campaigns and parties have formed complex joint fundraising committees that let them accept contributions in increments of hundreds of thousands of dollars. Both Obama and Trump fundraised jointly for their reelection

campaign committee and for various national and state party entities so that donors could contribute larger amounts of money. In the wake of the *McCutcheon* Supreme Court decision in 2014 that removed the aggregate cap on biennial
donations to federal candidates and party committees, these joint fundraising
committees engaged in even higher-dollar fundraising. State parties could then
transfer the funds received via these committees to the DNC or RNC. These legal
but controversial transfers effectively allowed national party committees to circumvent limits on direct contributions while raising money in increasingly large
amounts. In 2020 Trump headlined multiple events where the price of admission
was $290,300 per person.[4] In May 2021 the Democratic National Committee an-
nounced a joint fundraising committee to which an individual can contribute up
to $875,000 per year.[5]

Trump described the potential for corruption in a speech at a campaign rally
in October 2020. He made the case that if he wanted to, he could raise more
money than his Democratic rival, Joe Biden, and gave this example of what a
president could do:

> I called the head of Exxon. . . . "How are you doing? How's energy coming?
> When are you doing the exploration? Oh, you need a couple of permits?". . . .
> I'd love you to send me $25 million for the campaign. . . . But if I made the
> call, I will hit a home run every single call, I would raise $1 billion in one day
> if I wanted to. I don't want to do that. I don't want to do it.[6]

In the wake of Trump's speech, ExxonMobil issued this statement via Twitter:
"We are aware of the President's statement regarding a hypothetical call with our
CEO . . . and just so we're all clear, it never happened."[7]

While the example Trump gave in 2020 was conjectural, he openly discussed
the exchange of donations for political favors when he was a candidate for president in 2015: "I will tell you that our system is broken. I gave to many people.
Before this, before two months ago, I was a businessman. I give to everybody.
When they call, I give. And you know what? When I need something from them,
two years later, three years later, I call them. They are there for me. And that's a
broken system."[8]

The modern campaign finance system lets wealthy individual donors contribute a great deal. A report studying donor dynamics from 2009 through 2020 found
that nineteen people—twelve so-called megadonors and their spouses—contributed a total of $3.4 billion to candidates for federal office and political groups—
including both political parties and groups such as Super PACs. This represented
close to 7.5 percent of the total amount raised by all federal candidates and political groups over this period.[9] That concentration of financial influence is what
the campaign finance system, with its limits on contributions to candidates and
political parties, was designed to avoid.

Justice Stephen Breyer decried the changes to the campaign finance system wrought by the Supreme Court's decision to strike down the aggregate biennial limits on contributions to federal candidates and political parties in the 2014 *McCutcheon v. FEC* case. Breyer took the relatively unusual step of reading his dissent from the bench and declared that the Court majority's decision "creates a loophole that will allow a single individual to contribute millions of dollars to a political party or to a candidate's campaign." He argued that the ruling "eviscerates our Nation's campaign finance laws, leaving a remnant incapable of dealing with the grave problems of democratic legitimacy that those laws were intended to resolve." The central problem with the ruling, as Breyer saw it, was that "where enough money calls the tune, the general public will not be heard."[10] In response to the decision, Senator John McCain said, "If money is free speech, then the wealthiest people in America are those that get to speak the most freely."[11]

Special Access and Privileges for Donors

In the summer of 2016, leaked emails from the Democratic National Committee revealed some of the ways in which its staff sought to make the most of Obama's fundraising efforts. One message included this offer: "If [you] were willing to contribute $33,400 we can bump you up a level to the Fairmont. Additionally, your generous contribution would allow you to attend a small roundtable we are having with President Obama in DC on May 18th or a dinner in NYC on June 8th." The *Washington Post* described this as an example of "how the party has tried to leverage its greatest weapon—the president—as it entices wealthy backers to bankroll the convention and other needs." When questioned about the propriety of such appeals to donors, a White House spokesperson responded, "As presidents of both parties have done for decades, President Obama takes seriously his role as the head of the Democratic Party. To this end, the President participates in a range of events to raise awareness and support for the party, and to outline his priorities for making progress for the American people, in line with federal election and ethics laws."[12]

Obama's spokesperson was correct that many presidents of both parties have engaged in similar practices. Carter was reluctant to do so, though, when he took office only a few years after Watergate. Democrats were worried about another campaign finance scandal, and they responded by not offering special benefits for donors. One lobbyist described the DNC's trouble raising money in late 1977, and said, "It is a clean operation. There are no promises of access or hope of getting anything special done for you. Maybe we've reformed ourselves to a point where fund-raising can't be done."[13] But subsequent presidents were not as hesitant to set up donor rewards programs.

During the Reagan years, donors who gave $10,000 to the Republican National Committee each year were called Eagles. They and other top contributors were invited repeatedly to the White House for events with Reagan. At two such

White House events in 1985, Reagan said, "I hope I can count on all of you next time around," and he urged the donors to "redouble your efforts." In 1992 contributors who gave at least $92,000 in soft money to attend the RNC's "President's Dinner" had their photo taken privately with George H. W. Bush. The largest donors to the dinner, including one person who contributed $400,000, got to sit at the head table with the president or the vice president. When asked if donors were buying influence, White House press secretary Marlin Fitzwater replied candidly, "We don't believe it's buying influence, but it certainly . . . it's buying access to the system, yes. When you contribute to the political parties and the political system, you are supporting the process in America, you're supporting the political process, you're buying into the political process as a participant."[14]

Joan Baggett, who ran Clinton's political affairs office during his first two years, made the case that while donors did not buy access to the White House, they were rewarded with access for their prior contributions:

> Certainly we tried to make sure donors were included in state dinners and small dinners and other social activities at the White House. We would bring them in for briefings and the types of things that I just mentioned. But there was no quid pro quo there. It wasn't, you give money, you get to come to the White House. It was, you've supported the party all these years, and the President and we want to make sure you're included when there's an opportunity.[15]

But Clinton's donor rewards program during his reelection campaign drew substantial criticism for its frequent invitations of donors to the White House for coffees with the president, as well as for the practice of top donors staying overnight in the White House's Lincoln Bedroom. DNC chair Donald Fowler defended the propriety of the program, saying, "Our donor program corresponds in significant detail to every donor program used by both political parties since Dwight Eisenhower was president." Former Bush press secretary Fitzwater commented on the DNC's practices, "One of the cautions is that you don't promise government favors for money donated. The closer you get to that line, the more dangerous it gets. It sounds like they've just gotten a little closer to the line." Clinton had denounced "cliques of $100,000 donors" when he ran for president in 1992. In 1995 his fundraising practices led to this headline: "White House: $100,000 Meals Don't Mean Clinton's for Sale."[16]

George W. Bush, Obama, and Trump would also give special access to top donors. In 2004 Bush held a series of private "donor maintenance" lunches with leading contributors to the RNC at the historic Evermay mansion in Washington, DC. Lunch attendees included "Regents," who had given $50,000 to the RNC, and members of "Team 100," who had contributed $25,000. The amounts for each group had been $250,000 and $100,000, respectively, before the passage of campaign finance legislation in 2002 that limited donations to party committees and forced the RNC to adjust its donor reward program.[17] Obama, in addition to the donor rewards described above in leaked DNC emails, held a farewell party in January 2017 in the East Room of the White House "for close friends and major donors."[18] In 2019 Michael Hodges, an executive in the payday lending industry, talked about how the RNC gave him a hearing about policy issues because of his support of the president. "I've gone to [RNC chair] Ronna McDaniel and said, 'Ronna, I need help on something.' She's been able to call over to the White House and say, 'Hey, we have one of our large givers. They need an audience. . . . They need to be heard and you need to listen to them.'"[19]

In 1995 Ann McBride, the president of the organization Common Cause, shared criticism of the DNC's donor rewards program. "This high-priced access peddling is wrong and an insult to the millions of Americans who believe that their government should not be for sale. These kinds of fund-raising practices are indefensible and perpetuate the perception . . . that the wealthy have privileged access to elected officials." McBride's critique, which appeared in an article headlined "Parties Use Access to Elected Officials as Bait for Contributions," could easily apply to similar efforts by more recent presidents and their parties. While access for donors has played out in various ways during different presidencies, a recurring theme has been special privileges for a party's top contributors.[20]

Limiting Presidents' Exposure to Ordinary Americans

Spending substantial amounts of time fundraising gives presidents extended exposure to the wealthiest Americans and only a limited view of the public at large. In September 2018, as Trump was about to make his first presidential visit to South Dakota, the *Rapid City Journal* ran an editorial titled "Trump Fundraiser for Noem Shuts the Public Out." The paper cited the more than 200,000 South Dakotans who had voted for Trump in 2016 and asked:

> How many working-class South Dakotans with children or who work at two or three jobs can afford to spend $1,000 per couple just to get in the door? . . . Perhaps, however, this fundraising event is just a sign of the times. It's money that politicians seem to covet above all else. In just a few hours, Rep. Noem will likely rake in hundreds of thousands of dollars from party insiders and representatives of special interests. At the same time, the public will be shut out. The entire event smacks of the elitism that Trump and Noem point to when criticizing the status quo in Washington, D.C. But even though money is the jet fuel of political campaigns, it is difficult to understand why President Trump has yet to make time for his grassroots supporters in South Dakota. Since there is still time, we urge the president to open his arms to all South Dakotans—not just those with deep pockets.[21]

Presidents of both parties have faced similar critiques. In June 2013 a *San Francisco Chronicle* reporter decried a comparable situation when Obama traveled west to raise campaign cash in California:

> A scenario that's all too familiar: President Obama will visit Silicon Valley this week—but the only Californians who will see or hear from him will pay at least $2,500 for the privilege. As the president begins his 20th trip to California since entering office, the seemingly endless capacity of the White House to vacuum up California campaign checks—without scheduling any public events—is becoming a cause for concern.[22]

Frequent fundraising is certainly likely to put presidents in close contact with an elite and unrepresentative slice of the American people. Obama wrote about the consequences of these dynamics during his years as a senator in his 2006 book, *The Audacity of Hope*:

> I can't assume that the money chase didn't alter me in some ways. . . . Increasingly I found myself spending time with people of means—law firm partners and investment bankers, hedge fund managers and venture capitalists. As a rule, they were smart, interesting people, knowledgeable about public policy, liberal in their politics, expecting nothing more than a hearing of their opinions in exchange for their checks. But they reflected, almost uniformly, the perspectives of their class: the top 1 percent or so of the income scale that can afford to write a $2,000 check to a political candidate. . . . I know that as a consequence of my fundraising I became more like the wealthy donors I met, in the very particular sense that I spent more and more of my time above the fray, outside the world of immediate hunger, disappointment, fear, irrationality, and frequent hardship of the other 99 percent of the population—that is, the people that I'd entered public life to serve.[23]

This concern is not just a matter of extolling the virtues of presidents spending time with everyday Americans. Research by Raymond La Raja and Brian Schaffner has found that campaign donors are more ideologically polarized than other citizens.[24] Presidents who spend substantial time with and perhaps cater to these wealthy donors are interacting with people who are not just far wealthier than most Americans but who also tend to be more ideologically extreme.

The nature of the office means that presidents always live in what Obama called the presidential "bubble." Harry Truman described the White House in his diary as "this great white jail." Reagan explained that as president, "You're a bird in a gilded cage." And Clinton once joked that he didn't "know whether it's the finest public housing in America or the crown jewel of the prison system."[25] Frequent high-dollar fundraising can contribute to the substantial distance that separates presidents from the people they are elected to lead and serve.

Distracting Presidents from Their Job

Presidents who spend time fundraising invite criticism that they are neglecting their official duties as president. Time is indeed the president's most important asset. Former vice president and White House chief of staff Dick Cheney made the case that "you have to have somebody disciplined running the calendar because the president's time is the most valuable thing there is."[26] Obama's national security advisor Tom Donilon concurred when he discussed a key question that every administration faces when determining the president's schedule. "When you're talking about the president's time, which is the most precious resource in the White House, there's going to be a debate about whether or not this is worth the candle. Is it worth that amount of time?"[27]

In 2008 White House press secretary Dana Perino acknowledged the trade-offs that came with making decisions about how to allocate George W. Bush's time. "The President could be out doing—you know, out on the road almost every day doing fundraisers, but he also has responsibilities as Commander-in-Chief."[28] In the waning days of his presidency, Obama struck a similar note. When questioned about the Democratic Party's weakened standing in states across the country as compared to when Obama had taken office, he responded, "I take some responsibility on that. I couldn't be both chief organizer of the Democratic Party and function as commander-in-chief and president of the United States."[29]

And yet Bush, Obama, and other presidents received substantial criticism for the time that they did devote to presidential fundraising. In 2012 Obama's extensive fundraising made him a ready target of Republican condemnation. When he had headlined more than 100 reelection fundraisers, RNC spokesperson Sean Spicer said, "If you assume two hours per fund-raiser, which is conservative, that's 200 hours, the equivalent of five workweeks." Another spokesperson for the RNC added, "There's a feeling out there that the president is putting more time and energy into his campaign than putting forth solutions to help the country." The *New York Times* highlighted these critiques in an article titled "Obama Parries Criticism as Fund-Raising Eats into His Schedule."[30] Obama's press secretary defended his boss, declaring, "The President is still spending the vast preponderance of his time on his official duties."[31] Two years later, an April 2014 story in *The Atlantic* ran at a time when Obama had taken part in 373 fundraisers as president, close to one every five days. It was headlined "Obama's Real Job: Fundraiser in Chief."[32]

Campaign finance scholar Jessica Levinson captured these important dynamics this way:

> The downside of all this time spent away from office is the time the president is not doing his job as chief executive, promoting legislation or working with Congress. As more money is dropped into the political process it has become a self-perpetuating cycle, requiring politicians to spend ever

more time seeking donations rather than governing. It's an imperfect use of his time.[33]

Presidents often claim that they can balance the many elements of their most demanding of jobs. Clinton in his memoir did acknowledge that a president on the campaign trail can create the perception that he is neglecting his duties as president. Writing about his efforts for the 1994 midterms, Clinton addressed the tension between party leadership and national leadership. "My campaign riffs were effective for the party faithful, but not for the larger audience who saw them on television; on TV, the hot campaign rhetoric turned a statesman-like president back into the politician the voters weren't sure about. Going back on the campaign trail, while understandable and perhaps unavoidable, was a mistake."[34]

Funding Fundraising Travel

Presidential travel is a tremendously expensive proposition, and when presidents travel for official government business, the federal government pays the entirety of the costs. When presidents travel for electoral purposes, a campaign or political party must pay for a portion of the expense of the trip. Even if there are no official events to supplement a fundraising event, the taxpayer still pays a substantial portion of a trip's cost, as a president is always on the job no matter where he is and what he is doing. Any trip requires extensive advance work by both civilian and military personnel, and a large entourage, including aides focused on security and communications, accompanies a president at all times. A 1982 Associated Press article described the costs of presidential travel this way:

Even on Reagan's strictly political forays, the government pays those costs Reagan incurs solely because he is president. Those costs, which come from several agency budgets, include: Maintenance and operation of Air Force One, the presidential jet, and at least two Marine Corps helicopters. . . . On trips involving both official and political stops, the aides are treated as a political expense to be reimbursed from campaign funds. The use of a military transport plane to fly presidential limousines, specially equipped Secret Service vehicles, armored lecterns and other security gear to the places Reagan will visit. Installation and operation of sophisticated communications equipment that accompanies the president at all times for reasons of national security. The expenses of Reagan's personal physician, his military aide and the three shifts of Secret Service agents who guard him. There is no precise estimate of these costs. . . . In addition, the White House incurs tens of thousands of dollars in telephone bills, public address systems, hotel room charges, rental of staff and guest cars in the motorcade, advance planning staff and functionaries accompanying the president.[35]

How much of the expense of presidential fundraising travel is borne by the campaign or political party that benefits from the president's efforts? The exact costs of presidential travel are unknown, as administrations of both parties have declined to share how expensive it is to move the president and what is in effect a mobile White House around the country. Press secretaries for every recent presidential administration have insisted that they carefully follow both law and precedent when it comes to reimbursing the government for electoral travel. But they have consistently refused to disclose just how much of the cost of fundraising travel is paid for by a campaign or by the American taxpayer.

These issues have recurred in presidency after presidency. When George H. W. Bush engaged in what was then unprecedented fundraising travel in the 1990 midterm election cycle, the *Los Angeles Times* ran a story with the headline "White House Will Not Reveal Portion of Bush's Political Travel Paid for by GOP." FEC filings indicated that

> The Republican National Committee paid $740,603 to the government for White House travel and communications in 1990. But RNC officials say they have no way of knowing how those bills are calculated or precisely what they are intended to cover. Decisions on how much to bill are "all done at the White House, the formula and everything," said party spokesman Gary Koops. White House officials consistently have refused requests from The Times and other news organizations to explain how the costs were calculated or which of Bush's trips were considered "political" rather than "official" travel. "We don't have anything to add or anything more to tell you," Judy Smith, White House deputy press secretary, said Friday when asked about the subject.[36]

Similarly, when Clinton fundraised for the DNC in his second term, a party spokesperson gave this vague response when asked about the cost: "Whenever the president travels outside Washington, D.C., to raise money for the DNC, the DNC is fully responsible for paying the U.S. government the costs of transportation in accordance with government rules."[37] When George W. Bush traveled around the country fundraising for his 2004 reelection bid, his administration refused to disclose how much of the costs of presidential fundraising travel were borne by the campaign or the party. Instead, a White House spokesperson assured that "federal election laws set forth clear guidelines as to how costs should be incurred, and consistent with decades of past practices, we strictly adhere to those guidelines."[38]

Eight years later, as Obama sought a second term as president, a spokesperson for the campaign said, "The campaign will follow all rules and pay for the portion of travel that relates to political events, as has been true for previous incumbent presidential candidates." A White House spokesperson sounded a similar note: "As in other administrations, we follow all rules and regulations to ensure that the D.N.C. or other relevant political committee pays what is required for the president to travel to political events."[39] In 2017 Trump's press secretary was asked about taxpayers bearing the cost of a fundraising trip to North Carolina. She responded simply, "My understanding is that for a political event that that will be reimbursed for any political travel."[40] For decades, aides to presidents of both parties have assured the media and the public that they are handling expenses for fundraising travel appropriately—but they have declined to provide specifics. Meredith McGehee of the nonpartisan Campaign Legal Center said, "It's very opaque. You're kind of left in the position of, 'Trust us; we're doing it right.'"[41]

One piece of this unclear puzzle is that since the 1980s, taxpayers have paid more of the cost of fundraising travel when there is also an official presidential event as part of the trip. Presidents are criticized both for pairing a fundraiser with an official event and for not doing so. When presidents travel to fundraise and hold no accompanying official events, the other party regularly criticizes them for neglecting their official duties in favor of raising campaign cash. But an official event that takes place on a fundraising trip is often seen as window dressing, designed to allow the benefiting campaign or political party to pay less than it otherwise would have. When Trump flew to Dallas in October 2017 and raised about $4 million for his reelection bid, he was also briefed at the airport upon arrival on how Texas was faring in the wake of Hurricane Harvey. This official event, which took place hundreds of miles from the hurricane's main area of impact around Houston, led *Newsweek* to run a story about the trip that was headlined, "Trump Flies to Texas for His Re-election Fundraiser and Writes It Off as Taxpayer Expense."[42]

In July 2014, when Obama held five fundraisers over three days in and near Seattle, San Francisco, and Los Angeles, he also gave a speech on the economy at an official event in Los Angeles. The *Washington Examiner* story about the trip was headlined "How Obama Is Saving the DNC Money on His Fundraising Trips—at Your Expense."[43] Similar stories in 2002 and 2006 discussed these dynamics under the headlines "Taxpayers Pay for Bush's Campaign Travel" and "On the Way to the Fundraiser; Stopovers Let Bush Charge Taxpayers for Political Trips."[44] In 1995 an Associated Press headline declared, "Goal of Clinton Trip Is Fund-Raising, 'Official' Events an Afterthought."[45] Kathy Kiely of the Sunlight Foundation, which advocated for greater governmental transparency, said in 2013, "Every president does this. But it's pretty obvious that a lot of these public speaking events are tacked on to provide an excuse for him to be in town."[46]

Even given the rules change in 2010, described in chapter 3, that now requires the benefiting candidate or party committee to pay a greater share of the costs of presidential travel, these dynamics add up to a tremendous advantage for the party of the president. "Having a member of your party in the White House is a perk for any candidate in that party," declared a spokesperson for the Center for Responsive Politics. "He comes [to town to campaign] with all the trappings of the president." Some have proposed that campaigns and political parties bear all of the cost of presidential fundraising travel. But following that proposal "would bankrupt the campaign," according to the same spokesperson.[47] If a president's co-partisans had to pay the full, substantial costs of his fundraising travel, he likely would never fundraise outside of the Washington, DC, metropolitan area.

Michael Berman, who worked in the Carter White House and helped to formulate the rules that subsequent administrations would use when allocating travel expenses for political travel, talked in 2012 about the balance he thought would be appropriate. "You don't want to penalize the person who's in office" by compelling a campaign to cover all the expenses of presidential travel. "But they also shouldn't have an advantage."[48] Given the lack of information about just how much taxpayers, campaigns, and political parties pay to support the president's fundraising travel, it's hard to know if a reasonable balance has been struck.

Personal Profit for the President

The presidency of Donald Trump presented a new fundraising controversy that had not come up when his predecessors dedicated themselves to raising campaign cash—a president who profits personally from his fundraising efforts. In late October 2020 the *Washington Post* reported that, according to FEC filings, Trump's reelection campaign and the Trump Victory joint fundraising committee had paid $3.2 million to rent Trump properties for fundraising events.[49] Since Trump was the first president with extensive commercial real estate holdings, his business situation presented unprecedented issues. Throughout his four years in office Trump attended thirty-five fundraisers at his own properties.[50] An RNC official explained, "We hold some of our events at Trump properties because they are great venues that fit our needs."[51] The *Washington Post* reported, "RNC and campaign officials have said Trump has never ordered them to visit his clubs—but it was understood that he is more likely to attend if an event is at one of his properties."[52]

A spokesperson for Trump's reelection campaigned declared, "The campaign pays fair market value and abides by all FEC laws and regulations."[53] When Trump held his first reelection fundraiser at his own hotel in Washington, DC, a former White House ethics adviser to George W. Bush assessed the situation and said, "There's nothing flat-out illegal about it, but it's pay-to-play. The appearances are terrible."[54] For his part, Trump reportedly enjoyed playing what the *Washington Post* described as "the dual role of candidate and caterer" at his properties, regardless of the controversy it sparked. When he spoke at a fundraiser at his DC hotel in 2019, he said to the paying attendees, "I wonder who built this beautiful place." A former director of the federal Office of Government Ethics highlighted the issues that Trump's fundraising practices raised: "What's terrible about this is that it continues the pattern of President Trump finding ways to use the presidency—or his campaign—to profit himself at somebody else's expense."[55]

The practice of personally profiting from political fundraisers has continued into Trump's postpresidency. Trump, like many other former presidents, has engaged in fundraising after he left office. But while other former White House occupants have done so for fellow party members, Trump's main focus has been raising funds for his own political action committees, and those committees have directed funds back to Trump himself. A *New York Times* review of campaign finance filings found that "Trump's political committees spent more than $600,000 on Trump properties for rent, meals, meeting expenses and hotel stays" in 2021. At the same time, Trump's political committees have given relatively little to Republican candidates. One of his committees contributed $350,000 to candidates Trump supported in 2021, which was less than the approximately $375,000 that the committee paid to rent office space at Trump Tower that same year.[56]

Additionally, a *Washington Post* analysis revealed that Republican candidates in 2021 held even more fundraisers at Trump's properties than they did in any year when he was president. In an article with the headline "GOP Candidates Are Flocking to Mar-a-Lago to Pay Trump for the Privilege of Hosting Their Events," the *Post* reported that "Mar-a-Lago has become a hotbed for Republican fundraisers, with candidates jockeying to line the former president's pockets in hopes of winning his endorsement, get a photo with him or simply give donors a chance to be in his presence."[57]

Trump has even held fundraising events with proceeds that go not to a political committee but instead directly to the former president himself, according to the *New York Times*. In an article headlined "Selling Trump: A Profitable Post-Presidency Like No Other," the *Times* reported:

> In early December [2021], Donald J. Trump put on a tuxedo and boarded the private jet of a scrap-metal magnate and crypto-miner for a short flight across Florida, touching down at an airport in Naples. There, a long red carpet marked the pathway into a Christmas-decorated hangar filled with supporters of Mr. Trump who had paid $10,000 to $30,000 for the privilege of attending a party and taking a photo with him.
>
> The event had all the trappings of a typical high-end fund-raiser. . . . But the money raised did not go to Mr. Trump's political operation. Instead, Mr. Trump's share of the evening's proceeds went straight into his pocket, according to a person familiar with the arrangement.
>
> Multiple attendees said they bought their tickets from a private company, Whip Fundraising, whose founder, Brad Keltner, has asserted that "the lion's share" went to charity. But the website advertising the event listed no charitable cause. And Mr. Keltner, reached by phone, declined to discuss how money was distributed.[58]

With Trump teasing another potential run for the White House in 2024 and given his record of aggressively fundraising even when he is not a candidate, the controversies surrounding him profiting personally from fundraising efforts are not likely to go away anytime soon. While this is an issue that is unique to Trump, it does present important questions about the ethical standards the American people can and should expect from our political leaders.

Fundraising against Governing Partners

These presidential fundraising efforts may make it more difficult to cooperate with members of the opposite party with whom a president often must work in order to govern. In one prominent example, George W. Bush traveled to South Dakota in April 2002, where, at an official event focused on agriculture and trade issues, he praised the state's senior Democratic senator, saying, "I want to appreciate the Senate Majority Leader, Tom Daschle, for being here today. Tom, I'm honored, I'm honored you'd come. And Tom and I have spent some quality time together. I invite him to the Oval Office for breakfast. He doesn't eat much, I want you to know, which is good for my wallet. But I appreciate working with him."[59] Later that afternoon, Bush headed to a fundraiser for the Republican who hoped to unseat South Dakota's other Democratic senator, Tim Johnson, and, if Republicans gained control of the closely divided Senate, thereby oust Daschle from his post as majority leader. Headlines focused on the tension between Bush and Daschle, declaring, "Battle for the Senate Comes to the Prairie; Bush Takes on Daschle in S. Dakota"; "Bush Duels Daschle in Dakota"; and "Bush's South Dakota Visit Puts Democrats' Nerves on Edge."[60] Bush's understandable efforts to help his party take back control of the Senate likely complicated his ability to work across party lines with Majority Leader Daschle and other Senate Democrats.

These tensions arose early in Reagan's second term as well. As Reagan aggressively fundraised in an effort to defend his party's Senate majority, Senator George Mitchell of Maine took issue with Reagan's approach: "The president is preaching one thing and practicing another. In Washington, he is asking Democratic leaders for bipartisan support on his tax program. At the same time, his trips, which are billed as selling the tax program to the American people, are highly partisan. How can he ask for bipartisanship on the one hand and lead political pep rallies on the other?"[61]

Similarly, Obama sparked criticism when he opened his second term with what was called a "charm offensive" in which he reached out to Republicans, as well as an aggressive fundraising push that he hoped would defeat Republican candidates for office. Republican Representative Tim Griffin made the case that Obama's fundraising was getting in the way of governing. "I'll admit, it's very difficult to do both. That's why he shouldn't do both. He needs to put the campaign rhetoric aside, roll up his sleeves and demonstrate a willingness to work with House Republicans on tax reform, entitlement reform and the problems driving our debt." RNC chair Reince Priebus also took issue with Obama's approach. "He's doing a pretty lousy job of it. If he was someone who was as conciliatory as he proclaims to be, you would think he would have a few decent relationships with Republicans, but he doesn't. Instead, he spends most of his time campaigning." Obama spokesperson Josh Earnest responded that Obama could fundraise against Republicans while at the same time trying to collaborate with them to govern. "The president's appeal to his supporters won't interfere with his continued efforts to work with Republicans to move that agenda through the Congress."[62]

Given the current competitive political landscape, many political actors would rather wait until after the next election than strike a legislative compromise. Hope springs eternal, and politicians in both parties often believe that they are likely to be in a stronger position to get more of what they want after the next election. Thus they focus on campaigning instead of making a deal in the short term that gives them only part of what they want. A Trump tweet in June 2018 exemplified these dynamics: "Republicans should stop wasting their time on Immigration until after we elect more Senators and Congressmen/women in November. Dems are just playing games, have no intention of doing anything to solves [*sic*] this decades old problem. We can pass great legislation after the Red Wave!"[63]

Campaigning and governing are often in tension. It's difficult to cut legislative deals with people whom you're also working to defeat at the ballot box. As fundraising has become a frequently used tool of modern presidential leadership, complications arise alongside efforts to govern.

PROSPECTS

Frequent high-dollar presidential fundraising is here to stay. It has become a regular activity of modern presidents, who use fundraising as a means to an end and as a tool of presidential leadership. The rules of the political system create incentives that shape strategies and outcomes. Those rules have interacted with the political landscape to yield a situation where presidents devote substantial amounts of their scarce time to raising funds for themselves and for their fellow party members. Rising campaign costs, limits on contributions to candidates and political parties, the specter of groups like Super PACs raising funds in unlimited amounts, and fiercely competitive contests to control the presidency, the Senate, the House, and governors' offices across the country have incentivized presidents to embrace their role as fundraiser in chief.

Most presidents claim not to enjoy fundraising, but they do it anyway for a number of reasons. Presidents worry about whether they will win a second term in office. The forty years from 1980 through 2020 witnessed four successful presidential reelection bids, and three that ended a one-term president's tenure in the White House. The four successful efforts were not predestined to succeed. Indeed, there were points in the first terms of Reagan, Clinton, George W. Bush, and Obama when reelection for each president looked unlikely. Every president knows that a second term is far from guaranteed. Aggressive reelection fundraising efforts have become a key element of a president's bid for another four years in the White House.

There is also great demand for presidents to help their fellow party members raise campaign funds. As races for the House, the Senate, and governors' seats become more expensive, candidates and elected officials spend more and more time raising money to win or retain office. "Both parties have told newly elected members of the Congress that they should spend 30 hours a week in the Republican and Democratic call centers across the street from the Congress, dialing for dollars," said former Democratic House member Rick Nolan. "The simple fact is, our entire legislative schedule is set around fundraising."[64] Former Republican House member Dave Jolly concurred. "We're here three days a week, and half your time is spent raising money. In the face of growing crises around the globe, you've got a part-time Congress."[65] The fundraising pressure that these officials described is certainly tied to the potential to flip control of the House, Senate, and White House in most election cycles. As Thomas Mann of the Brookings Institution put it, "There is no question that partisan parity tends to raise the stakes of any particular election because of the potential for change in majority party control."[66] In the face of these dynamics, office holders and candidates across the country frequently seek the president's fundraising aid.

An Incoherent Campaign Finance System

Current presidential fundraising dynamics are tied inextricably to the disjointed campaign finance system. Limits on contributions to candidates and political parties were enacted in order to limit corruption or the appearance of corruption. That system exists side by side with nominally independent nonparty groups like Super PACs that are in actuality closely tied to campaigns and parties. This combination makes little sense. In 2020 a supporter of Trump could have contributed a total of $5,600 directly to his campaign committee but was able to give millions or tens of millions of dollars to America First Action, a Super PAC that supported Trump's reelection. In September 2020 one couple gave $21 million to the Super PAC, and another donor contributed $10 million.[67] Trump appeared at four fundraising events for the group between 2018 and 2020, and its efforts were focused on supporting Trump's bid for another term.

In the current system, Super PACs and other outside groups have financial advantages that parties and candidates cannot match, though they try. In the wake of the 2014 law that substantially increased the amounts of money that could be contributed to national party committees, campaign finance lawyer Robert Lenhard said, "I think politics is very entrepreneurial. And history has shown us that people are very creative and thoughtful in looking for ways they can succeed in a competitive environment."[68] Robert Farmer, a Democratic fundraiser, expressed a similar sentiment: "I've always believed that campaign finance reform creates a blueprint for how to game the system. . . . Any campaign is a competition. If you don't have the resources to wage a credible campaign, you're out of it."[69]

The creativity that Lenhard described has played out in the expansive use of complicated joint fundraising committees. Joint fundraising committees that benefit presidential reelection campaigns, multiple national party committees, and multiple state parties allow donors to make far larger contributions than had been possible previously under the campaign finance law passed in 2002. The ability of state and national parties to make unlimited transfers to each other then allows state parties to redirect the funds they receive through joint fundraising committees to their national party committee. Presidents and their fellow party members use these committees to collect donations in the hundreds of thousands of dollars as they seek to amass resources that they can control directly in an effort to keep up with outside groups that are not bound by contribution limits. As political scientist Jack Pitney put it, "This is one-stop giving. . . . If you're a rich person with money to spend, party organizations have a way of taking every penny you've got."[70]

The American campaign finance system was built around contribution limits in the low thousands of dollars to limit potential corruption. A series of legislative changes that sparked consequences that were both intended and unintended have combined with transformative court rulings to yield a system that is far removed from the one created in the 1970s. And while many would agree that the resulting framework of the current system does not fit together in a coherent way, prospects for systematic reform seem remote.

Reform Is Unlikely

The rules of the campaign finance system are of paramount importance. In the words of Steven Law, a former aide to Senator Mitch McConnell who prominently opposed campaign finance reform efforts, "Writing the rules of the games in campaigns and elections . . . can shift the playing field."[71] Advocates of tighter regulations on money in politics would like to regulate Super PACs and other similar groups. Those who believe that campaign finance regulations are ill-advised, ineffective, or both, often call for looser restrictions on campaigns and parties so that they can compete with the nonparty groups that can raise funds in unlimited amounts. Though either approach would make the campaign finance system more logically consistent, neither appears likely.

Many Republicans prefer fewer campaign finance regulations and less disclosure of donor information, and they often oppose public financing of campaigns. Many Democrats, in contrast, frequently advocate for tighter restrictions on money in politics, more donor disclosure, and public funding for federal candidates. Neither approach has drawn much recent support from the other party, including the Democrats' sweeping For the People Act, which passed the House in March 2021 with no Republican votes and, as of this writing in early 2022, seems unlikely to draw enough Republican support to advance in the Senate.[72]

Polling has frequently shown support for reducing the role of money in politics in general, and for reining in Super PACs in particular, but the issue is not one that shapes how many people vote.[73] While Obama, Trump, and Biden all initially claimed to oppose Super PACs—Trump in 2015 described them as "unfair," "horrible," and "scams"—all three eventually accepted the support they offered. Obama and Trump overcame their initial reluctance and chose to headline Super PAC fundraisers while president.[74] But the rulings in the Supreme Court's *Citizens United* and *McCutcheon* cases can only be reversed by a subsequent ruling of the Supreme Court or a constitutional amendment. The former seems improbable given the current composition of the Court. And the latter presents very significant challenges, as two-thirds of both chambers of Congress and legislatures in thirty-eight of the fifty states would need to approve an amendment to the Constitution. Indeed, these hurdles are so high that the Constitution has only been amended seventeen times since the initial ten amendments that comprise the Bill of Rights were adopted more than two centuries ago.[75] Campaign finance scholar Anthony Corrado summarized the few possibilities now open to those who would like to restrict the role of money in politics: "The limited options you have as a candidate are either overturning *Citizens United* or providing more disclosure or offering a matching plan for small contributions. It's hard to offer major alternatives because they are not considered constitutional or realistic."[76]

Some argue that because Super PACs are likely here to stay, the changes in 2014 that led to more high-dollar giving to political parties were a healthy corrective. "A lot of us would like to get the parties back in the game," said lobbyist Richard Hohlt. He made the case that allowing larger donations to political parties would offer "some transparency and oversight over an uncontrollable, Wild West fundraising atmosphere." Tony Herman, a chief attorney for the Federal Election Commission, agreed. "It will thus help recalibrate the balance away from secret contributions and from unaccountable super PACs and toward open contributions to the parties."[77]

These arguments align with the conclusions from Raymond La Raja and Brian Schaffner's research on the connections between campaign finance rules and partisan polarization. They contended that political parties tend to be run by pragmatists who want to maximize electoral victories, instead of by ideological purists. They drew on the idea that money in politics is like water running downhill, and they advocated "canals, not dams" to channel funds to political parties instead of trying to block money that will just find somewhere else to go. They acknowledged that better-funded parties raise concerns about corruption but argued that campaign finance rules have empowered ideological extremists in ways that are more problematic than concerns about potential corruption. If large amounts of money are bound to be spent in elections, they contended, better to have parties with what they described as their "moderating tendencies" and disclosure requirements as the central actors than nonparty groups like Super PACs.[78] Fred Wertheimer disagreed, calling the higher party contribution limits adopted in 2014 "the most destructive and corrupting campaign provisions ever enacted by Congress. They will create the opportunity for the wealthiest Americans to buy — and federal officeholders to sell — government influence and decisions."[79]

Although presidents of both parties have claimed to be dissatisfied with campaign finance rules, their allies use a common refrain to explain their frequent fundraising. In 1995 DNC chair Donald Fowler reconciled Clinton's support for campaign finance reform with his aggressive fundraising efforts by saying, "Until the system is changed, we will not unilaterally disarm."[80] In 2002 George W. Bush signed into law a campaign finance bill that would ban soft money donations to political parties effective the following year. Bush then promptly left Washington on a fundraising trip during which he raised soft money for his party. "I'm not going to lay down my arms," Bush explained in an article headlined "President Signs Bill on Campaign Gifts; Begins Money Tour."[81]

A key congressional ally of Obama, Steve Israel, in 2014 defended Democrats' fundraising practices following the Supreme Court's *McCutcheon* decision. "We're going to play by the same rules as the Republicans. We do not like those rules now, and we will seek to change those rules when we are in the majority. The only way we can get into the majority is if we have the resources we need to win elections."[82] And in 2018, former White House press secretary Sean Spicer explained Trump's decision to take part in a Super PAC fundraiser by saying, "He understands the nature of the political landscape today. You can't unilaterally disarm if the other side is going to utilize super PACs."[83] With substantial campaign finance reform unlikely, we can expect to hear this refrain in coming years as well, as presidents continue to make strategic decisions that are shaped by the rules of the campaign finance system, even as they decry the rules themselves.

CONCLUDING THOUGHTS

Presidential fundraising dynamics highlight competing concerns about potential corruption and the value of the president's time. The campaign finance system crafted in the 1970s was premised on the desire to limit corruption or the appearance of corruption by enacting strict contribution limits. When presidents work to raise millions of dollars in the increments set forth by campaign finance law, doing so involves a substantial amount of their scarce and valuable time. When presidents are allowed to work with their parties to raise money in larger amounts, they can raise greater sums with less impact on the time that they devote to important presidential duties, but with those larger contributions comes a greater concern about the role of money in politics. We saw these trade-offs in the Obama and Trump years. Obama had to raise money in smaller increments than did Trump and devoted more time to doing so. Trump was able to raise greater amounts in far less time due to changes in campaign finance rules in 2014 that sparked the pro-liferation of complicated joint fundraising committees. These new entities allow for more efficient high-dollar fundraising, but they also prompt questions about the possibility of corruption.

Campaign costs continue to increase. Presidential elections are quite compet-itive, as are contests for majority control of the House and Senate, and for gover-nors' seats across the country. Nonparty groups like Super PACs raise increasingly large sums of money that are not bound by contribution limits. When George W. Bush decided not to participate in the public funding program for the 2000 pres-idential nominating contest, he explained his choice by declaring, "I want to be in a position to respond."[84] Presidents have responded to these campaign finance dynamics by fundraising extensively for themselves and for their fellow party members, as they have followed the powerful incentives established by the rules of the campaign finance system and by the competitive electoral landscape.

Fundraising has become an important element of a president's leadership tool kit. Looking to the next election is not new. Indeed, one key aspect of the Amer-ican political experiment has been having terms of elected office that are long enough so that officials can govern but still brief enough that those who come up short in one election do not have to wait too long until they can run for office again. Cycles of campaigning and governing have long been part of the American political system. In the modern era, fundraising rarely stops, as it has become a frequent, ongoing endeavor throughout a president's term in office. Presidents and their allies have railed against the campaign finance system even as they fundraise creatively and aggressively to maximize their electoral advantages. As political scientist James Thurber put it, "You can't go to heaven without dying. You've got to have the money in order to run. . . . Even if you're a reformer, you have to get money, or you won't have the fuel to compete."[85]

When presidents raise campaign funds for themselves or for their co-parti-sans, their principal goal, of course, is to secure a second term in the White House or to help their fellow party members win elections. In so doing, they hope that having more fellow party members in the House of Representatives, Senate, gov-ernor's seats, and other elected offices across the country will empower them to enact more of their policy goals and bring the country closer to their vision of a more perfect union. There are no simple answers to the questions that presidential fundraising spurs about the workings of the American political system. But under-standing these dynamics provides important insights into the evolving electoral landscape and the nature of modern presidential leadership.

Appendix
Tracking Presidential Fundraisers

Building the data set of presidential fundraisers covering the forty-four years from the start of Jimmy Carter's presidency to the conclusion of Donald Trump's term was a years-long endeavor. Throughout the process, I aimed to apply consistent standards about what did and did not qualify as a fundraiser and about whether fundraising efforts should be counted as single or multiple events. I systematically consulted a wide range of sources as I gathered evidence about how much of each president's scarce time was spent raising campaign cash.

The resulting data set contains 2,190 fundraising events and is the most comprehensive record available of presidents' efforts to raise campaign funds for themselves and their political allies. Table A.1 presents a summary of the results of these efforts to track forty-four years of presidential fundraising—the number of fundraisers that each of these seven presidents participated in by term. This appendix discusses the processes I used and the principal questions I grappled with as I constructed the record of presidential fundraising that underpins the analysis in this book.

DATA SOURCES

My efforts to build a data set of presidential participation in fundraising events began late in George W. Bush's first term. For the rest of Bush's presidency and

Table A.1: Presidential Fundraisers by Term, 1977–2020

President	First Term	Second Term
Carter	104	
Reagan	83	105
GHW Bush	184	
Clinton	264	473
GW Bush	178	167
Obama	321	177
Trump	134	

Sources: Data compiled by the author from the *Public Papers of the Presidents*, the Digests of Other White House Announcements, White House schedules and press briefings, Reagan's personal diary, and Associated Press and other news articles.

during the tenures of Obama and Trump, I tracked presidential fundraisers as they occurred. For Carter, Reagan, George H. W. Bush, Clinton, and the first years of George W. Bush's administration, I endeavored to re-create the historical record of presidential fundraisers after the fact by consulting a wide range of sources.

I first documented presidential fundraising efforts in the course of constructing a data set of presidential travel drawn from the *Public Papers of the Presidents of the United States*, which are available on the website of the American Presidency Project. While many presidential fundraisers are recorded in the *Public Papers*, a substantial number are closed to the press or do not involve a speech by the president and thus are routinely excluded from the *Public Papers*. References in press briefings and news accounts to closed press presidential fundraisers led me to conduct LexisNexis searches of Associated Press articles that contained each president's name within twenty-five words of the words "fundraiser," "fundraising," or another of its variants in each year of this study. The resulting news stories were used to check the data set. Additionally, I drew frequently upon information from the discussion of the president's schedule by White House press secretaries in their gaggles and briefings with the press corps. These were the principal data sources for the data set of fundraisers I drew upon in my 2012 book, *The Rise of the President's Permanent Campaign*.

I subsequently learned of and reviewed additional data sources that enabled me to expand the data set and offer an even more comprehensive record of presidential fundraising efforts. The Digests of Other White House Announcements, which are released by the White House press office and provide supplemental information on presidential activities, included mentions of some closed press fundraisers that I had not previously captured. For some of the years covered by this study, these could be reviewed electronically, which allowed keyword searches to be used. For other years, only print copies of the digests were available. In those cases, I spent many months manually reviewing these documents in their entirety.

Additionally, I reviewed the recently available minute-by-minute daily White House schedules for Carter, Reagan, the first two years of George H. W. Bush (the only years of his presidency for which the schedules are available online), and Clinton, as well as Reagan's personal diary, which is available online and is conveniently paired with his daily White House schedules. Finally, I often cross-referenced information from these many sources with additional news stories in order to find further information about presidential fundraisers.

All of these efforts to expand and check my data set yielded additional fundraisers that my previous research had not captured. In all, I found an additional nineteen fundraisers for Carter, eight for Reagan, forty-six for George H. W. Bush, ninety-nine for Clinton, and seventeen for George W. Bush. A list of the principal data sources I drew upon, including web links when available, is provided below.

WHAT COUNTS AS A FUNDRAISER?

The data set for this book includes political fundraisers but excludes fundraising events for charities, such as Carter attending a fundraiser for the Hubert Humphrey Center at the University of Minnesota, Reagan taking part in a fundraiser for Nicaraguan refugees, and Trump attending a charity event focused on cancer research. It also excludes events with donors that were declared not to be fundraisers, but instead donor maintenance, donor courting, or donor reward events.

Various administrations described fundraisers in different ways, and these practices changed at times within a presidency as well. Helpfully, some fundraising events were actually identified as such. For example, on May 25, 1982, Reagan took part in an event titled "Remarks in Los Angeles at a California Republican Party Fund-raising Dinner." In George W. Bush's presidency, fundraisers were often described as a "dinner for" or a "reception for" a certain beneficiary, such as "Remarks by the President at Scott McCallum for Governor Reception," on February 11, 2002. The Obama White House often used the term *fundraiser* during its first two years. During Obama's reelection campaign, however, his White House website unhelpfully described both a fundraiser and a campaign rally as a "Campaign Event," such as Obama's "Remarks by the President at a Campaign Event—Tampa, FL" on September 20, 2012. I then had to determine which campaign events were fundraisers and which were not. In Obama's second term, a fundraiser was often described simply as a "DNC event" or a "DCCC event," such as "Remarks by the President at a DNC Event—Chicago, IL," on October 20, 2014. A Trump fundraiser was sometimes called a "Roundtable with Supporters," such as his fundraiser in New Jersey on June 13, 2020.[1]

I had to ascertain what each of the various terms usually meant in each presidency and then determine whether many individual events were fundraisers or not. While I often consulted news accounts and White House press briefings to do so, no source was more helpful in this respect than Mark Knoller of CBS News. Knoller covered the White House for decades and tracked the daily activities of each president beginning during Clinton's reelection bid. His tweets about the president's schedule frequently shared important information about presidential fundraising events. He also generously answered many of my questions over the years as I tried to determine whether certain events were or were not fundraisers. I am quite appreciative and owe him a debt of gratitude.

Distinguishing Fundraisers from Other Events with Donors

The data set does not include presidential meetings with supporters that were classified as donor courting, donor reward, or donor maintenance events instead of fundraising events. What is the difference? Over the years, various White House or campaign officials explained that there was no price of admission for certain presidential events with donors. While these events do not directly generate campaign funds, presidential aides and allies often hope that a session with the president will encourage these supporters to give more in the future. Nevertheless, including them in this analysis would be problematic. Many of these gatherings take place at the White House itself, where actual fundraising is prohibited by federal law. Others are avowed to be meetings of the president with key supporters and friends with no price tag for admission attached. Presidents meet with large numbers of people for a wide variety of reasons, and many of these people have contributed to the campaigns of the president and his fellow party members. While one might suspect that donations are important to many of these political relationships, an attempt to categorize any meeting of a president with a campaign donor as a fundraising effort would be problematic. Thus, this data set is restricted to actual fundraising events.

Terry McAuliffe, a long-time Democratic fundraiser who also served as DNC chair, described donor courting events during the Clinton administration in his memoir as "warm-up sessions . . . lunches or dinners where you give the pitch and try to get people to commit." These were not actual fundraisers but instead attempts to get people to promise to raise money for an upcoming gala fundraising event.[2] In 2018 Trump attended a dinner in the Georgetown neighborhood of Washington, DC, "with wealthy donors who are expected to play crucial roles in financing his re-election campaign." Reporting indicated that a supportive Super PAC organized the dinner, but there was no price of admission. The dinner itself was declared not to be a fundraising event.[3] An Associated Press article described these kinds of events in August 2000:

> The White House and Democratic Party officials say many of Clinton's appearances are unofficial "thank-you" sessions with past donors. Although organizers hope that face time with the president will help free up more dollars in the future, there is no admission price for the sessions. Clinton's official public schedule includes one event apiece designed to lure or honor Jewish, black and labor donors and two events with a mostly Hispanic audience.[4]

In some instances, a lack of definitive information about whether a specific presidential event was a fundraiser or a donor maintenance event required judgment calls. This was particularly the case during the reelection cycles of George H. W. Bush and Clinton. In 1992, Bush attended a series of closed press "Victory '92" events that were noted in the Digests of Other White House Announcements. Some of these were explicitly called fundraisers. Others were labeled as "receptions," "lunches," or "dinners." Still others were called "Meetings with Victory '92 supporters." Victory '92 was described in the press as a Republican soft money account. Federal Election Commission records indicated that there was a federal Victory '92 committee that raised very little money, but that substantial amounts of money were raised by various state Victory '92 committees. I did extensive checking of White House briefings and news accounts of Bush's campaigning and fundraising efforts. The evidence I found suggested that I should code the receptions, lunches, and dinners as fundraising events but treat the events labeled "Meetings with Victory '92 supporters" as donor maintenance or reward events.

During Clinton's reelection campaign, the DNC organized an extensive donor courting and reward program that included lunches, dinners, and receptions with the president. Many of these took place at the White House itself, where fundraising is not allowed, and there was no price of admission for these events. Clinton also attended a number of DNC events at hotels close to the White House. I reached out to then-DNC chair Donald Fowler and Clinton White House aide Doug Sosnik, who was often listed as the staff contact for these events on the White House schedules. Both told me that these were usually donor maintenance or donor targeting events and that there was usually not a price of admission at these gatherings, though the attendees were often subsequently asked to make a contribution. Based on this information and on media coverage of these events, I separated those events that were explicitly referred to as fundraisers in White House schedules, by the White House press office, or in media coverage, from those that were not, and then categorized the latter as likely donor courting or maintenance events.

While this approach might not be perfect, it reflects my good-faith effort to consult a wide range of data sources to make the best determination I could about which events were actual fundraisers and which were not. The ambiguity involved in the 1992 and 1996 reelection campaigns made me quite grateful whenever a White House press secretary would provide a clear, straightforward answer about whether an event was a fundraiser or not, as White House press secretary Joe Lockhart did on February 25, 2000: "The President will attend a DNC lunch Wednesday, March 1st, at the Hay Adams Hotel. This is actually a meeting with some Democratic fundraisers, it is not an actual fundraiser."[5]

ONE OR MULTIPLE FUNDRAISERS?

One challenge of coding presidential fundraisers was grappling with the question of whether a president's fundraising activities on a given day constituted one fundraising event or multiple fundraisers. Many fundraising events include a range of admission prices. Donors who pay more might be seated closer to the president or might get their photo taken with him as well. For example, Reagan frequently participated in a photo line for major donors as part of a larger fundraising event. It is also common for a president to attend a brief reception for the head table at a fundraiser or for the organizers of the event before or after the principal event. In these instances, the receptions were part of a single event but involved a select subset of attendees. In the words of Democratic strategist Tim Lim:

It's a regular fundraising practice where you'll have a VIP reception before-hand, and that's for people who are hosts, who have gotten other people to donate, or who have donated a lot themselves, and it's a smaller, kind of more intimate setting for the donors and the candidate or the executive director or the special guest, whoever that is. And then after that you'll have the more general event with everybody else.[6]

For example, in September 2017, a news outlet described a Trump fundraiser in New York City that offered additional benefits for donors who had contributed greater amounts:

President Donald Trump on Tuesday evening huddled at an upscale restaurant here with some of his wealthiest donors and New York City friends, pulling in about $5 million for his campaign and the GOP. Republican donors attending the dinner at the ritzy French restaurant Le Cirque spent at least $35,000 per couple. A $100,000 donation got a couple of donors "VIP access," while anything over $250,000 earned the donors a seat at a table with the President ahead of his remarks, an RNC official said.[7]

This practice is not a new one. In April 1992, George H. W. Bush attended a fundraiser called "The President's Dinner." The *New York Times* offered this description of the multiple admission prices and benefits for this single fundraising event. The "black tie gala in Washington . . . attracted 4,300 guests who paid from $1,500 to $400,000 apiece—for a sliding scale of privileges. A contribution of $15,000 entitled the donor to sit with a Congressman; $92,000 bought a photo with the President. All told, the dinner brought in $8 million."[8] While each of these fundraisers had specific elements for different tiers of donors, they comprised one fundraising event.

Presidents sometimes attend multiple fundraising events that are held on the same day in separate venues with different groups of people and distinct admission and ticketing processes. For example, on June 13, 2011, Obama took part in three fundraisers in Miami that each benefited the Democratic National Committee. The notes at the end of the event transcripts posted at the American Presidency Project indicated that two of the fundraisers took place at two different private homes, and the third was held at a performing arts center. Thus, these were coded as three distinct fundraising events.[9]

When it was unclear whether a president attended one fundraiser or multiple fundraising events, I checked to see how these events were described in the *Public Papers*, on the White House schedule, by the press secretary, and by the media. For recent presidents, Mark Knoller of CBS News was very helpful in resolving some of these questions, especially on the rare occasions when some of the other sources offered conflicting information. While it can be challenging to sort out years or decades after the fact whether a presidential fundraiser consisted of one event or multiple events, I have carefully reviewed the entire data set and applied a consistent standard in an effort to do so.

DETERMINING BENEFICIARIES

Each of this study's fundraisers was coded for its beneficiary or beneficiaries. Fundraisers for specific candidates were categorized according to the office that each beneficiary was seeking. Many of these candidates held one office while running for another position, such as a House member running for the Senate, or a senator running for governor or president. My interest was in the kinds of contests that presidents tried to aid with their fundraising. Thus, a fundraiser for a Senate candidate who was a sitting member of the House of Representatives was coded as benefiting a race for the Senate. Similarly, when George W. Bush attended several fundraisers in May 2008 to aid Senator John McCain's presidential candidacy, they were coded as fundraisers for the party's next presidential nominee, not as fundraisers for a senator.

Many fundraising events had multiple beneficiaries. Some state party fundraisers were described as aiding a specific candidate for governor, senator, or another office. If so, I coded that event as benefiting both the state party and that candidate. Similarly, a fundraiser benefiting a Super PAC focused on Senate races was coded both as benefiting a Super PAC and as aiding Senate contests, such as Obama's fundraiser for the Senate Majority PAC in June 2014. Joint fundraising committees have proliferated in recent years. Some of these include just two beneficiaries, while others aid dozens of candidates and party committees. For such events, I worked to determine which political entities comprised and benefited from the joint committees.

Most fundraising events had a clear beneficiary. When an event's beneficiary was not evident, I reviewed the many sources described above to see whether I could determine which candidate or party entity the fundraiser aided. I was able to ascertain who the specific beneficiaries were for all but eleven of the 2,190 fundraisers from 1977 through 2020.

LIST OF DATA SOURCES

The American Presidency Project
Presidential remarks at fundraisers from the *Public Papers of the Presidents of the United States*: https://www.presidency.ucsb.edu/documents/app-categories /presidential/spoken-addresses-and-remarks

White House Press Briefings
https://www.presidency.ucsb.edu/documents/app-categories/pressmedia/press
-briefings

Digests of Other White House Announcements
Reviewed printed copies of the digests for Carter, Reagan, and George H. W.
Bush. They are included as appendices in the annual compilations of the hard-
copy versions of the *Public Papers of the Presidents of the United States* that are
available in the United States Naval Academy's Nimitz Library.

Reviewed the digests online for Clinton and George W. Bush. They are available
as appendices at the end of the Books of Presidential Documents within the *Public Papers*, which are provided in six-month increments via this website: https://
www.govinfo.gov/app/collection/PPP/president-57/2008/02;A;July%201%20to
%20December%2031,%202008

Reviewed the digests online for Obama, Trump, and Biden. Various years dating
back to 2009 can be viewed by substituting a given year for the two occurrences
of "2021" in this URL: https://www.govinfo.gov/content/pkg/DCPD-2021DIGEST
/html/DCPD-2021 DIGEST.htm

Minute-by-Minute Presidential Schedules
These detailed schedules are only released to the public years after a president
leaves office.
Carter's White House schedules: https://www.jimmycarterlibrary.gov/assets/doc
uments/diary
Reagan's White House schedules and personal diary: https://www.reaganfounda
tion.org/ronald-reagan/white-house-diaries/diary-entry-01201981
George H. W. Bush's White House schedules for 1989 and 1990, formerly available at: https://millercenter.org/scripps/archive/documents/ghb/diary
Clinton's White House schedules: https://clinton.presidentiallibraries.us/collec
tions/show/39

White House Websites
These sites offer records of presidential events as well as transcripts of White
House press briefings.
https://clintonwhitehouse4.archives.gov
https://georgewbush-whitehouse.archives.gov
https://obamawhitehouse.archives.gov
https://trumpwhitehouse.archives.gov
https://www.whitehouse.gov

Notes

PREFACE

1. Mark A. Uhlig, "Jesse Unruh, a California Political Power, Dies," *New York Times,* August 6, 1987, http://www.nytimes.com/1987/08/06/obituaries/jesse-unruh-a-california -political-power-dies.html.

CHAPTER 1: FUNDRAISING AS A PRESIDENTIAL LEADERSHIP TOOL

1. "FEC Form 1, Statement of Organization for Protect the House," August 3, 2018, https://docquery.fec.gov/cgi-bin/forms/C00669622/1254365/.

2. Ronald Powers, "Clinton's Primary-Eve Fund-Raiser Irks State Democrats," Associated Press, September 4, 1998.

3. William F. Connelly Jr. and John J. Pitney Jr., *Congress' Permanent Minority?: Republicans in the U.S. House* (Lanham, MD: Rowman & Littlefield, 1994).

4. Frances E. Lee, *Insecure Majorities: Congress and the Perpetual Campaign*, (Chicago: University of Chicago Press, 2016).

5. "Elections," National Governors Association, accessed March 16, 2017, https:// www.nga.org/cms/elections.

6. "2017 and 2018 Special Elections," OpenSecrets, accessed June 13, 2018, https:// www.opensecrets.org/races/special-elections.

7. Barack Obama, "Remarks by the President at a DCCC Event—San Francisco, CA," April 4, 2013, https://obamawhitehouse.archives.gov/the-press-office/2013/04/04/remarks -president-dccc-event-san-francisco-ca-0.

8. Mark Knoller, "Twitter Post," @markknoller, April 4, 2013, https://twitter.com /markknoller/status/319679692930170880.

9. Robert Biersack, Paul S. Herrnson, and Clyde Wilcox, "Seeds for Success: Early Money in Congressional Elections," *Legislative Studies Quarterly* 18, no. 4 (1993): 535– 551, https://doi.org/10.2307/439854; James Gerstenzang, Associated Press, April 29, 1983.

10. David Siders, Maggie Severns, and Natasha Korecki, "'It's Too Much': Democrats Shudder at Trump's Money Machine," *Politico*, October 21, 2019, https://www .politico.com/news/2019/10/21/trump-money-democrats-2020-election-050962.

11. James Gerstenzang, "Bush Still a Fundraising Magnet for GOP Donors," *Los Angeles Times*, February 25, 2006, https://www.latimes.com/archives/la-xpm-2006-feb-25 -na-fundraise25-story.html; Scott Detrow, "One Year in, DNC Turnaround Has a Long Way to Go," NPR, February 22, 2018, https://www.npr.org/2018/02/22/587722316/one

-year-in-dnc-turnaround-has-a-long-way-to-go; Ari Shapiro, "Despite Low Ratings, Obama Remains a Democratic Money Magnet," NPR, November 19, 2013, https://www .npr.org/2013/11/19/246201774/obamas-still-a-democratic-money-magnet-despite-low -ratings; Julie Bykowicz, "Trump's Fundraising Prowess Keeps Republican Party Close," *AP News*, August 2, 2017, https://apnews.com/d9154939959f4015a9ff54ae54ea3813 /Trump%27s-fundraising-prowess-keeps-Republican-Party-close.

12. Nancy Benac, "Clinton Raising Money for Democrats on Four-State Tour," Associated Press, September 24, 1994.

13. Gerstenzang, "Bush Still a Fundraising Magnet for GOP Donors."

14. Julie Bykowicz and Tarini Parti, "Big Donors Spent Heavily on Failed Election Efforts," *Wall Street Journal*, November 23, 2020, https://www.wsj.com/articles/big-do nors-spent-heavily-on-failed-election-efforts-11606147552.

15. "House Campaign Expenditures: Major Party General Election Candidates, 1974– 2018" and "Senate Campaign Expenditures: Major Party General Election Candidates, 1974–2018," Campaign Finance Institute, accessed April 26, 2021, http://www.cfinst.org /data.aspx.

16. "Archive of Contribution Limits," accessed February 16, 2021, https://www .fec.gov/help-candidates-and-committees/candidate-taking-receipts/archived-contribution -limits/.

17. US Government Publishing Office, "Tributes to Hon. Ernest F. Hollings," accessed April 29, 2021, https://www.govinfo.gov/content/pkg/CDOC-108sdoc26/html /CDOC-108sdoc26.htm.

18. Clinton Digital Library, "President Clinton's Daily Schedule for March 1998," accessed April 29, 2021, https://clinton.presidentiallibraries.us/items/show/12698.

19. Tracy Jan, "For Freshman in Congress, Focus Is on Raising Money," *Boston Globe*, May 12, 2013, http://www.bostonglobe.com/news/politics/2013/05/11/freshman -lawmakers-are-introduced-permanent-hunt-for-campaign-money/YQMMMoqCNxGKh 2h0tOIF9H/story.html.

20. Steve Israel, "Steve Israel: Confessions of a Congressman," *New York Times*, January 8, 2016, https://www.nytimes.com/2016/01/09/opinion/steve-israel-confessions-of-a -congressman.html.

21. "'Steve Israel'—ObamaWhiteHouse Search Results," accessed April 29, 2021, https://search.archives.gov/search?utf8=%E2%9C%93&affiliate=obamawhitehouse&sort _by=&query=%22steve+israel%22.

22. Paul Blumenthal, "Chris Murphy: 'Soul-Crushing' Fundraising Is Bad for Congress," *Huffington Post*, May 7, 2013, http://www.huffingtonpost.com/2013/05/07/chris -murphy-fundraising_n_3232143.html.

23. Jan, "For Freshman in Congress, Focus Is on Raising Money."

24. Lee Drutman, "Yet Another Retiring Member of Congress Complains about the Misery of Fundraising," *Vox*, January 8, 2016, https://www.vox.com/polyarchy/2016 /1/8/10736402/congress-fundraising-miserable.

25. Richard McGregor, "Democrats Tell Obama to Send Money but Stay Home," *Financial Times*, October 10, 2014, https://www.ft.com/content/efa6dee4-4ffc-11e4-a0a4 -00144feab7de; Eric S. Heberlig and Bruce A. Larson, "U.S. House Incumbent Fundraising and Spending in a Post-Citizens United and Post-McCutcheon World," *Political Science Quarterly* 129, no. 4 (2014): 613–642; Alan Rappeport, "Donald Trump's Debate Weapon: Checks Written to His Rivals," *New York Times*, August 4, 2015, https://www

.nytimes.com/politics/first-draft/2015/08/04/donald-trump-debate-weapon-checks-writ ten-to-his-rivals/.

26. James Madison, "The Federalist Papers No. 10," 1788, http://avalon.law.yale.edu /18th_century/fed10.asp.

27. "Press Gaggle by Principal Deputy Press Secretary Josh Earnest aboard Air Force One en Route Seattle, Washington," November 24, 2013, https://obamawhitehouse .archives.gov/the-press-office/2013/11/24/press-gaggle-principal-deputy-press-secretary -josh-earnest-aboard-air-fo.

28. Ron Fournier, "Clinton Strategy for Democratic Victory in November: Money, Money, Money," Associated Press, June 11, 1998.

29. Marc Lacey, "Noncandidate Clinton's Steady Refrain: I Believe in Fund-Raising," *New York Times*, September 25, 2000.

30. Herbert E. Alexander, *Financing the 1976 Election* (Washington, DC: CQ Press, 1979); Michael J. Malbin, *The Election after Reform: Money, Politics, and the Bipartisan Campaign Reform Act* (Lanham, MD: Rowman & Littlefield, 2006); David B. Magleby and Anthony Corrado, *Financing the 2008 Election: Assessing Reform* (Washington, DC: Brookings Institution, 2011).

31. David B. Magleby, Jay Goodliffe, and Joseph A. Olsen, *Who Donates in Campaigns?: The Importance of Message, Messenger, Medium, and Structure* (Cambridge: Cambridge University Press, 2018); Bruce E. Cain, *Democracy More or Less: America's Political Reform Quandary* (New York: Cambridge University Press, 2014); Raymond J. La Raja, *Small Change: Money, Political Parties, and Campaign Finance Reform* (Ann Arbor: University of Michigan Press, 2008); Richard L. Hasen, *Plutocrats United: Campaign Money, the Supreme Court, and the Distortion of American Elections* (New Haven, CT: Yale University Press, 2016); Victoria A. Farrar-Myers and Diana Dwyre, *Limits and Loopholes: The Quest for Money, Free Speech, and Fair Elections* (Washington, DC: CQ Press, 2007); Lawrence Lessig, *Republic, Lost: How Money Corrupts Congress—and a Plan to Stop It*, rev. ed. (New York: Twelve, 2015); Nicholas Carnes, *The Cash Ceiling: Why Only the Rich Run for Office—and What We Can Do about It* (Princeton, NJ: Princeton University Press, 2018); Raymond J. La Raja and Brian F. Schaffner, *Campaign Finance and Political Polarization: When Purists Prevail*, illustrated ed. (Ann Arbor: University of Michigan Press, 2015).

32. Henry Kissinger, *Years of Renewal* (New York: Simon & Schuster, 1999), 74.

33. Jimmy Carter, "Dinner Honoring Senator Robert C. Byrd of West Virginia," May 17, 1978, http://www.presidency.ucsb.edu/ws/index.php?pid=30812&st=&st1=.

34. Olivier Knox, "Inside President Obama's Secret Schedule," *Yahoo News*, July 7, 2014, http://news.yahoo.com/inside-president-obama-s-secret-schedule-183756327.html.

35. David Frum, *The Right Man: The Surprise Presidency of George W. Bush* (New York: Weidenfeld & Nicolson, 2003).

36. Eliana Johnson and Daniel Lippman, "9 Hours of 'Executive Time': Trump's Unstructured Days Define His Presidency," *Politico*, October 29, 2018, https://politi.co /2AxP4TN.

37. Michael Weisskopf and Charles R. Babcock, "Donors Pay and Stay at White House; Lincoln Bedroom a Special Treat," *Washington Post*, December 15, 1996.

38. Jeffrey E. Cohen, Michael A. Krassa, and John A. Hamman, "The Impact of Presidential Campaigning on Midterm U.S. Senate Elections," *American Political Science Review* 85, no. 1 (March 1, 1991): 165–178, https://doi.org/10.2307/1962883.

39. Matthew Hoddie and Stephen R. Routh, "Predicting the Presidential Presence: Explaining Presidential Midterm Elections Campaign Behavior," *Political Research Quarterly* 57, no. 2 (June 1, 2004): 257–265, https://doi.org/10.2307/3219869; Matthew Lang, Brandon Rottinghaus, and Gerhard Peters, "Revisiting Midterm Visits: Why the Type of Visit Matters," *Presidential Studies Quarterly* 41, no. 4 (December 1, 2011): 809–818, https://doi.org/10.1111/j.1741–5705.2011.03919.x.

40. Matthew Eshbaugh-Soha and Sean Nicholson-Crotty, "Presidential Campaigning in Midterm Elections," *American Review of Politics* 30 (2009): 35–50; Rob Mellen Jr. and Kathleen Searles, "Predicting Presidential Appearances during Midterm Elections: The President and House Candidates, 1982–2010," *American Politics Research* 41, no. 2 (March 1, 2013): 328–347, https://doi.org/10.1177/1532673X12461827; Rob Mellen Jr. and Kathleen Searles, "Midterm Mobilization: The President as Campaigner-in-Chief during Midterm House Elections, 1982–2006," *White House Studies* 13, no. 2 (2015): 187–199.

41. Michael A. Julius, *Midterm Campaigning and the Modern Presidency: Reshaping the President's Relationship with Congress* (Santa Barbara, CA: Praeger, 2018).

42. Patrick J. Sellers and Laura M. Denton, "Presidential Visits and Midterm Senate Elections," *Presidential Studies Quarterly* 36, no. 3 (2006): 410–432.

43. Gary C. Jacobson, Samuel Kernell, and Jeffrey Lazarus, "Assessing the President's Role as Party Agent in Congressional Elections: The Case of Bill Clinton in 2000," *Legislative Studies Quarterly* 29, no. 2 (May 1, 2004): 159–184; Paul S. Herrnson and Irwin L. Morris, "Presidential Campaigning in the 2002 Congressional Elections," *Legislative Studies Quarterly* 32, no. 4 (November 2007): 629–648.

44. Daniel J. Galvin, *Presidential Party Building: Dwight D. Eisenhower to George W. Bush* (Princeton, NJ: Princeton University Press, 2010).

45. Brendan J. Doherty, *The Rise of the President's Permanent Campaign* (Lawrence: University Press of Kansas, 2012).

46. Bill Turque, "Obama Raises Millions for 2012 Campaign within Spitting Distance of White House," *Washington Post*, July 27, 2012, https://www.washingtonpost.com/politics/obama-raises-millions-for-2012-campaign-within-spitting-distance-of-white-house/2012/07/26/gJQAbkdeBX_story.html.

47. Mike McIntyre, "Reagan Lights Up $6.5 Million Dinner," *Washington Post*, April 30, 1987, https://www.washingtonpost.com/archive/lifestyle/1987/04/30/reagan-lights-up-65-million-dinner/d7e23c1b-f3f5–44b5–84d4–7b2819f80e17/.

48. Jonathan D. Salant, "Unions, Lobbyists Help Democrats Break Money Record," Associated Press, May 23, 2000.

49. Weisskopf and Babcock, "Donors Pay and Stay at White House."

50. Sandra Sobieraj, "Campaigning Again: Clinton and Gore's Day Together," Associated Press, August 10, 1999.

51. Bill Clinton, "Remarks at a Democratic Senatorial Campaign Committee Dinner for Senator Barbara Boxer," September 28, 1998, https://www.presidency.ucsb.edu/documents/remarks-democratic-senatorial-campaign-committee-dinner-for-senator-barbara-boxer; Patricia Sullivan, "Smith Bagley Dies at 74; Democratic Fundraiser, Socialite," *Washington Post*, January 4, 2010, http://www.washingtonpost.com/wp-dyn/content/article/2010/01/03/AR2010010302036.html.

52. Rebecca Keegan, "George Clooney's Obama Fundraiser Uses Star Power with a Twist," *Los Angeles Times*, May 10, 2012, https://www.latimes.com/la-xpm-2012-may-10

-la-et-clooney-obama-20120510-story.html; Sam Metz, "Trump to Visit Larry Ellison's California Estate for Fundraising Event," *Desert Sun*, February 12, 2020, https://www.des ertsun.com/story/news/politics/2020/02/12/trump-visit-larry-ellisons-rancho-mirage-es tate-fundraising-event/4743576002/.

53. Richard Johnson, "Obama Slams Billionaires at the Home of a Guy Named Rich Richman," *New York Post*, October 8, 2014, https://pagesix.com/2014/10/08/obama -slams-republicans-as-party-of-billionaires/.

54. Michael Putzel, "With Carter Fundraisers, What You Get Is What You Pay For," Associated Press, July 22, 1980.

55. Jennifer Epstein, "Obama's 5-Fundraiser Day," *Politico*, March 17, 2012, https:// www.politico.com/story/2012/03/obamas-five-fundraisers-day-074133; Becky Brittain, "POTUS's Schedule for Friday, March 16, 2012," March 16, 2012, https://whitehouse .blogs.cnn.com/2012/03/16/potuss-schedule-for-friday-march-16–2012/.

56. Savannah Behrmann, "Trump Campaign Pulls in $20 Million during the President's First Virtual Re-Election Fundraiser," *USA Today*, July 21, 2020, https://www.usa today.com/story/news/politics/elections/2020/07/21/trump-campaign-pulls-20-million -during-first-virtual-fundraiser/5484473002/; Shane Goldmacher and Maggie Haberman, "How Trump's Billion-Dollar Campaign Lost Its Cash Advantage," *New York Times*, September 7, 2020, https://www.nytimes.com/2020/09/07/us/politics/trump-election-cam paign-fundraising.html.

CHAPTER 2: ESCALATION AND COMPLICATION

1. Michael Putzel, "Carter Says He's 'Turned the Tide' on America's Problems," Associated Press, May 29, 1980; "Carter Makes First, and Last, Primary Campaign Trip," Associated Press, May 30, 1980.

2. "We Are One/Estamos Unidos with Obama for Obama Victory Fund," Political Party Time, accessed July 24, 2017, http://politicalpartytime.org/party/33679/; Barack Obama, "Remarks at an Obama Victory Fund 2012 Fundraiser in Miami, Florida," October 11, 2012, http://www.presidency.ucsb.edu/ws/?pid=102368.

3. Matea Gold, "President Trump Tells the FEC He Qualifies as a Candidate for 2020," *Washington Post*, January 20, 2017, https://www.washingtonpost.com/local/2017 /live-updates/politics/live-coverage-of-trumps-inauguration/president-trump-tells-the-fec -he-qualifies-as-a-candidate-for-2020/?utm_term=.640bf8e3146d; Julie Bykowicz and Jill Colvin, "Trump Rakes in $10 Million at First Re-Election Fundraiser," *US News & World Report*, June 28, 2017, https://www.usnews.com/news/politics/articles/2017–06–28/with -40-months-to-go-trump-holds-re-election-fundraiser.

4. Josh Dawsey and Michelle Ye Hee Lee, "Trump to Headline a $580,600-per-Couple Fundraiser, the Most Expensive of His Reelection Bid," *Washington Post*, February 13, 2020, https://www.washingtonpost.com/politics/trump-to-headline-a-580600-per-couple-fund raiser-the-most-expensive-of-his-reelection-bid/2020/02/13/144b75b2–4e7a-11ea-a4ab -9f389ce8ad30_story.html; Josh Dawsey and Michelle Ye Hee Lee, "Trump Set to Headline High-Dollar Fundraising Dinner at a Private Florida Home Next Week," *Washington Post*, July 1, 2020, https://www.washingtonpost.com/politics/trump-set-to-headline-high -dollar-fundraising-dinner-at-a-private-florida-home-next-week/2020/07/01/3568ff28 -bbce-11ea-86d5–3b9b3863273b_story.html.

5. Ronald Campbell, "Cash Is What Presidential Candidates Really Want in California," *Orange County Register*, October 12, 2012, https://www.ocregister.com/2012/10/12/cash-is-what-presidential-candidates-really-want-in-california/.

6. Libby Watson, "How Political Megadonors Can Give Almost $500,000 with a Single Check," Sunlight Foundation, June 1, 2016, https://sunlightfoundation.com/2016/06/01/how-political-megadonors-can-give-almost-500000-with-a-single-check/.

7. "FEC Form 1, Statement of Organization for Hillary Victory Fund," June 23, 2016, https://docquery.fec.gov/cgi-bin/forms/C00586537/1080677/.

8. "FEC Form 1, Statement of Organization for Trump Victory," September 21, 2016, https://docquery.fec.gov/cgi-bin/forms/C00618389/1100963/.

9. Watson, "How Political Megadonors Can Give Almost $500,000 with a Single Check."

10. "FEC Form 1, Statement of Organization for Trump Victory," March 31, 2017, https://docquery.fec.gov/cgi-bin/forms/C00618389/1154503/.

11. "FEC Form 1, Statement of Organization for Trump Victory," January 15, 2020, https://docquery.fec.gov/cgi-bin/forms/C00618389/1370480/; "FEC Form 1, Statement of Organization for Trump Victory," September 23, 2020, https://docquery.fec.gov/cgi-bin/forms/C00618389/1440807/.

12. Dawsey and Lee, "Trump to Headline a $580,600-per-Couple Fundraiser, the Most Expensive of His Reelection Bid"; Dawsey and Lee, "Trump Set to Headline High-Dollar Fundraising Dinner at a Private Florida Home Next Week."

13. "Archive of Contribution Limits," accessed February 16, 2021, https://www.fec.gov/help-candidates-and-committees/candidate-taking-receipts/archived-contribution-limits/.

14. Carrie Levine, "Comeback for 'Legalized Money Laundering' in Party Politics?," Center for Public Integrity, August 4, 2017, https://publicintegrity.org/politics/comeback-for-legalized-money-laundering-in-party-politics/.

15. *Buckley v. Valeo*, 424 U.S. 1, January 30, 1976, https://www.fec.gov/resources/legal-resources/litigation/Buckley.pdf.

16. "Table 2–4," CQ Press Electronic Library, Vital Statistics on American Politics Online Edition, originally published in Harold W. Stanley and Richard G. Niemi, *Vital Statistics on American Politics 2007–2008* (Washington, DC: CQ Press, 2008), accessed at http://library.cqpress.com/vsap/.

17. Karen Gullo, "1996: The Year in Which Campaign Finance Went Broke?," Associated Press, November 10, 1996.

18. Don McLeod, "Carter Campaign Off and Running," Associated Press, December 5, 1979.

19. Bill Allison, "Trump Raises $30M for 2020—More Than Any Democratic Candidate," *Fortune*, April 15, 2019, https://fortune.com/2019/04/15/trump-2020-campaign-fundraising/.

20. David Hoffman, "Reelection Bid Announcement Pushed Back," *Washington Post*, October 18, 1983, https://www.washingtonpost.com/archive/politics/1983/10/18/reelection-bid-announcement-pushed-back/d1dee43a-dc58-48c8-957a-2539461c9dac/; "Two White House Aides Affirm Reagan Will Run for Re-election," *New York Times*, October 17, 1983.

21. Tom Raum, "Bush Triggers Re-Election Fund Raising," Associated Press, Oc-

tober 11, 1991; Tom Raum, "Bush Hoping to Tap Texas for $2 Million in Two Days," Associated Press, October 31, 1991.

22. Gold, "President Trump Tells the FEC He Qualifies as a Candidate for 2020."

23. Jessica Taylor, "Trump Set to Officially Launch Reelection Bid, But Hasn't He Been Running All Along?," NPR, June 18, 2019, https://www.npr.org/2019/06/18/733 505037/trump-set-to-officially-launch-reelection-but-hasnt-he-been-running-all-along.

24. Joe Biden, "Remarks by President Biden in Press Conference," March 25, 2021, https://www.whitehouse.gov/briefing-room/speeches-remarks/2021/03/25/remarks-by -president-biden-in-press-conference/.

25. Michael Scherer, "Biden Shifts His Operation to DNC ahead of 2022 Midterm Elections," *Washington Post*, February 23, 2021, https://www.washingtonpost.com/poli tics/biden-dnc-politics/2021/02/23/ba11c3da-75f6–11eb-8115–9ad5e9c02117_story.html.

26. Robert Schmuhl, "The Last Time America Had So Many Two-Term Presidents Was the 1820s," History News Network, September 18, 2012, http://historynewsnetwork .org/article/148379.

27. Greg Giroux, "Final Tally Shows Obama First Since '56 to Win 51% Twice," *Bloomberg*, January 4, 2013, https://www.bloomberg.com/news/articles/2013–01–03/final -tally-shows-obama-first-since-56-to-win-51-twice.

28. "Presidential Job Approval," American Presidency Project, accessed June 15, 2016, http://www.presidency.ucsb.edu/data/popularity.php.

29. US Senate Historical Office, "Party Division in the Senate, 1789-Present," accessed July 26, 2016, http://www.senate.gov/history/partydiv.htm; Office of the Clerk of the US House of Representatives, "Party Divisions of the House of Representatives (1789 to Present)," accessed August 3, 2016, http://history.house.gov/Institution/Party-Divisions /Party-Divisions/; Roger H. Davidson, Walter J. Oleszek, and Frances E. Lee, *Congress and Its Members*, 13th ed. (Washington, DC: CQ Press, 2011), 94.

30. Robert E. Mutch, *Campaign Finance: What Everyone Needs to Know* (New York: Oxford University Press, 2016), 13–14, 25–26.

31. Nelson W. Polsby et al., *Presidential Elections: Strategies and Structures of American Politics*, 13th ed. (Lanham, MD: Rowman & Littlefield, 2012), 59–64.

32. Christopher Connell, "Reagan Nomination Fund Shows Big Surplus," Associated Press, September 21, 1984.

33. Mutch, *Campaign Finance*, 103–106.

34. Mutch, 106–108.

35. Elizabeth Shogren, "Democratic Fund-Raising King Has 26 Million Reasons to Gloat," *Los Angeles Times*, May 23, 2000, https://www.latimes.com/archives/la-xpm-2000 -may-23-mn-33107-story.html.

36. Don Van Natta, "Bush Forgoes Federal Funds and Has No Spending Limit," *New York Times*, July 15, 1999.

37. "Table 2-4," Vital Statistics on American Politics 2007–2008; "Table 3-29," Lyn Ragsdale, *Vital Statistics on the Presidency: The Definitive Source for Data and Analysis on the American Presidency*, 3rd ed. (Washington, DC: CQ Press, 2008).

38. "Presidential Spending Limits 2008," accessed July 7, 2011, http://www.fec.gov /pages/brochures/pubfund_limits_2008.shtml; Peter Wallsten, "Obama Pushing behind Scenes to Win over Big-Dollar Donors," *Washington Post*, June 27, 2011; "Table 2=4," Vital Statistics on American Politics 2007–2008.

39. David Jackson, "Obama vs. Bush—'More Fundraisers, Less Funds,'" USA Today.com, July 8, 2010, http://content.usatoday.com/communities/theoval/post/2010/07/obama-vs-bush—more-fundraisers-less-funds/1; Jonathan Weisman, "Obama Races for Cash," *Wall Street Journal*, October 26, 2009, https://www.wsj.com/articles/SB12565 1404955107091.

40. "McCain: 'Soft Money' Ruling 'a Victory for the People,'" CNN, December 12, 2003, https://www.cnn.com/2003/ALLPOLITICS/12/11/cnna.mccain/index.html.

41. Michael Janofsky, "Advocacy Groups Spent Record Amount on 2004 Election," *New York Times*, December 17, 2004, https://www.nytimes.com/2004/12/17/politics/advocacy-groups-spent-record-amount-on-2004-election.html.

42. Michael J. Malbin, *Life after Reform: When the Bipartisan Campaign Reform Act Meets Politics* (Lanham, MD: Rowman & Littlefield, 2003), 3.

43. Susan Walsh, "Bush Says He's Committed to Environment," *USA Today*, April 23, 2004, https://usatoday30.usatoday.com/news/politicselections/nation/president/2004–04–23-bush-environment_x.htm; personal communication with Mark Knoller, CBS News, May 24, 2012.

44. "Citizens United v. Federal Election Commission," January 21, 2010, https://www.law.cornell.edu/supct/html/08–205.ZO.html.

45. "Independent Expenditure-Only Committees," accessed June 6, 2013, http://www.fec.gov/press/press2011/ieoc_alpha.shtml.

46. Mutch, *Campaign Finance*, 75–88, 112–117.

47. Kenneth P. Vogel, Dave Levinthal, and Tarini Parti, "Barack Obama, Mitt Romney Both Topped $1 Billion in 2012," *Politico*, December 7, 2012, http://www.politico.com/story/2012/12/barack-obama-mitt-romney-both-topped-1-billion-in-2012-84737.html#ixzz2ENPPvAKu.

48. Campbell, "Cash Is What Presidential Candidates Really Want in California"; "Archive of Contribution Limits."

49. "Contribution Limits for 2011–2012," March 1, 2011, https://www.fec.gov/updates/contribution-limits-for-2011–2012/.

50. "McCutcheon et al. v. Federal Election Commission," April 2, 2014, https://www.supremecourt.gov/opinions/13pdf/12–536_e1pf.pdf.

51. "McCutcheon et al. v. Federal Election Commission."

52. Kenneth P. Vogel, "Budget Rider Would Expand Party Cash," *Politico*, December 10, 2014, http://www.politico.com/story/2014/12/budget-rider-would-expand-party-cash-113459.html; Matea Gold, "Fundraising Expansion Slipped into Spending Deal Could Power Financial Bonanza for Parties," *Washington Post*, December 10, 2014, https://www.washingtonpost.com/news/post-politics/wp/2014/12/10/fundraising-expansion-slipped-into-spending-deal-could-power-financial-bonzana-for-parties/.

53. Watson, "How Political Megadonors Can Give Almost $500,000 with a Single Check."

54. "FEC Form 1, Statement of Organization for Hillary Victory Fund."

55. OpenSecrets, "Fundraiser with Barack Obama for Hillary Victory Fund," Political Party Time, accessed June 7, 2019, http://politicalpartytime.org/party/41847/.

56. Watson, "How Political Megadonors Can Give Almost $500,000 with a Single Check"; "FEC Form 1, Statement of Organization for Trump Victory," May 25, 2016, https://docquery.fec.gov/cgi-bin/forms/C00618389/1074535/; "FEC Form 1, Statement of Organization for Trump Victory," September 4, 2016, https://docquery.fec.gov/cgi-bin

/forms/C00618389/1097858/; "FEC Form 1, Statement of Organization for Trump Victory," September 21, 2016.

57. Kenneth P. Vogel and Isaac Arnsdorf, "Clinton Fundraising Leaves Little for State Parties," *Politico*, May 2, 2016, http://politi.co/2hxUy6W; Kenneth P. Vogel and Isaac Arnsdorf, "DNC Sought to Hide Details of Clinton Funding Deal," *Politico*, July 26, 2016, http://politi.co/2afvQq6; "Contribution Limits for 2019–2020," n.d., https://www.fec.gov/resources/cms-content/documents/contribution_limits_chart_2019–2020.pdf.

58. Savannah Behrmann, "Trump Campaign Pulls in $20 Million during the President's First Virtual Re-Election Fundraiser," *USA Today*, July 21, 2020, https://www.usatoday.com/story/news/politics/elections/2020/07/21/trump-campaign-pulls-20-million-during-first-virtual-fundraiser/5484473002/; Shane Goldmacher and Maggie Haberman, "How Trump's Billion-Dollar Campaign Lost Its Cash Advantage," *New York Times*, September 7, 2020, https://www.nytimes.com/2020/09/07/us/politics/trump-election-campaign-fundraising.html; Shane Goldmacher and Maggie Haberman, "Trump's Cash Crunch Limits His Options and Prompts Finger-Pointing," *New York Times*, October 22, 2020, https://www.nytimes.com/2020/10/22/us/politics/trump-campaign-money.html.

59. "FEC Form 99, Donald J. Trump for President, Inc.," January 20, 2017, https://docquery.fec.gov/pdf/569/201701209041436569/201701209041436569.pdf; "Trump Rakes in $10 Million at First Re-Election Fundraiser," CNBC, June 29, 2017, https://www.cnbc.com/2017/06/29/trump-takes-10-million-at-first-re-election-fundraiser.html; Maggie Haberman, "A Trump Friend, under Scrutiny by Prosecutors, Appears at California Fund-Raisers," *New York Times*, September 18, 2019, https://www.nytimes.com /2019/09/18/us/politics/thomas-barrack-trump.html; "FEC Form 1, Statement of Organization for Trump Victory," January 15, 2020; "FEC Form 1, Statement of Organization for Trump Victory," September 23, 2020.

60. "Obama Hosts Six Fundraisers Friday in Minneapolis, Chicago," ABC News Radio, June 1, 2012, http://abcnewsradioonline.com/politics-news/obama-hosts-six-fundraisers-friday-in-minneapolis-chicago.html.

61. Mark Knoller, "Twitter Post," @markknoller, June 11, 2020, https://twitter.com/markknoller/status/1270869185309085696; Meredith Yeomans, "Trump Fundraiser Held at Home of Dallas Billionaire," June 11, 2020, https://www.nbcdfw.com/news/politics/trump-fundraiser-held-at-home-of-dallas-billionaire/2387378/.

62. "Archive of Contribution Limits"; "FEC Form 1, Statement Organization for Biden Victory Fund," April 24, 2020, https://docquery.fec.gov/cgi-bin/forms/C00744946/1403427/; "FEC Form 1, Statement Organization for Biden Victory Fund," May 16, 2020, https://docquery.fec.gov/cgi-bin/forms/C00744946/1405948/; "FEC Form 1, Statement Organization for Biden Victory Fund," July 20, 2020, https://docquery.fec.gov/cgi-bin/forms/C00744946/1426972/; "FEC Form 1, Statement Organization for Biden Victory Fund," August 31, 2020, https://docquery.fec.gov/cgi-bin/forms/C00744946/1435913/.

63. Shane Goldmacher, "The Big Role That Big Donors Still Play, Quietly, for Joe Biden," *New York Times*, October 20, 2020, https://www.nytimes.com/2020/10/20/us/politics/joe-biden-donors.html.

64. Shane Goldmacher, "Joe Biden Starts General Election Nearly $187 Million behind Trump," *New York Times*, April 21, 2020, https://www.nytimes.com/2020/04/21/us/politics/biden-2020-fundraising.html.

65. Goldmacher and Haberman, "Trump's Cash Crunch Limits His Options and Prompts Finger-Pointing."

66. Matea Gold, "It's Bold, but Legal: How Campaigns and Their Super PAC Backers Work Together," *Washington Post*, July 6, 2015, https://www.washingtonpost.com/politics/here-are-the-secret-ways-super-pacs-and-campaigns-can-work-together/2015/07/06/bda78210–1539–11e5–89f3–61410da94eb1_story.html.

67. "DNC and State Parties Announce Historic Agreement," democrats.org, May 12, 2021, https://democrats.org/news/dnc-and-state-parties-announce-historic-agreement/.

68. Daniel Strauss, "Sanders Campaign Slams Clinton-DNC Fundraising Agreement," *Politico*, April 8, 2016, http://politi.co/1YDzZCY.

69. Matea Gold and Tom Hamburger, "Political Parties Go after Million-Dollar Donors in Wake of Looser Rules," *Washington Post*, September 19, 2015, https://www.washingtonpost.com/politics/political-parties-go-after-million-dollar-donors-in-wake-of-looser-rules/2015/09/19/728b43fe-5ede-11e5–8e9e-dce8a2a2a679_story.html.

70. Bill Allison, "Millions From Maxed-Out Clinton Donors Flowed through Loophole," *Bloomberg*, August 26, 2016, https://www.bloomberg.com/politics/graphics/2016-dnc-contributions/; Levine, "Comeback for 'Legalized Money Laundering' in Party Politics?"

71. Gold and Hamburger, "Political Parties Go after Million-Dollar Donors in Wake of Looser Rules."

72. Gold and Hamburger.

73. Levine, "Comeback for 'Legalized Money Laundering' in Party Politics?"

74. Dave Levinthal, "Donald Trump Created a Permanent Presidential Campaign. Here's How," Center for Public Integrity, February 18, 2019, https://publicintegrity.org/federal-politics/donald-trump-president-campaign-money-fundraising/.

75. Zeke Miller and Catherine Lucey, "The $1 Billion Ask: Trump All-In on Fundraising for 2020," *US News & World Report*, April 4, 2019, https://www.usnews.com/news/politics/articles/2019–04–04/the-1-billion-ask-trump-is-all-in-on-fundraising-for-2020.

CHAPTER 3: NATIONALIZATION

1. Daniel J. Hopkins, *The Increasingly United States: How and Why American Political Behavior Nationalized* (Chicago: University of Chicago Press, 2018).

2. Mike Allen, "DNC Amps Up Fundraising," *Politico*, March 29, 2013, http://www.politico.com/story/2013/03/dnc-fundraising-89456.html.

3. Daniel Newhauser, "How State Political Parties Helped Big Money Pay for the 2020 Election," Maryland Matters, November 30, 2020, https://www.marylandmatters.org/2020/11/30/how-state-political-parties-helped-big-money-pay-for-the-2020-election/.

4. M. Margaret Conway, "Republican Political Party Nationalization, Campaign Activities, and Their Implications for the Party System," *Publius* 13, no. 1 (1983): 1–17, https://doi.org/10.2307/3330068.

5. Matt Grossmann and David A. Hopkins, "Ideological Republicans and Group Interest Democrats: The Asymmetry of American Party Politics," *Perspectives on Politics* 13, no. 1 (2015): 119–139.

6. Daniel J. Hopkins, Eric Schickler, and David Azizi, "From Many Divides, One? The Polarization and Nationalization of American State Party Platforms, 1918–2017," SSRN Scholarly Paper (Rochester, NY: Social Science Research Network, December 21, 2020), https://doi.org/10.2139/ssrn.3772946.

7. Adam Nagourney and James Dao, "As Clinton Eats Up Contributions, New York Party Says It's Starving," *New York Times*, January 9, 1998, https://www.nytimes.com /1998/01/09/nyregion/as-clinton-eats-up-contributions-new-york-party-says-it-s-starving .html; Ronald Powers, "Clinton's Primary-Eve Fund-Raiser Irks State Democrats," Associated Press, September 4, 1998.

8. R. G. Ratcliffe, "Some Dems Fear More of Same after Obama Visit," *Houston Chronicle*, August 9, 2010, http://www.chron.com/disp/story.mpl/metropolitan/7145208 .html.

9. Scott Lindlaw, "Money Swings Offer Presidential Candidates a Narrow View of California," Associated Press, October 12, 2000.

10. "Clinton Trip Upsets Gov Candidate," United Press International, September 23, 1994.

11. Karen Ball, "We Need Dough Too, Reps Tell Prez," *New York Daily News*, September 15, 1996.

12. Karl Rove, "I'm Impressed by Your Fundraising, Mr. Obama—But Not as Much as I Thought I'd Be," Foxnews.com, July 18, 2011, http://www.foxnews.com/opinion/2011 /07/18/im-impressed-by-your-fundraising-mr-obama-but-not-as-much-as-thought-id-be/.

13. "Archive of Contribution Limits," accessed February 16, 2021, https://www .fec.gov/help-candidates-and-committees/candidate-taking-receipts/archived-contribu tion-limits/.

14. "Press Gaggle by Dana Perino," July 25, 2008, http://georgewbush-whitehouse .archives.gov/news/releases/2008/07/20080725-7.html.

15. "FEC Form 1, Statement of Organization for Take Back the House 2020," September 11, 2019, https://docquery.fec.gov/cgi-bin/forms/C00695585/1351546/; "Trump Attends Fundraiser for House Republicans," October 29, 2019, https://abcnews.go.com /Politics/wireStory/trump-attends-fundraiser-house-republicans-66622477.

16. Jackie Calmes, "'Presidential' vs. 'Political' Trips: A Blurry Line, and Tricky Math," *New York Times*, April 22, 2012, https://www.nytimes.com/2012/04/22/us/politics /presidential-vs-political-trips-a-blurry-line-for-obama.html.i

17. Nancy Benac, "Who Pays When the President Politicks?," *Seattle Times*, April 28, 2012, https://www.seattletimes.com/nation-world/who-pays-when-the-president-poli ticks/.

18. Benac, "Who Pays When the President Politicks?"; "Democratic National Committee Travel Offset Account Disbursements," accessed February 18, 2021, https://www .fec.gov/data/disbursements/?committee_id=C00460147&two_year_transaction_peri od=2012&cycle=2012&line_number=F3X-21B&data_type=processed.

19. "Archive of Contribution Limits."

20. Karen Tumulty, "Can Democrats Hold the Senate by Running Away from Obama—and Their Own Records?," *Washington Post*, October 28, 2014, https://www .washingtonpost.com/politics/can-democrats-hold-the-senate-by-running-away-from -obama—and-their-own-records/2014/10/28/35f0f670-5eb5-11e4-9f3a-7e28799e0549 _story.html; Ed O'Keefe, "Joe Manchin: 'There's Nothing' Obama Can Do to Help At-Risk Democrats," *Washington Post*, October 21, 2014, https://www.washingtonpost.com /news/post-politics/wp/2014/10/21/joe-manchin-theres-nothing-obama-can-do-to-help-at -risk-democrats/.

21. "2014 Senate Race Ratings," Cook Political Report, November 3, 2014, https:// cookpolitical.com/ratings/senate-race-ratings/139256.

22. Charles Babington, "Some Dems Keep Distance as Obama Popularity Drops," *Associated Press*, December 2, 2013.

23. "Gallup Presidential Job Approval Center," accessed February 19, 2021, https://news.gallup.com/interactives/185273/presidential-job-approval-center.aspx; "Udall Skipping Obama Fundraiser," *Politico*, July 9, 2014, https://www.politico.com/story/2014/07/mark-udall-skipping-obama-fundraiser-for-his-campaign-108713; Colby Itkowitz, "Julian Castro Easily Confirmed for HUD Job Today," *Washington Post*, July 9, 2014, https://www.washingtonpost.com/blogs/in-the-loop/wp/2014/07/09/julian-castro-expected-to-be-easily-confirmed-for-hud-today/.

24. "Gallup Presidential Job Approval Center."

25. John Heinz, "Letter to James A. Baker III," Ronald Reagan Presidential Library, March 9, 1982.

26. Richard S. Williamson, "Memorandum to James A. Baker III Re: Senator Heinz's Request for the President to Attend a Fund Raiser for the Senator in Pennsylvania in 1982," Ronald Reagan Presidential Library, December 8, 1981; Pete Domenici et al., "Letter to Senator Howard Baker," Ronald Reagan Presidential Library, April 2, 1982; Ronald Reagan, "Letter to Senator Howard Baker," Ronald Reagan Presidential Library, April 6, 1982.

CHAPTER 4: PRIORITIES AND STRATEGIES

1. "Press Briefing by Ari Fleischer," April 24, 2001, https://georgewbush-white house.archives.gov/news/briefings/20010424.html.

2. Barack Obama, "Remarks by the President at DNC Event," November 4, 2015, https://obamawhitehouse.archives.gov/the-press-office/2015/11/04/remarks-president-dnc-event.

3. Daniel J. Galvin, *Presidential Party Building: Dwight D. Eisenhower to George W. Bush* (Princeton, NJ: Princeton University Press, 2010), 2, 17–38.

4. Sidney M Milkis, Jesse H. Rhodes, and Emily J. Charnock, "What Happened to Post-Partisanship? Barack Obama and the New American Party System," *Perspectives on Politics* 10, no. 1 (March 2012): 57–76.

5. Brendan J. Doherty, *The Rise of the President's Permanent Campaign* (Lawrence: University Press of Kansas, 2012), 42–88.

6. "2020 Gubernatorial Elections Map," accessed March 16, 2022, https://www.270towin.com/2020-governor-election/.

7. Steve Peoples and Jonathan Lemire, "In NH and Iowa, Trump Eyes 2020 Re-Election as Midterms Loom," *Associated Press*, March 20, 2018.

8. Kenneth P. Vogel, "As Other Republican Candidates Struggle Financially, Trump Stockpiles Cash," *New York Times*, October 17, 2018, https://www.nytimes.com/2018/10/17/us/politics/trump-campaign-finance-midterms.html.

9. Anita Kumar and Ben Wieder, "Trump Raised $135M at 29 Fundraisers. But Nearly Half the Events Were for Himself," *McClatchy DC Bureau*, August 7, 2018, https://www.mcclatchydc.com/news/politics-government/election/campaigns/article215903015.html.

10. US Senate Historical Office, "Party Division in the Senate, 1789-Present," accessed July 26, 2016, http://www.senate.gov/history/partydiv.htm; Office of the Clerk of the US House of Representatives, "Party Divisions of the House of Representatives (1789

to Present)," accessed August 3, 2016, http://history.house.gov/Institution/Party-Divisions/Party-Divisions/.

11. Jonathan Weisman, "Obama Races for Cash," *Wall Street Journal*, October 26, 2009, https://www.wsj.com/articles/SB125651404955107091; Jonathan Martin and Julie Hirschfeld Davis, "On Campaign Road, Uneasy Democrats Show Obama Their Tail Lights," *New York Times*, October 26, 2014, https://www.nytimes.com/2014/10/26/us/politics/on-campaign-road-uneasy-democrats-show-obama-their-tail-lights.html; Alex Isenstadt, "Republicans Warn Trump of 2018 Bloodbath," *Politico*, December 22, 2017, http://politi.co/2kVzXdR.

12. William J. Clinton, "Remarks at a Michigan Victory 2000 Reception in Livonia, Michigan," American Presidency Project, September 21, 2000, https://www.presidency.ucsb.edu/documents/remarks-michigan-victory-2000-reception-livonia-michigan.

13. Gary C. Jacobson, *The Politics of Congressional Elections*, 7th ed. (New York: Longman, 2008).

14. "Interview with Bruce Reed," William J. Clinton Presidential History Project, February 2004, https://millercenter.org/the-presidency/presidential-oral-histories/bruce-reed-oral-history-february-2004.

15. Maureen Santini, "Reagan Campaign Strategy: From Black Tie to Hard Hat," Associated Press, July 15, 1982.

16. Scott Lindlaw, "New Campaign Finance Law Doesn't Stop Bush from Fund Raising," Associated Press, March 28, 2002.

17. Susanne M. Schafer, "Reagan Heads South to Work for GOP Candidates," Associated Press, July 23, 1986.

18. Dudley Clendinen, "After Suicide, Speculation Focuses on Broyhill for Senate Seat," *New York Times*, July 1, 1986, http://www.nytimes.com/1986/07/01/us/after-suicide-speculation-focuses-on-broyhill-for-senate-seat.html.

19. Kyle Kondik and Geoffrey Skelley, "2018 Senate: The Democrats Are Very Exposed — Sabato's Crystal Ball," December 8, 2016, https://centerforpolitics.org/crystalball/articles/2018-senate-democrats-are-very-exposed/.

20. "Presidential Job Approval," American Presidency Project, accessed June 15, 2016, http://www.presidency.ucsb.edu/data/popularity.php.

21. "Presidential Job Approval."

22. "Presidential Job Approval."

23. Aaron Blake, "Which Election Was Worse for Democrats: 2010 or 2014? It's a Surprisingly Close Call," *Washington Post*, November 5, 2014, https://www.washingtonpost.com/news/the-fix/wp/2014/11/05/which-election-was-worse-for-democrats-2010-or-2014/.

24. Personal communication with Geoffrey Skelley, University of Virginia Center for Politics, July 19, 2017.

25. Calvin Woodward, "Clinton Raising Cash as Congress Moves toward Impeachment Inquiry," Associated Press, October 6, 1998; Ron Fournier, "Clinton Strategy for Democratic Victory in November: Money, Money, Money," Associated Press, June 11, 1998; Alison Mitchell and Eric Schmitt, "G.O.P. in Scramble over Blame for Poor Showing at the Polls," *New York Times*, November 5, 1998, https://www.nytimes.com/1998/11/05/us/1998-elections-congress-overview-gop-scramble-over-blame-for-poor-showing-polls.html.

26. "Interview with Joan N. Baggett," William J. Clinton Presidential History Project,

October 27, 2016, https://millercenter.org/the-presidency/presidential-oral-histories/joan-n-baggett-oral-history.

27. "Election Statistics: 1920 to Present," US House of Representatives: History, Art & Archives, accessed October 18, 2021, https://history.house.gov/Institution/Election-Statistics/.

28. Edward-Isaac Dovere, "Obama Looks to Help Elect Dem Govs," *Politico*, December 3, 2013, https://www.politico.com/story/2013/12/obama-republican-governors-blue-states-2014-100549.

29. "Elections," National Governors Association, accessed March 16, 2017, https://www.nga.org/cms/elections; Rick Ganley, "Should New Hampshire's Governor Serve a Four-Year Term?," January 28, 2015, https://www.nhpr.org/post/should-new-hampshires-governor-serve-four-year-term.

30. William M. Welch, "Reapportionment Puts Focus on Three Sunbelt Governors Races," Associated Press, January 11, 1990.

31. Rita Beamish, "President Heads Out On Behalf of GOP Candidates," Associated Press, September 18, 1990.

32. "'This Week' Transcript: President Barack Obama," ABC News, January 8, 2017, https://abcnews.go.com/Politics/week-transcript-president-barack-obama/story?id=44630949.

33. Alexander Burns and Jonathan Martin, "Eric Holder to Lead Democrats' Attack on Republican Gerrymandering," *New York Times*, January 11, 2017, https://www.nytimes.com/2017/01/11/us/eric-holder-to-lead-democrats-attack-on-republican-gerrymandering.html.

34. Schafer, "Reagan Heads South to Work For GOP Candidates."

35. Personal communication with Eric Ostermeier, University of Minnesota Smart Politics, April 21, 2021.

36. "States with Gubernatorial Term Limits," accessed March 17, 2022, https://ballotpedia.org/States_with_gubernatorial_term_limits.

37. Fredreka Schouten, "Governors Associations Fill Coffers at Conventions," ABC News, September 5, 2008, https://abcnews.go.com/Politics/story?id=5731629&page=1.

38. Ed O'Keefe and Matea Gold, "DNC Plans to Pump Up House, Senate Campaign Funds in Push toward Election Day," *Washington Post*, October 11, 2014, https://www.washingtonpost.com/news/post-politics/wp/2014/10/11/dnc-plans-to-pump-up-house-senate-campaign-funds-in-push-toward-election-day/; Alex Isenstadt, "Trump Intervenes to Save the House," *Politico*, July 26, 2018, https://politi.co/2LrP5Q6.

39. Marc Lacey, "Clinton Keeps a Frenetic Fund-Raising Pace," *New York Times*, June 25, 2000.

40. "President Bush Meets with Senator John McCain," March 5, 2008, https://georgewbush-whitehouse.archives.gov/news/releases/2008/03/20080305-4.html.

41. Eun Kyung Kim, "Obama Apologizes to Kamala Harris for 'Best-Looking Attorney General' Comment," April 5, 2013, http://www.today.com/news/obama-apologizes-kamala-harris-best-looking-attorney-general-comment-1B9237348.

42. "Fundraising for Super PACs by Federal Candidates," accessed April 13, 2021, https://www.fec.gov/help-candidates-and-committees/making-disbursements-pac/fundraising-super-pacs-federal-candidates-nonconnected-pac/.

CHAPTER 5: FUNDRAISING BEHIND CLOSED DOORS

1. Fred I. Greenstein, *The Hidden-Hand Presidency: Eisenhower as Leader* (New York: Basic, 1982), 5.

2. Thomas E. Cronin and Michael A. Genovese, *The Paradoxes of the American Presidency* (New York: Oxford University Press, 2004).

3. Julia R. Azari, Lara M. Brown, and Zim G. Nwokora, *The Presidential Leadership Dilemma: Between the Constitution and a Political Party* (Albany: State University of New York Press, 2013).

4. Lloyd Grove, "Oh, That Party of Change! Behind Closed Doors, Clinton Mixes with Democratic Fat Cats," *Washington Post*, October 6, 1993; "Fundraiser in Chief," *Washington Post*, February 6, 2002.

5. Ron Fournier, "Bush White House Deeply Entangled in State GOP Politics, Hoping for Gains in Congress," Associated Press, March 15, 2002.

6. Karl Rove, "The President Who Hates to Govern," *Wall Street Journal*, October 27, 2011, http://online.wsj.com/article/SB10001424052970203687504576655183399057512 .html?mod=googlenews_wsj.

7. Sheryl Gay Stolberg, "Presidential Face Time Isn't Everything, Except to Big Donors," *New York Times*, September 26, 2006, https://www.nytimes.com/2006/09/26/us /politics/26bush.html.

8. Donovan Slack, "Obama Attends Secretive Fundraiser," *Politico*, May 7, 2013, https://www.politico.com/blogs/politico44/2013/05/obama-attends-secretive-fundraiser -163450; Ron Fournier, "Democrats Like Those Big Bucks, but Wary of Clinton Record," Associated Press, October 4, 1994.

9. "President Trump Remarks at National Republican Congressional Committee Dinner," C-SPAN, April 2, 2019, https://www.c-span.org/video/?459408–1/president-trump-re marks-national-republican-congressional-committee-dinner. Quotation at 1 hour, 5 minute mark.

10. Anne E. Kornblut, "Democrats Map out Midterm Campaign Strategy for Obama," *Washington Post*, April 2, 2010, https://www.washingtonpost.com/wp-dyn/content/article /2010/04/01/AR2010040103754_2.html.

11. Sheryl Gay Stolberg, "Bush Winds Up Last Fund-Raising Appeal," *New York Times*, October 21, 1988, http://thecaucus.blogs.nytimes.com/2008/10/21/bush-winds-up -last-fund-raising-appeal.

12. Deb Riechmann, "Bush Still Raking in Cash for GOP," Associated Press, August 15, 2008.

13. "Press Gaggle by Dana Perino," July 25, 2008, http://georgewbush-whitehouse .archives.gov/news/releases/2008/07/20080725–7.html.

14. "Democrats Accuse GOP of Hiding President Bush's N.J. Visit," Associated Press, September 11, 2008, https://www.nj.com/news/2008/09/democrats_accuse_gop_of _hiding.html.

15. "Gallup Presidential Job Approval Center," accessed June 6, 2013, http://www .gallup.com/poll/124922/presidential-approval-center.aspx.

16. Ian Brodie, "Democratic Candidates Steer Clear of Clinton," *The Times* (London), October 13, 1994; Ann Devroy, "President Campaigns without Candidates; At Ford, Clinton Starts Drive Against GOP," *Washington Post*, October 12, 1994; Michael Wines, "Clinton Lauds His Policies, But Listeners Are Sparse," *New York Times*, October 12,

1994; "Clinton Boosts Party—or Does He?," *Atlanta Journal and Constitution*, October 12, 1994.

17. "Press Briefing by Dee Myers," October 12, 1994, http://www.presidency.ucsb.edu/ws/index.php?pid=59878&st=&st1=.

18. Richard Benedetto, "Some Candidates Not Shying Away from Clinton," *USA Today*, September 23, 1994.

19. Richard McGregor, "Democrats Tell Obama to Send Money but Stay Home," *Financial Times*, October 10, 2014, https://www.ft.com/content/efa6dee4-4ffc-11e4-a0a4-00144feab7de.

20. Ernie Freda, "Clinton to Drop Secrecy from Fund-Raising Events," *Atlanta Journal and Constitution*, October 13, 1993.

21. Peter Baker, "Open-Door Fund-Raisers?," *Washington Post*, December 11, 1996.

22. James Rowley, "Clinton Says Having Donors at the White House Was 'Entirely Appropriate,'" Associated Press, February 26, 1997; Terence Hunt, "Gore: Made Fund-Raising Calls from Office, Won't Any More," Associated Press, March 3, 1997; Edward-Isaac Dovere and Josh Gerstein, "Barack Obama Locks Out the Press—Again," *Politico*, July 23, 2014, https://www.politico.com/story/2014/07/barack-obama-locks-out-the-press-again-109316.

23. Julia Malone, "Speak Softly, Carry a Golf Club and Raise Money; Hoarse Clinton Enjoys a Holiday with the Rich," *Atlanta Journal and Constitution*, November 2, 1997.

24. Marc Lacey, "Bush Accused of Stealing Clinton's Oratory," *New York Times*, August 6, 2000, https://www.nytimes.com/2000/08/06/us/the-2000-campaign-the-speech-bush-accused-of-stealing-clinton-s-oratory.html.

25. "Press Gaggle by Tony Snow," September 25, 2006, http://georgewbush-whitehouse.archives.gov/news/releases/2006/09/20060925-3.html.

26. "Press Gaggle by Dana Perino," May 27, 2008, https://georgewbush-whitehouse.archives.gov/news/releases/2008/05/20080527-6.html; "McCain Does Tricky Dance with Unpopular Bush," May 27, 2008, https://www.cnn.com/2008/POLITICS/05/27/mccain.bush/index.html.

27. Christopher Beam, "The TMI Presidency: How Much Transparency Do We Really Want from Obama?," Slate, November 12, 2008, http://www.slate.com/articles/news_and_politics/politics/2008/11/the_tmi_presidency.html; Jonathan Easley, "Obama Says His Is 'most Transparent Administration' Ever," *The Hill*, February 14, 2013, http://thehill.com/blogs/blog-briefing-room/news/283335-obama-this-is-the-most-transparent-administration-in-history.

28. "Press Briefing by Press Secretary Robert Gibbs," October 12, 2010, https://obamawhitehouse.archives.gov/the-press-office/2010/10/12/press-briefing-press-secretary-robert-gibbs-10122010.

29. Dovere and Gerstein, "Barack Obama Locks Out the Press—Again."

30. Dovere and Gerstein.

31. "Press Briefing by Press Secretary Robert Gibbs."

32. Mark Knoller, "A Fundraiser That Isn't a Fundraiser," CBS News, July 27, 2010, http://www.cbsnews.com/news/a-fundraiser-that-isnt-a-fundraiser/; "Press Briefing by Press Secretary Jay Carney, 4/19/12," April 19, 2012, https://obamawhitehouse.archives.gov/the-press-office/2012/04/19/press-briefing-press-secretary-jay-carney-41912.

33. "Press Gaggle by Principal Deputy Press Secretary Eric Schultz—En Route Los

Angeles, California," July 23, 2014, https://obamawhitehouse.archives.gov/the-press-of
fice/2014/07/23/press-gaggle-principal-deputy-press-secretary-eric-schultz-en-route-los-.

34. "Press Gaggle by Principal Deputy Press Secretary Eric Schultz—En Route Los Angeles, California."

35. "Press Briefing by the Press Secretary Josh Earnest, 10/22/2014," October 22, 2014, https://obamawhitehouse.archives.gov/the-press-office/2014/10/22/press-briefing -press-secretary-josh-earnest-10222014.

36. "Press Briefing by the Press Secretary Josh Earnest, 10/22/2014."

37. "Press Briefing by the Press Secretary Josh Earnest, 10/22/2014."

38. "Press Briefing by Press Secretary Josh Earnest, 8/24/16," August 24, 2016, https://obamawhitehouse.archives.gov/the-press-office/2016/08/24/press-briefing-press -secretary-josh-earnest-82416.

39. "Press Gaggle by Principal Deputy Press Secretary Sarah Sanders En Route Orlando, Florida," March 3, 2017, https://trumpwhitehouse.archives.gov/briefings-state ments/press-gaggle-principal-deputy-press-secretary-sarah-sanders-en-route-orlando-flor ida/; "Press Briefing by Principal Deputy Press Secretary Sarah Sanders and Treasury Secretary Mnuchin," June 29, 2017, https://trumpwhitehouse.archives.gov/briefings-state ments/press-briefing-principal-deputy-press-secretary-sarah-sanders-treasury-secretary -mnuchin-062917/; Karen Yourish and Jasmine C. Lee, "The Demise of the White House Press Briefing under Trump," *New York Times*, January 22, 2019, https://www.nytimes .com/interactive/2019/01/22/us/politics/white-house-press-briefing.html.

40. Dovere and Gerstein, "Barack Obama Locks Out the Press—Again."

41. Josh Dawsey and Michelle Ye Hee Lee, "Trump to Headline a $580,600-per-Couple Fundraiser, the Most Expensive of His Reelection Bid," *Washington Post*, February 13, 2020, https://www.washingtonpost.com/politics/trump-to-headline-a-580600-per-couple -fundraiser-the-most-expensive-of-his-reelection-bid/2020/02/13/144b75b2-4e7a-11ea -a4ab-9f389ce8ad30_story.html.

42. Paul M. Barrett, "Obama Joins Romney Sharing Secrets with Donors at Closed Din-ners," *Bloomberg*, July 12, 2012, https://www.bloomberg.com/news/articles/2012-07-12 /obama-joins-romney-sharing-secrets-with-donors-at-closed-dinners.

43. Natasha Korecki, "Biden Opens Big-Donor Fundraisers to Press," *Politico*, May 3, 2019, https://politi.co/2PNcU48.

44. Korecki.

CHAPTER 6: CONTROVERSIES AND PROSPECTS

1. Robert E. Mutch, *Campaign Finance: What Everyone Needs to Know* (New York: Oxford University Press, 2016), 10–15; Dan Eggen, "Post-Watergate Campaign Finance Limits Undercut by Changes," *Washington Post*, June 16, 2012, https://www.washingtonpost .com/politics/post-watergate-campaign-finance-limits-undercut-by-changes/2012/06/16 /gJQAinRrhV_story.html; "Statement by President Gerald Ford," October 15, 1974, https://www.fordlibrarymuseum.gov/library/document/0248/whpr19741015–011.pdf.

2. Interviewed in a video accompanying "The Cost of Campaigns," *New York Times*, October 19, 2014, https://www.nytimes.com/2014/10/20/us/the-cost-of-campaigns.html.

3. "Fundraising for Super PACs by Federal Candidates," FEC, accessed April 13,

2021, https://www.fec.gov/help-candidates-and-committees/making-disbursements-pac/fundraising-super-pacs-federal-candidates-nonconnected-pac/.

4. Josh Dawsey and Michelle Ye Hee Lee, "Trump to Headline a $580,600-per-Couple Fundraiser, the Most Expensive of His Reelection Bid," *Washington Post*, February 13, 2020, https://www.washingtonpost.com/politics/trump-to-headline-a-580600-per-couple-fundraiser-the-most-expensive-of-his-reelection-bid/2020/02/13/144b75b2–4e7a-11ea-a4ab-9f389ce8ad30_story.html.

5. "DNC and State Parties Announce Historic Agreement," democrats.org, May 12, 2021, https://democrats.org/news/dnc-and-state-parties-announce-historic-agreement/.

6. "Speech: Donald Trump Holds a Campaign Rally in Prescott, Arizona—October 19, 2020," Factba.se, October 19, 2020, https://factba.se/transcript/donald-trump-speech-campaign-rally-prescott-arizona-october-19–2020.

7. ExxonMobil, "Twitter Post," Twitter, October 19, 2020, https://twitter.com/exxonmobil/status/1318324411146141701.

8. Andrew Prokop, "Donald Trump Made One Shockingly Insightful Comment during the First GOP Debate," *Vox*, August 6, 2015, https://www.vox.com/2015/8/6/9114565/donald-trump-debate-money.

9. Michael Beckel, "12 Political Megadonors Are Responsible for $1 of Every $13 in Federal Elections since Citizens United and 25% of All Giving from the Top 100 ZIP Codes—a Total of $3.4 Billion," n.d., 5.

10. "McCutcheon et al. v. Federal Election Commission," April 2, 2014, https://www.supremecourt.gov/opinions/13pdf/12–536_e1pf.pdf.

11. Haberman, "The Cost of Campaigns."

12. Matea Gold, "Leaked DNC Emails Reveal the Inner Workings of the Party's Finance Operation," *Washington Post*, July 24, 2016, https://www.washingtonpost.com/politics/inside-the-democratic-partys-scramble-for-big-money/2016/07/24/0f02b56c-51c0–11e6-b7de-dfe509430c39_story.html.

13. Walter Pincus, "Democrats Fall Way behind Money-Making GOP," *Washington Post*, December 18, 1977.

14. Rita Beamish, "Huge Contributions Roll In as GOP Holds Biggest Fundraiser Ever," Associated Press, April 28, 1992.

15. "Interview with Joan N. Baggett," William J. Clinton Presidential History Project, October 27, 2016, https://millercenter.org/the-presidency/presidential-oral-histories/joan-n-baggett-oral-history.

16. Tom Raum, "White House Defends Donors' $100,000 Meals with Clinton," The Associated Press, July 6, 1995; Tom Raum, "White House: $100,000 Meals Don't Mean Clinton's for Sale," Associated Press, July 7, 1995.

17. Adam Ashton, "Bush Meets with Elite GOP Contributors for the Third Time in a Month," Associated Press, February 2, 2004.

18. Helena Andrews-Dyer, "President Obama to Host a Goodbye Party at the White House on Friday," *Washington Post*, January 3, 2017, https://www.washingtonpost.com/news/reliable-source/wp/2017/01/03/president-obama-to-host-a-good-bye-party-at-the-white-house-on-friday/.

19. Renae Merle, "Payday Lenders Discussed Raising Money for Trump's Campaign to Fend Off Regulation, Audio Reveals," *Washington Post*, October 29, 2019, https://

www.washingtonpost.com/business/2019/10/29/payday-lenders-discussed-raising-money
-trumps-campaign-fend-off-regulation-audio-reveals/.

20. Richard Keil, "Parties Use Access to Elected Officials As Bait for Contributions,"
Associated Press, December 8, 1995.

21. "Trump Fundraiser for Noem Shuts the Public Out," *Rapid City* (SD) *Journal*,
September 6, 2018, https://rapidcityjournal.com/opinion/editorial/ours-trump-fundraiser
-for-noem-shuts-the-public-out/article_08b56499–7319–51d2–82b4-fe01919c8d5c.html.

22. Carla Marinucci, "Fans Resent Lack of Public Events on Obama Visits," *San
Francisco Chronicle*, June 3, 2013.

23. Barack Obama, *The Audacity of Hope: Thoughts on Reclaiming the American
Dream* (New York: Crown, 2006), 113–115.

24. Raymond J. La Raja and Brian F. Schaffner, *Campaign Finance and Political
Polarization: When Purists Prevail*, illustrated ed. (Ann Arbor: University of Michigan
Press, 2015).

25. Garance Franke-Ruta, "The Big House," *Atlantic*, February 21, 2013, https://
www.theatlantic.com/magazine/archive/2013/03/the-white-house-list/309225/.

26. David Bauder, "Documentary Brings Together 20 Presidential Chiefs," Associated Press, September 10, 2013.

27. Thomas Donilon, "President Obama's Asia Policy and Upcoming Trip to the
Region," November 15, 2012, csis.org/files/attachments/121511_Donilon_Statesmens
_Forum_TS.pdf.

28. "Press Gaggle by Dana Perino," July 25, 2008, http://georgewbush-whitehouse
.archives.gov/news/releases/2008/07/20080725–7.html.

29. Gabriel Debenedetti, "Where Is Barack Obama?," *New York Magazine*, June 25,
2018, https://nymag.com/intelligencer/2018/06/where-is-barack-obama.html.

30. Mark Landler, "Obama Parries Criticism as Fund-Raising Eats Into His Schedule," *New York Times*, March 17, 2012, https://www.nytimes.com/2012/03/17/us/politics
/obama-faces-criticism-over-time-spent-fund-raising.html; Jackie Calmes, "'Presidential'
vs. 'Political' Trips: A Blurry Line, and Tricky Math," *New York Times*, April 22, 2012,
https://www.nytimes.com/2012/04/22/us/politics/presidential-vs-political-trips-a-blurry
-line-for-obama.html.

31. "Press Briefing by Press Secretary Jay Carney, 3/15/2012," March 15, 2012, 12,
https://obamawhitehouse.archives.gov/the-press-office/2012/03/15/press-briefing-press
-secretary-jay-carney-3152012.

32. James Oliphant, "Obama's Real Job: Fundraiser in Chief," *Atlantic*, April 14,
2014, https://www.theatlantic.com/politics/archive/2014/04/obamas-real-job-fundraiser-in
-chief/360610/.

33. Dan Roberts and Kenton Powell, "Revealed: Obama's Record-Breaking Effort to
Tap Wealthy Donors for Cash," *The Guardian*, November 12, 2013, http://www.theguard
ian.com/world/2013/nov/12/obama-wealthy-donors-fundraising-drive-democrats.

34. Karen Tumulty, "Obama Plans Major Fall Campaign Rallies," *Washington Post*,
September 10, 2010, http://www.washingtonpost.com/wp-dyn/content/article/2010/09/09
/AR2010090903597.html.

35. Michael Putzel, "As Election Nears, Who Pays Reagan's Tab on the Road?," Associated Press, October 24, 1982.

36. David Lauter, "White House Will Not Reveal Portion of Bush's Political Travel

Paid for by GOP," *Los Angeles Times*, April 27, 1991, https://www.latimes.com/archives /la-xpm-1991–04–27-mn-647-story.html.

37. Anne Gearan, "President Begins Three-Day Money Marathon in the West," Associated Press, June 22, 2000.

38. Scott Lindlaw, "Bush Campaigns Heavily on Air Force One," Associated Press, May 30, 2004.

39. Calmes, "'Presidential' vs. 'Political' Trips."

40. "Press Briefing by Press Secretary Sarah Sanders," October 5, 2017, https:// trumpwhitehouse.archives.gov/briefings-statements/press-briefing-press-secretary-sar ah-sanders-100517/.

41. Calmes, "'Presidential' vs. 'Political' Trips."

42. Chris Riotta, "Trump Flies to Texas for His Re-Election Fundraiser and Writes It off as Taxpayer Expense," *Newsweek*, October 25, 2017, https://www.newsweek.com /trump-flies-texas-taxpayer-expense-campaign-2020-reelection-692656; Todd J. Gillman and Gromer Jeffers Jr., "Awaiting Trump in Dallas: Love, Protests and Campaign Cash," *Dallas Morning News*, October 25, 2017, https://www.dallasnews.com/news/politics/2017 /10/25/awaiting-trump-in-dallas-love-protests-and-campaign-cash/.

43. Susan Crabtree, "How Obama Is Saving the DNC Money on His Fundraising Trips—at Your Expense," *Washington Examiner*, July 23, 2014, https://www.washington examiner.com/tag/barack-obama.

44. Mike Allen, "On the Way to the Fundraiser; Stopovers Let Bush Charge Taxpayers for Political Trips," *Washington Post*, May 20, 2002; "Taxpayers Pay for Bush's Campaign Travel," NBC News, August 30, 2006, https://www.nbcnews.com/id/wbna14588025.

45. Tom Raum, "Goal of Clinton Trip Is Fund-Raising, 'Official' Events an Afterthought," Associated Press, September 15, 1995.

46. Roberts and Powell, "Revealed."

47. "Taxpayers Pay for Bush's Campaign Travel."

48. Allen, "On the Way to the Fundraiser."

49. David Fahrenthold et al., "Ballrooms, Candles and Luxury Cottages: During Trump's Term, Millions of Government and GOP Dollars Have Flowed to His Properties," *Washington Post*, October 27, 2020, https://www.washingtonpost.com/politics/ball rooms-candles-and-luxury-cottages-during-trumps-term-millions-of-government-and -gop-dollars-have-flowed-to-his-propertiesmar-a-lago-charged-the-government-3-apiece -for-glasses-of-water-for-trump-and-the-japanese-leader/2020/10/27/186f20a2–1469-11eb -bc10–40b25382f1be_story.html.

50. Nicholas Confessore et al., "The Swamp That Trump Built," *New York Times*, October 10, 2020, https://www.nytimes.com/interactive/2020/10/10/us/trump-properties -swamp.html.

51. Brian Schwartz, "Trump Properties Have Made over $17 Million from the Campaign and the RNC since 2016," July 17, 2020, https://www.cnbc.com/2020/07/17/trump -properties-made-over-17-million-from-campaign-rnc-since-2016.html.

52. Fahrenthold et al., "Ballrooms, Candles and Luxury Cottages."

53. Schwartz, "Trump Properties Have Made over $17 Million from the Campaign and the RNC since 2016."

54. Peter Overby, "Mixing Business and the Presidency, Trump to Hold Fundraiser at His Washington Hotel," NPR, June 27, 2017, http://www.npr.org/2017/06/27/534327346 /mixing-business-and-the-presidency-trump-to-hold-fundraiser-at-his-washington-ho.

55. David Fahrenthold et al., "'Who Built This Beautiful Place?' Despite Trump's Visits to His Properties, Some of His Businesses Show New Signs of Financial Decline," *Washington Post*, November 5, 2019, https://www.washingtonpost.com/politics/who-built-this-beautiful-place-despite-trumps-visits-to-his-properties-some-of-his-businesses-show-new-signs-of-financial-decline/2019/11/05/819869cc-f691–11e9–8cf0–4cc99f74d127_story.html.

56. Alex Isenstadt and Meredith McGraw, "Trump Political Groups Have over $100M in the Bank," *Politico*, July 31, 2021, https://www.politico.com/news/2021/07/31/trump-political-groups-82-million-501958; Shane Goldmacher and Eric Lipton, "Selling Trump: A Profitable Post-Presidency Like No Other," *New York Times*, February 12, 2022, https://www.nytimes.com/2022/02/12/us/politics/donald-trump-business-interests.html.

57. Josh Dawsey and David Fahrenthold, "GOP Candidates Are Flocking to Mar-a-Lago to Pay Trump for the Privilege of Hosting Their Events," *Washington Post*, December 16, 2021, https://www.washingtonpost.com/politics/2021/12/16/trump-gop-candidates-fund raisers/.

58. Goldmacher and Lipton, "Selling Trump."

59. "President Discusses Ag, Trade in South Dakota," April 24, 2002, http://georgew bush-whitehouse.archives.gov/news/releases/2002/04/20020424–3.html.

60. David Von Drehle, "Battle for the Senate Comes to the Prairie; Bush Takes on Daschle in S. Dakota," *Washington Post*, April 25, 2002; Deborah Orin, "Bush Duels Daschle in Dakota," *New York Post*, April 25, 2002; Matthew Tully, "Bush's South Dakota Visit Puts Democrats' Nerves on Edge," *Congressional Quarterly Daily Monitor*, April 24, 2002.

61. W. Dale Nelson, "Reagan's Campaigns for Tax Plan," Associated Press, June 5, 1985.

62. Josh Lederman and Jim Kuhnhenn, "Obama Raises California Cash for Democrats," Associated Press, April 4, 2013.

63. Donald Trump, "Twitter Post," @realdonaldtrump, June 22, 2018, https://twitter.com/realDonaldTrump/status/1010116816998490113.

64. Ciara Torres-Spelliscy, "Netflix for Democracy," Brennan Center for Justice, January 17, 2019, https://www.brennancenter.org/our-work/analysis-opinion/netflix-democracy.

65. Dana Milbank, "Lawmakers Could Do This to Fight Corruption. But They Won't," *Washington Post*, May 16, 2016, https://www.washingtonpost.com/opinions/an-isolated-crusade-to-clean-up-congress/2016/05/16/983a3264–1b9d-11e6–9c81–4be1c14fb8c8_story.html.

66. Carl Hulse, "As Aisle Gets Wider, Arms Get Shorter," *New York Times*, 2009.

67. Brian Schwartz, "Pro-Trump Super PAC America First Action Raised over $42 Million in September," October 20, 2020, https://www.cnbc.com/2020/10/20/pro-trump-super-pac-america-first-action-raised-over-42-million-in-september.html.

68. Eliza Newlin Carney, "Parties Poised to Exploit Broad New Rules," *Roll Call*, January 6, 2015, http://blogs.rollcall.com/beltway-insiders/parties-poised-to-exploit-broad-new-rules.

69. Interviewed in a video accompanying "The Cost of Campaigns."

70. Ronald Campbell, "Cash Is What Presidential Candidates Really Want in California," *Orange County Register*, October 12, 2012, https://www.ocregister.com/2012/10/12/cash-is-what-presidential-candidates-really-want-in-california/.

71. David Catanese, "Mitch McConnell's Outside Man, Steven Law, Plays the Long Game," *Lexington Herald-Leader*, July 22, 2021, https://www.kentucky.com/news/poli tics-government/article252947403.html.

72. "Actions—H.R.1—117th Congress (2021–2022): For the People Act of 2021," 2021/2022, accessed July 29, 2021, https://www.congress.gov/bill/117th-congress/house -bill/1/actions.

73. Nicholas Confessore and Megan Thee-Brenan, "Poll Shows Americans Favor an Overhaul of Campaign Financing," *New York Times*, June 2, 2015, https://www.nytimes .com/2015/06/03/us/politics/poll-shows-americans-favor-overhaul-of-campaign-fi nancing.html; Matea Gold, "Big Money in Politics Emerges as a Rising Issue in 2016 Campaign," *Washington Post*, April 19, 2015, https://www.washingtonpost.com/poli tics/big-money-in-politics-emerges-as-a-rising-issue-in-2016-campaign/2015/04/19/c695 cbb8-e51c-11e4-905f-cc896d379a32_story.html.

74. Dave Levinthal, "Actions, Not Words, Tell Trump's Political Money Story," Center for Public Integrity, January 19, 2018, https://publicintegrity.org/politics/actions-not -words-tell-trumps-political-money-story/.

75. Robert Harding, "John Katko, Democrats Aim to Overturn Supreme Court's Citizens United Decision," *Auburn Citizen*, January 22, 2021, https://auburnpub.com /news/local/govt-and-politics/john-katko-democrats-aim-to-overturn-supreme-courts-citi zens-united-decision/article_b8087ec3-fdc8-5af8-9ca5-a6edd9a6d61e.html.

76. Kate Ackley, "Candidates Decry Political Money, but Change Is Unlikely," *Roll Call*, February 25, 2016, https://www.rollcall.com/2016/02/25/candidates-decry-political -money-but-change-is-unlikely-2/.

77. Matea Gold and Tom Hamburger, "Party Fundraising Provision, Crafted in Secret, Could Shift Money Flow in Politics," *Washington Post*, December 10, 2014, https://www .washingtonpost.com/politics/party-fundraising-provision-crafted-in-secret-could-shift -money-flow-in-politics/2014/12/10/f6856ed0-808d-11e4-9f38-95a187e4c1f7_story .html.

78. La Raja and Schaffner, *Campaign Finance and Political Polarization*, 134.

79. Gold and Hamburger, "Party Fundraising Provision, Crafted in Secret."

80. John M. Broder, "For the Really Big Donors, It's Dinner with Clinton," *Los Angeles Times*, July 7, 1995, http://articles.latimes.com/1995-07-07/news/mn-21053_1_big -donors.

81. Elizabeth Bumiller, "President Signs Bill on Campaign Gifts; Begins Money Tour," *New York Times*, March 28, 2002.

82. Nicholas Confessore, "Ruling Spurs Rush for Cash in Both Parties," *New York Times*, April 4, 2014, https://www.nytimes.com/2014/04/05/us/politics/ruling-sets-off-a -bipartisan-rush-for-campaign-cash.html?emc=edit_th_20140405&nl=todayshead lines&nlid=15178127&_r=0.

83. Michelle Ye Hee Lee, "Trump Has Embraced the Big-Money Donor World He Once Shunned," *Washington Post*, July 2, 2018, https://www.washingtonpost.com/politics/trump -has-embraced-the-big-money-donor-world-he-once-shunned/2018/06/30/0ef53478 -7630-11e8-9780-b1dd6a09b549_story.html.

84. Don Van Natta, "Bush Forgoes Federal Funds and Has No Spending Limit," *New York Times*, July 15, 1999.

85. Dan Morain, "Obama Wags Finger at Fundraising, but His Hand's Out," *Los An-*

geles Times, February 23, 2007, https://www.latimes.com/archives/la-xpm-2007-feb-23
-na-obama23-story.html.

APPENDIX: TRACKING PRESIDENTIAL FUNDRAISERS

1. Ronald Reagan, "Remarks in Los Angeles at a California Republican Party Fund-Raising Dinner," May 25, 1982, https://www.presidency.ucsb.edu/documents/remarks-los-angeles-california-republican-party-fund-raising-dinner; George W. Bush, "Remarks by the President at Scott McCallum for Governor Reception," February 11, 2002, https://georgewbush-whitehouse.archives.gov/news/releases/2002/02/20020211–9.html; Barack Obama, "Remarks by the President at a Campaign Event—Tampa, FL," September 20, 2012, https://obamawhitehouse.archives.gov/the-press-office/2012/09/20/remarks-president-campaign-event-tampa-fl; Barack Obama, "Remarks by the President at a DNC Event—Chicago, IL," October 20, 2014, https://obamawhitehouse.archives.gov/the-press-office/2014/10/20/remarks-president-dnc-event-chicago-il; Daniel Dale, "Twitter Post," @ddale8, June 13, 2020, https://twitter.com/ddale8/status/1271874479183089666.

2. Terry McAuliffe and Steve Kettmann, *What A Party!: My Life among Democrats: Presidents, Candidates, Donors, Activists, Alligators and Other Wild Animals* (New York: Thomas Dunne, 2007), 213.

3. Kenneth P. Vogel, "Venturing into the Swamp, Trump Dines with Major Donors," *New York Times*, March 8, 2018, https://www.nytimes.com/2018/03/08/us/politics/trump-donor-dinner-georgetown.html.

4. Anne Gearan, "Clinton Hits All Democratic Bases in L.A.," Associated Press, August 13, 2000.

5. "Press Briefing by Joe Lockhart," February 25, 2000, https://www.presidency.ucsb.edu/documents/press-briefing-joe-lockhart-15.

6. Scott Bland, "Fundraising Remix: The Zoom Where It Happens," Politico's Nerdcast, August 14, 2020, https://politicos-nerdcast-874ac64d.simplecast.com/episodes/fundraising-remix-the-zoom-where-it-happens-XpqXa67m.

7. Jeremy Diamond, "Trump Freewheels at RNC Fundraiser, Talks Trade Dealings with Trudeau," September 26, 2017, https://www.cnn.com/2017/09/26/politics/donald-trump-rnc-fundraiser-new-york-city/index.html.

8. "The Blank-Blank '92 Ticket," *New York Times*, April 30, 1992.

9. Barack Obama, "Remarks at a Democratic National Committee Fundraiser in Miami Beach, Florida," June 13, 2011, https://www.presidency.ucsb.edu/documents/remarks-democratic-national-committee-fundraiser-miami-beach-florida; Barack Obama, "Remarks at a Democratic National Committee Fundraiser in Miami, Florida," June 13, 2011, https://www.presidency.ucsb.edu/documents/remarks-democratic-national-committee-fundraiser-miami-florida; Barack Obama, "Remarks at a Democratic National Committee Fundraiser in Miami," June 13, 2011, https://www.presidency.ucsb.edu/documents/remarks-democratic-national-committee-fundraiser-miami.

Index

Page references in *italics* indicate a figure; page references in **bold** indicate a table.

corruption concerns, 48
creation of, 40
distribution of funds to state parties, 49
donations to, 24, 43
proliferation of, 45, 163
Jolly, Dave, 152
Julius, Michael, 15

Kappel, Brett, 56
Keltner, Brad, 149
Kennedy, Anthony, 39
Kerry, John, 36
Kiely, Kathy, 147
Kissinger, Henry, 13
Knoller, Mark, 15, 37, 38, 119, 128, 129, 162
Koops, Gary, 146

Lance, Leonard, 124
Landrieu, Mary, 72
La Raja, Raymond, 143, 154
Larson, Bruce, 12
Lee, Frances, 3
Lenhard, Robert, 152, 153
Levinson, Jessica, 144
Lim, Tim, 161
Lockhart, Joe, 161
Longoria, Eva, 22

Madison, James, 12, 32
Magleby, David, 13
Maine Democratic Party, 44
Malbin, Michael, 13
Manchin, Joe, 72
Mann, Thomas, 152
McAuliffe, Terry, 117, 160
McBride, Ann, 142
McCain, John
  on campaign finance system, 136, 140
  legislative initiative, 11
  presidential candidacy, 36, 112, 124, 128, 163
McCain-Feingold law. *See* Bipartisan Campaign Reform Act of 2002 (BCRA)
McConnell, Mitch, 38, 59, 153
McCurry, Mike, 14
McCutcheon, Shaun, 41, 49

McCutcheon v. Federal Election Commission, 41–42, 48, 68, 139, 140, 154, 155
McDaniel, Ronna, 142
McGehee, Meredith, 147
McIntyre, Thomas, 69
McLarty, Mack, 14
megadonors, 139
Mellen, Rob, 15
Menendez, Bob, 87
Michigan Republican Party, 56
midterm elections, 4, 33, 76, 104, 109
Miers, Harriet E., 9
Mikulski, Barbara, 12
Milkis, Sidney M., 78, 115
Minnesota Republican Party, 56
Mitchell, George, 150
Monroe, James, 32
Morris, Irwin, 15
Moynihan, Daniel Patrick, 97
Murphy, Chris, 12
Myers, Chris, 124
Myers, Dee, 125

nationalization of presidential fundraising
  benefits of, 71–73
  consequences of, 95
  contrasting Reagan and Obama, 65–66
  geographic element of, 58
  growth of, 52–53, 73, 136–137
  key factors of, 66–67
  scholarly studies of, 20, 57
national party committees, **53**
  fundraising for, 28, 35, 42–43, 53–58, *54*, 68, 111
National Republican Congressional Committee (NRCC), 1, 42, **53**
  as beneficiary of presidential fundraising, 59, 70, 101, 103, 111
National Republican Senatorial Committee (NRSC), 42, **53**
  as beneficiary of presidential fundraising, 59, 95, 110, 111
Netsch, Dawn Clark, 62
Nicholson-Crotty, Sean, 15
Nixon, Richard, 33, 135
Nolan, Rick, 152